Donald Thompson in Russia

AMERICANS IN REVOLUTIONARY RUSSIA

Vol. 1
Albert Rhys Williams, *Through the Russian Revolution*,
edited by William Benton Whisenhunt (2016)

Vol. 2
Princess Julia Cantacuzène, Countess Spéransky, née Grant, *Russian People: Revolutionary Recollections*, edited by Norman E. Saul (2016)

Vol. 3
Ernest Poole, *The Village: Russian Impressions*, edited by Norman E. Saul (2017)

Vol. 4
John Reed, *Ten Days That Shook the World*,
edited by William Benton Whisenhunt (2017)

Vol. 5
Louise Bryant, *Six Red Months in Russia: An Observer's Account of Russia Before and During the Proletarian Dictatorship*, edited by Lee Farrow (2017)

Vol. 6
Edward Alsworth Ross, *Russia in Upheaval*, edited by Rex A. Wade (2017)

Vol. 7
Donald Thompson, *Donald Thompson in Russia*, edited by David H. Mould (2018)

Series General Editors: Norman E. Saul and William Benton Whisenhunt

Donald Thompson in Russia

Donald Thompson

Edited and Introduction by
David H. Mould

ANTHEM PRESS

Anthem Press
An imprint of Wimbledon Publishing Company
www.anthempress.com

First published by Slavica Publishers, Indiana University, USA, 2018

This edition first published in UK and USA 2026
by ANTHEM PRESS
75–76 Blackfriars Road, London SE1 8HA, UK
or PO Box 9779, London SW19 7ZG, UK
and
244 Madison Ave #116, New York, NY 10016, USA

Copyright © 2026 David H. Mould editorial matter and selection;
individual chapters © individual contributors

The moral right of the authors has been asserted.

All rights reserved. Without limiting the rights under copyright reserved above,
no part of this publication may be reproduced, stored or introduced into
a retrieval system, or transmitted, in any form or by any means
(electronic, mechanical, photocopying, recording or otherwise),
without the prior written permission of both the copyright
owner and the above publisher of this book.

British Library Cataloguing-in-Publication Data
A catalogue record for this book is available from the British Library.

Library of Congress Cataloging-in-Publication Data
A catalog record for this book has been requested.

ISBN-13: 978-1-83999-673-3 (Hbk)
ISBN-10: 1-83999-673-0 (Hbk)

ISBN-13: 978-1-83999-674-0 (Pbk)
ISBN-10: 1-83999-674-9 (Pbk)

This title is also available as an eBook.

Contents

Editor's Introduction ix

Editor's Note xxvii

Donald Thompson in Russia 1

Illustrations 153

Index 217

Illustrations

Map of Petrograd .... Figure 1

Map of Kronstadt and Tsarskoe Selo .... Figure 2

Map of the Russian front, 1917 .... Figure 3

Just before the Russian Revolution .... Figure 4

Demonstration against peace .... Figure 5

Gun and ammunition cart .... Figure 6

Merry-go-round at the Russian front .... Figure 7

Rasputin surrounded by admirers .... Figure 8

A bread line in Petrograd .... Figure 9

Three generations of Cossacks .... Figure 10

Russian front at Riga .... Figure 11

Nicolas Romanoff and his son, June, 1917 .... Figure 12

Men shooting from a motor .... Figure 13

The first red flags on the Nevsky Prospekt,
Sunday, March 11, 1917 .... Figure 14

Petrograd police station after the Revolution .... Figure 15

Half a million people demonstrating on the Nevsky .... Figure 16

Street scene in Petrograd .... Figure 17

A captured car, Monday night, March 12 .... Figure 18

Picking up the dead and wounded
after a street fight in Petrograd .... Figure 19

Types of Bolsheviks .... Figure 20

The Reds of Petrograd .... Figure 21

My room at the Hotel Astoria .... Figure 22

A deserted prison .... Figure 23

Soldiers' and workmen's deputies sitting .... Figure 24

A Russian nurse .... Figure 25

Women lined up for inspection .... Figure 26

Effects of street-fighting during the Revolution .... Figure 27

Armored cars in Petrograd .... Figure 28

CONTENTS

Funeral procession in Petrograd .... Figure 29

Catherine Breshkovskaya .... Figure 30

Cossack general reviewing Bochkareva's Death Battalion .... Figure 31

Sole survivors of an entire regiment after gas attack .... Figure 32

Wounded Russian soldiers walking back from the front .... Figure 33

Demonstration by loyal Russians .... Figure 34

Mobs meeting at the Nevsky and Sadovaia .... Figure 35

Trotsky and Lenin .... Figure 36

Women making a demonstration against the war .... Figure 37

Russian soldiers leaving the front .... Figure 38

Russian Cossacks .... Figure 39

Kerensky just about to salute regiment
passing on its way to the front .... Figure 40

Mobs listening to Kerensky near the Russian Admiralty .... Figure 41

Mobs on the Field of Mars in Petrograd .... Figure 42

Bochkareva and one of the companies of women soldiers .... Figure 43

Russian soldiers who had tried to cut this
barbed wire of the Germans .... Figure 44

Russian soldiers advancing through the grass .... Figure 45

Left to right: Bolshevik, German agent, and Kronstadt [sailor] ..... Figure 46

Russian army on the retreat .... Figure 47

Dr. Eugene Hurd, of Seattle, Washington .... Figure 48

House used by me at the front .... Figure 49

Women who joined the Women's Death Battalion .... Figure 50

Blessing of the Women's Death Battalion .... Figure 51

Florence Harper and Maria Bochkareva .... Figure 52

Bochkareva and Emmeline Pankhurst .... Figure 53

Lenin addressing a Petrograd mob, Monday, July 16, 1917 .... Figure 54

Emmeline Pankhurst and Bochkareva reviewing
Women's Death Battalions .... Figure 55

Mutinous soldiers .... Figure 56

Russian soldiers abandoning their positions
during the great retreat in July 1917 .... Figure 57

Lenin's arrival in Petrograd .... Figure 58

A Russian Death Battalion .... Figure 59

A crowded street tram in Petrograd .... Figure 60

Cattle cars were used to haul the wounded in .... Figure 61

With my camera in front line trenches on the Dvinsk front .... Figure 62

Low bridge on Russian front line .... Figure 63

A soldier's funeral .... Figure 64

Petrograd mobs .... Figure 65

Editor's Introduction
David H. Mould

"Well, I came to Russia against your wish and I am paying the price," Donald Thompson wrote to his wife Dorothy (Dot) from Petrograd in late July 1917. "If I ever get back home safely, this is the last trip I shall make.... Today I feel as you always want me to feel—sick and tired of being a war photographer" (July 21).[1]

Thompson had been away from home for almost eight months, and in Russia since mid-February. Over the next six months, he photographed demonstrations and street fighting in Petrograd, was caught in crossfire between protesters and troops, and was arrested and thrown in jail. He traveled to Moscow and to the Russian front lines in Latvia. He met and photographed Tsar Nicholas II, political and military leaders, and prominent foreign visitors. He witnessed political maneuverings, the power struggle between the Provisional Government and the Petrograd Soviet, and the breakdown of discipline in the army. Often working late into the night, Thompson suffered from exhaustion, stress, and poor diet. With food shortages, even in the hotels and restaurants patronized by foreigners, Thompson—already a lean 120 pounds—lost weight. Although he claimed he could live on bread and coffee, "the black bread that one gets now in Petrograd is one of the major horrors of war," he wrote (March 6). A few weeks later, he fell ill with a stomach infection and spent two weeks in the hospital.

In late July, Thompson was ready to go home but not ready to abandon the life of the "photographer-adventurer" that had taken him to every front in Europe since August 1914. After telling Dot that this would be his last trip, Thompson wrote: "But there is no use in saying this. I shall be the way I always have been. A few weeks at home and then I'll pick up the paper at breakfast and read about something happening somewhere and I'll want to go there" (July 21).

Donald Thompson in Russia is a compilation of letters to Thompson's second wife in Topeka, Kansas, written between December 12, 1916, and August 21, 1917[2]

---

[1] *Donald Thompson in Russia* (New York: Century, 1918). All references to the text are by date of letter.

[2] Thompson's letters are dated by the Western Gregorian calendar, which ran thirteen days ahead of the old-style Julian calendar used in Russia in this period. According to the Gregorian calendar, the events of the February Revolution actually took place in March, and those of the

and published in 1918. It is impossible to know whether the letters are exactly what Thompson wrote at the time, or whether he edited them later to fill out the narrative and reinforce his central theme—that the major cause of Russia's revolution and withdrawal from the war was German intrigue. He claims in the introduction that "at the time they were penned the idea of writing a book had never entered my head." But he asked Dot to keep the letters and his motive for publication is clear. "When I came back from Russia, after one of the most exciting trips of my life, I was glad that I could show the whole world the proofs that German intrigue was the cause of Russia's downfall. German intrigue, working among the unthinking masses, has brought Russia to her present woeful condition." The letters, he added, "tell a story that I know a great many people may doubt. Fortunately, the details are largely substantiated by the motion-picture film I have shown in this country [*The German Curse in Russia*] supplemented by thousands of photographs which have appeared in *Leslie's Weekly* and in newspapers throughout the world."[3]

Thompson's letters are one of the few first-hand accounts by an American of events in Russia from late February to early August 1917. The photographer's experiences feature prominently in Helen Rappaport's recent book, *Caught in the Revolution*, which recounts the testimonies of foreign journalists, diplomats, businessmen, nurses, and others living in Petrograd in 1917. "It is a matter of considerable regret," writes Rappaport, "not to mention a loss to history and scholarship, that Thompson's original photographic negatives do not appear to have survived."[4] The title of the book testifies to Thompson's zeal for self-promotion. Other expatriates wrote about their experiences in books with titles such as *Runaway Russia* (Florence MacLeod Harper), *Six Red Months in Russia* (Louise Bryant), *Inside the Russian Revolution* (Rheta Childe Dorr), *Diary of the Russian Revolution* (James L. Houghteling), *Unchained Russia* (Charles Edward Russell), *Russia's Agony* (Robert Wilton), and, of course, *Ten Days that Shook the World* (John Reed). Thompson's is one of only a few to include the name of the author in its title; in *Donald Thompson in Russia*, the author portrays himself not only as a witness to history, but as an actor in the drama.

Born in Topeka in 1885, Thompson worked as a freelance photographer, covering the 1903 Kansas River flood, the 1912 Democratic Convention, and the 1913 Colorado miners' strike. When war broke out in Europe, he was commissioned by a Montreal newspaper to film Canadian troops. It was his big break. "As a photographer," he wrote, "I knew it would be the greatest story in history and I determined

---

October Revolution in November. The introduction retains Thompson's dating but refers to the February and October Revolutions, because this is how they are commonly termed.

[3] Introduction to *Donald Thompson in Russia*.

[4] Helen Rappaport, *Caught in the Revolution: Petrograd, Russia, 1917* (London: Hutchinson, 2016), 332–33.

that I was going to cover it. I sold everything I had, bought a complete photographic outfit and my steamship ticket."[5] He sailed to Europe in August 1914.

The rapid growth of American mass media—newspapers, illustrated weekly magazines, and motion pictures—in the first two decades of the twentieth century created new opportunities for news photographers. Most, like Thompson, began their careers shooting stills for newspapers and magazines, and later shot film footage, using bulky, hand-cranked cameras mounted on tripods. The main customers for their films were the international newsreel companies, based in New York, Chicago, London, and Paris; several newspaper groups, notably the Hearst papers and the *Chicago Tribune*, also had interests in the newsreel business, as owners or part-owners of weekly reels. Footage was sometimes compiled into feature-length films. The rapid growth of the Hollywood movie industry gave newsreels and topical films thousands of theater outlets, and an audience for whom moviegoing was becoming a way of life.

The popular image of the brave, free-spirited news photographer, who defied danger, death, the elements, and the censors to get the picture, was largely fashioned during World War I, when photographers faced all these obstacles. It was, like most such images, a composite of fact and fiction, so it is hardly surprising that, in recalling their exploits, photographers such as Thompson often added colorful details and dramatic turns. Thompson compensated for his less-than-imposing physical presence by portraying himself as a pioneer war photographer. He was proud to tell people he was from Kansas, a state which, with its rich and bloody history, seemed to symbolize the American frontier. The trade and popular press were willing accomplices in this reconstruction of reality, accepting the stories at face value, and often adding their own spice to the narrative.[6] "Nearly every reader of news of the great European war is familiar with the name of Donald C. Thompson, known the world over as 'The War Photographer from Kansas,'" reported the trade newspaper *Moving Picture World*. "He is of a kind we sometimes read about but rarely collide with in the flesh."[7] In Belgium, Thompson worked on both sides of the lines with Edward Alexander Powell, war correspondent of the *New York World*, covering the Battle of Mons and the German siege of Antwerp. "He was a slim, wiry little fellow, as hard as nails and as tough as rawhide," wrote Powell. "He wore riding breeches and leggings and was as bow-legged as though he had spent his life astraddle of a horse."[8] The *Chicago Tribune* celebrated "Shrimp Thompson," the "young Topeka corn-fed product who has writ-

---

[5] Introduction to *Donald Thompson in Russia*.

[6] David H. Mould and Gerry Veeder, "The 'Photographer-Adventurers': Forgotten Heroes of the Silent Screen," *Journal of Popular Film and Television* 16 (Fall 1988): 127.

[7] *Moving Picture World*, February 6, 1915, 812.

[8] Edward Alexander Powell, *Slanting Lines of Steel* (New York: Macmillan, 1933), 46.

ten K-A-N-S-A-S across the war map of Europe."⁹ *Chicago Tribune* London bureau chief Charles Wheeler admired "this devil-may-care, easy going, fear immune, quick witted, 120 pounds of human being," who was "equally at home on a gun carriage or in the swellest hotels of Europe ... joking with a king or getting joyously drunk with a trooper."¹⁰ Powell described their first meeting in Antwerp:

> He blew into the Consulate wearing an American army shirt, a pair of British officer's riding breeches, French puttees, and a Highlander's forage cap, and carrying a camera the size of a parlor phonograph. Thompson is a little man, hard as nails, tough as raw-hide, his face perpetually wreathed in what he called his sunflower smile. He has more chilled-steel nerve than any man I know, and before he had been in Belgium a month his name became a synonym throughout the army for coolness and daring.[11]

Thompson's personal life enhanced his maverick image. He went through four marriages, and got into fistfights in hotel rooms and restaurants. He won and lost at the gaming tables,[12] and was once arrested in Chicago for impersonating a naval officer and passing bad checks.[13]

Photographers such as Thompson presented themselves as experts on political and military matters. When his films were shown in major cities, Thompson appeared in military uniform (although he held no military rank) and told audiences that armies throughout Europe knew him as "le capitaine Thompson."[14] His souvenirs—passports, letters of authority, and medals—were displayed in the theater lobby, or in the window of a nearby store. He was a showman, often appearing in his own films. This device not only enhanced the film's authenticity—the image proved he was there—but showed its maker in suitable poses, preparing the camera for action, meeting the military brass, donning a gas mask.

World War I was the first major conflict to be covered by motion picture photographers. It was difficult, dangerous work. Thompson had to depend on the armies

---

[9] "Tribune Staff Men Off to War Zones," *Chicago Daily Tribune*, February 11, 1915, 5.

[10] Charles N. Wheeler, "Kansas Boy Likes the War," reprinted in *Kansas City Star*, January 29, 1915.

[11] Edward Alexander Powell, *Fighting in Flanders* (New York: Charles Scribner and Sons, 1916), 13–14.

[12] En route to Russia in early 1917, he claimed to have made $8,000 on the roulette tables in a Shanghai casino, after starting with a $120 stake. "That will buy a lot of nice presents for you," he wrote to Dot (January 22, 1917).

[13] "Don Thompson, a Globe Trotter and Erstwhile Topekan, Under Arrest," *Topeka State Journal*, June 5, 1923, 1.

[14] "Thompson Tells Tales of Battle," *Topeka Daily Capital*, December 30, 1915, 3.

he worked with for access to the war zone, and faced a military bureaucracy that regarded photographers at worst as spies and at best as dangerous nuisances. Military censors confiscated his cameras, or took out exposed film and held it up to the light to inspect it. Somehow, Thompson always managed to talk his way out of trouble and resorted to elaborate schemes to smuggle his film back to London or New York.[15] In the war zone, he was subject to military authority—the army that provided him with food and transportation determined where he traveled, and what he shot. He was in as much danger as a regular soldier, sometimes more, because a camera could be mistaken for a new-fangled gun, and invite an artillery barrage. Several photographers were killed, and others, including Thompson, wounded. Most of his footage was taken behind the lines; it shows military parades and ceremonies, the build-up of troops and supplies, airplanes and observation balloons, artillery barrages, and prisoner-of-war camps. The few front-line scenes show a featureless landscape, broken only by the distant explosion of artillery shells. Indeed, the best times for fighting—in the dark or under smokescreen—were the worst times for photography; when the sun was shining and the light was good, there was not much going on. World War I, as Thompson saw and filmed it, was nothing like the Hollywood version, full of cavalry charges and desperate hand-to-hand combat.[16]

During the first year of the war, Thompson shot stills for American and British newspapers and magazines—the *New York World*, the *Chicago Tribune, Leslie's Illustrated Weekly*, the London *Daily Mail*, the *Illustrated London News*—and film for the major newsreel companies. His early experiences on the Western Front set the tone for the rest of his career. In his attempts to reach the front lines, he was frequently arrested. At the Battle of Mons, he filmed under heavy fire for seven days, was again arrested, and ordered to leave the country. Fearing his film would be confiscated, he persuaded a Russian countess traveling to England to carry it in her baggage. In London, he sold the film to the highest bidder, and then went back to the front.[17] On his return to London, Thompson was hired by the newspaper magnate Lord Northcliffe to go to Germany. They made up a fake newspaper clipping from a non-existent American newspaper, in which Thompson praised the German army in Belgium. He managed to reach Berlin, but a German spy in London tipped off the secret service, and Thompson had to make a quick getaway. He looked up a girlfriend, and proposed

---

[15] Powell, *Fighting in Flanders*, 15; "A Kansan Snapshots War," *Kansas City Star*, September 6, 1914, 8.

[16] David H. Mould, *American Newsfilm, 1914–1919: The Underexposed War* (New York: Routledge, 2014), 100–14.

[17] Powell, *Fighting in Flanders*, 15.

they elope; she got a passport for her "brother" and they drove to the border. There, the ungallant Thompson confessed that he was not in love after all, and left her.[18]

Thomson made his first trip to Russia in 1915. In February, he sailed to Europe with Robert R. McCormick, editor of the *Chicago Tribune*, and Edwin Weigle, a *Tribune* photographer. After a brief stay in England and France, Weigle went to Germany while McCormick and Thompson traveled east via Greece, Bulgaria, and Romania, arriving in Petrograd in early April 1915. McCormick was granted a short audience with Tsar Nicholas II, which he remembered mostly for the pomp and circumstance—the coaches, liveried footmen, uniforms, furniture, paintings of Louis XIV. "I felt like Marco Polo at the court of the Chinese emperor," he wrote later.[19] Then the pair traveled to the front in Galicia and the Carpathian Mountains, where in late 1914 the Russians had launched a successful offensive against the Austro-Hungarian army and laid siege to the strategic fortress of Przemysl on the road to Krakow. The fort surrendered in March 1915 with the Russians taking 120,000 prisoners and capturing 1,000 artillery pieces. The victory was short-lived. By the time McCormick and Thompson reached the front, the Russians were facing a combined German-Austrian offensive that ended with victory at the Battle of Gorlice-Tarnow in May. This turned into a strategic retreat, with the Russians withdrawing from Poland and removing the threat of an invasion of Germany or Austria-Hungary. The Russians had welcomed the well-connected McCormick, whose father had been U.S. ambassador in Petrograd, as an unofficial U.S. emissary. As Thompson noted: "Mr. McCormick had letters of introduction, passes to every country in Europe, and was received as no other war correspondent has ever been received during this war. Wherever he appeared the government officials went out of their way to assist him."[20] McCormick's memoir recounts meetings with politicians, strategy discussions with the General Staff, and lavish dinners with caviar and French wine. Traveling with him, Thompson would have had little opportunity to observe the conditions of the regular troops.

Thompson's footage was released by the *Chicago Tribune* as a feature-length film, *With the Russians at the Front*, in August 1915, followed a week later by the premiere of Weigle's *The German Side of the War*. Neither made any pretense of neutrality. Although the Russian army was in general retreat from Poland, *With the Russians at the Front*

---

[18] "Thompson Tells Tales of Battle," *Topeka Daily Capital*, December 30, 1915, 3; introduction to *Donald Thompson in Russia*.

[19] Robert R. McCormick, *With the Russian Army, Being the Experiences of a National Guardsman* (New York: MacMillan, 1915), 37.

[20] Introduction to *Donald Thompson in Russia*.

portrayed it as a formidable war machine.[21] The *Chicago Tribune* full-page display ads promised exclusive footage:

> Positively the only motion pictures taken within Russian lines made under the personal supervision of R. R. McCormick, war correspondent, and Donald C. Thompson, staff photographer. *The Chicago Tribune* received the **EXCLUSIVE PERMISSION** of the Russian government to photograph the very recent Russian campaigns in the Carpathians, on the Rawka River, at Przemysl, Warsaw. Be an eye-witness of the Russian armies in the field—*under fire*—in the rain-soaked trenches of the Polish front—taking up positions in the mountains. Approach *within a few feet* of the Czar of All the Russias. See that spectacle—the Imperial Guard *in battle before Lomza*.[22]

Only twenty-three minutes of the film have survived, and some scenes promoted in the advertising are missing.[23] Thompson faced the same logistical problems he had encountered on the Western Front—lack of access to the war zone and, even if he reached it, lack of action. Consequently, most of the footage was taken behind the lines. The film opens with Thompson and McCormick posing by a car with a *Chicago Tribune* banner. There are scenes from staff headquarters showing Grand Duke Nicholas, the commander in chief, the Tsar reviewing troops, General Aleksei Brusilov, commander of the 8th Army, artillery batteries in action in the Carpathian Mountains, Cossack cavalry on parade, field hospitals and kitchens, and refugees. The only "front-line" scene features the Semyonovsky Regiment of the Imperial Guard at Lomza. It shows soldiers running past a building and firing from a parapet; some fall back, apparently wounded, and are carried away on stretchers. As McCormick noted, Thompson filmed during a break in the fighting, and all the scenes were staged for the camera.[24] Given the difficulty of obtaining combat footage, such staging, with the willing assistance of military officers, was common during World War I. To satisfy audience demand for war footage, Thompson organized infantry to march, cavalry to charge, artillery to fire, and airplanes to take off and land.

---

[21] Historians attribute Russia's defeat on the Eastern Front not so much to strategy as to lack of artillery, ammunition, and supplies as well as the corruption and incompetence of Russian officers. McCormick refers to the lack of railways as an infrastructure problem, but in the film's titles and in his later memoir, *With the Russian Army*, provides positive assessments of the Russian army and the competence of its officers.

[22] *Chicago Daily Tribune*, August 22, 1915, 10.

[23] A print of the film is in the Film Study Center at the Museum of Modern Art in New York.

[24] The Papers of Colonel Robert R. McCormick, Cantigny Park, Illinois, I-62, Foreign Correspondents, 1914–1955, Box 11, Donald Thompson. Notes for lecture at film premiere at Studebaker Theater, Chicago.

Like McCormick, Thompson left Russia in 1915 with a positive view of its military command and government. He also made contacts he would use in 1917, including his interpreter, Boris. He was aware of supply problems, commenting later that munitions production had improved. "I find the Russian troops much better equipped now than in 1915, and ammunition is plentiful, artillery ammunition, especially. Shells are stacked up wherever you go" (February 28, 1917). If he was aware of corruption and incompetence in the army, he did not mention them in interviews with the motion picture and popular press. Reflecting on the 1915 trip in the introduction to *Donald Thompson in Russia,* Thompson says that he did not understand why the Russian armies with their "millions of men" did not "push the German army aside and go where they pleased." The reason, he was told, was German intrigue. A Cossack officer in the Carpathians said Russia was "paying the price" for not locking up its German-born citizens, whose bribery and intrigue were undermining the war effort. "Their generals were bought, their ammunition was going astray, and they were losing thousands of men in fruitless battles.... They caused thousands to die in hospitals, for while millions had been appropriated for field hospitals, German intrigue had diverted that money into other channels."[25]

Thompson goes on to attribute most setbacks in the Allied war effort to German intrigue. In Bucharest, Germany had "thousands of spies on her pay-roll"; Serbia was defeated "partly by the devious methods that Germans love and excel in"; in Rome, an Italian officer told him that Italy's "wonderful army" would be thrown back "because there were too many Germans running loose in the country, doing the dirty work of the Kaiser." Every Allied country Thompson had visited that "had not locked up its Germans, has since felt the disastrous effect of the Teutonic spy system."[26]

While McCormick returned to the U.S. from Russia via Sweden, Thompson traveled south to the Balkans. On July 23, 1915, the U.S. legation in Athens wired McCormick, relaying Thompson's request for $500 to travel home. McCormick, already frustrated by Thompson's cockiness, insubordination, and occasional drunkenness, refused. He wired back the next day: "Please take all moving picture apparatus film and cameras from Thompson. Buy him third class ticket to America and give him ten dollars. Don't lend Thompson any money." A week later the legation reported, "Thompson refused your offer. Got money somewhere and left for France with apparatus."[27]

Thompson spent the next few weeks filming with the Serbian army. By fall 1915, he was back in France, still posing as a *Tribune* photographer and running up hotel

---

[25] Introduction to *Donald Thompson in Russia.*

[26] Introduction to *Donald Thompson in Russia.*

[27] The Papers of Colonel Robert R. McCormick, Cantigny Park, Illinois, I-62, Foreign Correspondents, 1914–1955, Box 11, Donald Thompson.

bills that McCormick eventually had to pay. He released his first feature-length film, *Somewhere in France* (the title is an allusion to the censors' ban on revealing place names), in December 1915, then returned to the Balkans, where the Allies had opened a new front at Salonika. Then he joined the French army as an official cinematographer; although his status provided access to the front, he had to submit his film for censorship, and claimed he lost 70 percent of his footage.[28] He filmed at the siege of Verdun and Battle of the Somme, where he was wounded. His second feature, the immodestly titled *War As It Really Is*, was released in December 1916. Its premiere at the Rialto Theater in New York City broke the box office record.[29] By the end of 1916, Thompson had worked on every front in Europe, claimed to have witnessed thirty-eight battles, and had been wounded three times. His hometown newspaper, the *Topeka Daily Capital*, sponsoring the local premiere of *War As It Really Is*, praised him as "the photographic hero of the war."[30]

In December 1916, shortly after the release of *War As It Really Is*, Thompson, on assignment to shoot film for Paramount and stills for *Leslie's Weekly*, left Seattle on the liner *Empress of Russia* for Japan, accompanied by *Leslie's* staff correspondent Florence Harper. He found plenty of evidence to support his German conspiracy thesis on the long journey to Petrograd. On the ship, a Russian army officer told him that intrigue in the Imperial Court had undermined military assistance to Romania, forcing its armies to retreat and abandon Bucharest (December 12, 1916); in Manila, Thompson filed a libel suit against a newspaper editor who he suspected of being paid by the Germans over an article claiming that Thompson and Harper were impostors (January 5, 1917); Shanghai was "a regular pest-hole for German spies" (January 22); in Peking, he punched a hotel manager when he surprised him going through his baggage and papers (February 14); on the Trans-Siberian Railway, fellow passengers told him that German agents were creating food shortages in Petrograd to foment riots (February 24).

Thompson and Harper worked together for six turbulent months as the country plunged into political and social chaos. They covered the protests and street fighting of the February Revolution that ended with the Tsar's abdication and the establishment of the Provisional Government, and the abortive Bolshevik coup in July. They traveled to the front line, where discipline was breaking down and soldiers' committees were being formed. They left Russia in August, missing the main event—the October Revolution.

---

[28] "Real Thrills in Battle Pictures," *Moving Picture World*, November 11, 1916, 857.

[29] "War Films on State Rights from Thompson Company," *Motion Picture News*, December 2, 1916, 3453. For a review of *War As It Really Is*, see "Real Thrills in Battle Pictures," *Moving Picture World*, November 11, 1916, 857. A copy of the film is in the National Archives.

[30] *Topeka Daily Capital*, December 21, 1915.

Thompson sensed that he was in Russia at a historic time. "So far, Dot," he wrote on March 8, "I have guessed this war to a T. The people can say what they please, but I smell trouble. And thank God I am here to get the photographs of it! If there is a revolution I hope it comes now, for although I should hate to see bloodshed, if it has to be it might as well come while I am on the ground with plenty of film." On March 18, after the Tsar's abdication and the declaration of a republic, he wrote: "Just imagine if someone had had the French Revolution in motion pictures! Well, I have thousands of feet of film of the Russian Revolution. I have worked every day and have followed the mobs day and night. I went seventy-two hours without any sleep at all to speak of ... but I got my film and hundreds of still pictures."

His letters recounted daring photographic exploits under fire. With his flair for self-promotion, he may have exaggerated the stories, but there is corroboration from other sources, particularly the accounts of newspaper correspondents who worked with him. His closest associate, Harper, wrote articles describing the same incidents, and published a memoir on her Russian experiences, *Runaway Russia*.[31] In an article for the London *Daily Mail*, reprinted in American newspapers, she recounted a typical piece of Thompson derring-do during the abortive Bolshevik uprising in July:

> Tuesday morning the Nevsky was said to be very unsafe, so Thompson piled his camera into a big auto, and said, "Come on." He was in khaki; on the front seat his orderly and the chauffeur were both in uniform. I wore a blue Italian army cape, so we looked rather military. The tripod of the camera sticking up in the *tonneau* looked not unlike a new kind of gun. In fact it looked so dangerous that it gave us a clear passage up the Nevsky. As we neared the corner of the Liteiny the crowds were thick, and soon the trouble started. The Bolsheviki met the Cossacks, both armed and with machine guns on both sides. Thompson set up the camera and began to crank. One minute the street was a mass of people, the next they had fallen flat to escape the bullets or were running for cover. All the time Thompson cranked away. His coat was off, and strapped to his belt was an Army colt. The chauffeur showed signs of panic. Thompson drew his gun, and said, "You do as I tell you, or you'll get shot, too."[32]

Accounts of this incident appear in several sources, delivered in the same kind of breathless prose and with only minor variations in detail; if it seems a little far-

---

[31] Florence MacLeod Harper, *Runaway Russia* (New York: Century, 1918).

[32] "Thompson Risks Life to Film Russian Revolution Scenes," *Topeka Daily Capital*, September 30, 1917, 18.

fetched, at least everyone was telling the same story.[33] This was just one of many incidents recounted by Thompson and Harper, but unfortunately, there are few surviving stills to document them.

Thompson's accounts are rich in detail; he almost always included the date, the time of day, and locations, noting, for example, the direction in which a crowd was moving, or where he was when an incident occurred. Most events happened in central Petrograd, and so, by referring to a map of the city (see figure 1), it is possible to plot the action. However, Thompson's estimates of crowd size are unreliable. Describing a demonstration by women and factory workers on March 8, he noted that the crowd "soon numbered at least 2,000." A week later, on the Liteiny, he wrote that he "found a mob of about a million people, it seemed to me; and this mob was out for blood" (March 18). "There were fully 75,000 people packed in the square in front of the Duma," he reported the next day. "There were half a million people in line, men and women and soldiers" in the May Day parade, and "in one division 15,000 anarchists." The next day, on the Sadovaia, Thompson and his interpreter Boris "met a mob of about 10,000." He estimated that "about a million people" attended the funeral for Cossack soldiers killed during the abortive July coup (July 28). Estimating crowd size is a professional skill, and is best done from a vantage point. At street level, it is virtually impossible to estimate numbers, yet Thompson consistently did so, even when he was lying prone on the ground. Caught in crossfire near the Summer Palace during the abortive coup in July, Thompson and Boris threw themselves to the ground. "We had company, however," wrote Thompson, "between these two points, there must have been between 1,800 and 2,000 people lying flat on the street" (July 15).

Thompson spoke only a few words of Russian so relied on his interpreter, Boris, and other English speakers, not only to translate but to interpret events and reports. Of course, Thompson had other sources—fellow journalists and photographers, military officers at the Astoria Hotel, and American embassy staff. Harper spoke French, which allowed her to converse with some military officers and government officials. Boris, however, was with Thompson most of the time. On the streets of Petrograd, Boris told him what people were saying, what their banners and signs meant, what the newspapers were reporting.

We know little about Boris, except that he was conscripted into the Russian army in 1916 and wounded on the Romanian front. He complained to Thompson about lack of munitions and food at the front, and the disorderly retreat. Clearly, Boris was disillusioned with the Tsarist government, and warned Thompson that food shortages and strikes in Petrograd would lead to trouble. He told Thompson that secret police were acting as provocateurs, mingling with the crowds and inciting demon-

---

[33] A similar account of the incident described Thompson's actions as in character. "Americans who saw Mr. Thompson shouted to him that he must be crazy. But he had gone all over Europe taking war pictures and he wasn't going to be balked here." "Lenine Anti-American as Well as Pro-German," *New York Times Magazine*, November 18, 1917, 8.

strators to violence and looting to provoke an armed response by the Cossack cavalry or Imperial Guard. On April 4, Boris reported that "German spies are spending money here in Petrograd as they never spent it before" and "thousands of Germans are coming into Russia now from Sweden on forged passports and by bribing officials at the border."

Boris was most reliable in reporting what was happening on the streets of Petrograd. His assessments of the political and military situation or the maneuverings between rival factions were more speculative, yet Thompson frequently included them in his letters. "The revolution isn't two weeks old yet and already they are fighting amongst themselves," he wrote on March 21. "As things stand now, all are in favor of the republican form of government, such as we have in the United States. I hear through Boris that this is the sentiment in all the large cities." Boris told him that most people on the streets had no idea of why they were protesting. "I ran across one mob of 10,000 workmen, 80 percent of them armed; when Boris asked a few of them what they were out for, they didn't know; they only showed him a printed slip, telling them to be at a certain place at a certain time. Take it from me, this Lenin has certainly got these people well trained considering the short time he has been back in Russia" (May 9).

Just before the abortive Bolshevik coup in July, Thompson wrote that he had "made photographs of Lenin and a man named Trotsky who has come from New York" at the Bolshevik headquarters, the Kschessinskaya Mansion. Lenin is mentioned in three photograph captions in the book. "Lenin addressing a Petrograd mob, Monday, July 16, 1917" and "Lenin's arrival in Petrograd" are crowd shots in which the Bolshevik leader cannot be identified. The photograph captioned "Trotsky and Lenin" shows a group of six men and two women, with soldiers in the background. Trotsky and Lenin are not identified but part of the photograph, reproduced in the *Illustrated London News*, December 15, 1917, names the men on the far right as Trotsky and Lenin. This image, writes Mike Carey, appeared "in large-circulation journals ... most often alongside the argument that the two revolutionary leaders were either working for Germany or were even secretly Germans themselves."[34]

The men pictured are not Trotsky and Lenin, and bear little physical resemblance to them. Few images of the Bolshevik leaders were in circulation at the time, so Thompson's photograph was accepted for what it purported to be. As his earlier career indicates, Thompson had few qualms about staging and even faking scenes, and he would have known that a picture of the mysterious Bolshevik leaders would

---

[34] Mike Carey, "Definitely Not Lenin and Trotsky: Donald C. Thompson's Photographs of 1917," European Studies blog, British Library, January 4, 2016. According to Carey, a French series on Soviet history published in the early 1920s identifies the "Trotsky" figure as Mikhail Martynov, chair of the Kronstadt Soviet, and the "Lenin" figure as Christian Rakovsky, a Bulgarian socialist revolutionary who moved to Petrograd and joined the Bolsheviks in spring 1917.

be a scoop for *Leslie's*. Yet he may simply have been deceived by Boris or one of the Bolsheviks. Or perhaps, as Carey suggests, Lenin and Trotsky were "using body doubles, political decoys." We may never know.

Many of Thompson's letters mixed personal experiences with what he learned, often second or third hand. Almost every day, he heard unconfirmed reports and rumors, and freely admitted that sometimes he did not know what to believe. Soon after his arrival in Petrograd, he wrote: "Boris says a revolution is coming and he has heard that Protopopov has sold Russia to Germany, that he is going to make peace and that there will be lots of food in a few days. I asked him where he got this information and be said he couldn't tell me but that I would hear it from other people" (March 7). "The papers are full of what the members of the Duma and the different committees are saying, what they want, and what Russia should have, until you never know what to believe," he wrote on April 4. "It seems that every political party has a paper now. Since Russia is a republic everyone lets off steam." Shortly before his departure (August 4), he wrote: "I hear that Kerensky had a fight with one of the ministers of the cabinet, and that for a while we had no government at all, and that Kerensky had even rushed away to Finland in an automobile. How true this is I don't know, but I do know that all the ministers resigned but later reconsidered and withdrew their resignations."

Despite the rumors and his reliance on Boris and other sources, Thompson correctly interpreted, in his own homespun style, several key issues. He grasped that the future of the February Revolution would be decided in a power struggle between the Provisional Government, backed by the Duma, and the Petrograd Soviet of Soldiers' and Workmen's Deputies. He described the members of the Soviet as "the orneriest bunch of devils I have ever met. I will bet $1,000 to a cent that 90 percent of them cannot read or write, but they are being led by some pretty smart people. They are handing out proclamations every five minutes to appeal to the rabble they represent" (March 19). He understood the crucial linking role that Kerensky played as the only political leader to serve both as a minister and an elected member of the Soviet; later, he predicted that the rivalry between Kerensky and General Lavr Kornilov, the army commander in chief, would be a deciding factor. However, his deference to royalty (he had met and photographed the Tsar in 1915) clouded his judgment. Learning of the Tsar's abdication, he wrote (March 20): "I believe that if he could have been in the city Monday and had driven down the main street of Petrograd, the Nevsky Prospekt, and stood up in the back of his automobile with his hat off and talked, as Teddy Roosevelt would have done, he would still be the Tsar of Russia. He could have had the people with him and all that he would have had to do would have been to grant what the people wanted, to see to it that bread was brought into Petrograd, and to appoint new ministers.... As it was, he did nothing; why, I do not know. Probably because royalty doesn't do things that way."

Thompson reserved his sharpest criticism for Lenin and Trotsky—the two principal villains in the plot. Lenin had returned from exile in Switzerland in April. "Lenin might say that he is not in the pay of the Germans," he wrote (May 1), "but take it from me, Germany is not giving a special car to anyone to travel through Germany and back to Russia who is at war with them." At the same time, he grudgingly admired Lenin's political acumen. "Lenin is a brilliant man and is smart enough to know what the poor Russian wants to hear. These poor fellows believe that if Lenin is put in power the war will stop, the land and all the money will be divided amongst them, and they will never have to work again" (May 1). He wrote that Lenin was gaining support, and predicted that if he was not killed or jailed, he would soon be running Russia—a pretty accurate forecast for six months before the October Revolution.

Thompson made several trips to the front line which, after the retreat from Poland, ran roughly north–south—from Riga in Latvia, three hundred miles southwest of Petrograd, to northern Romania (see figure 3). He blamed German propaganda for disaffection and desertion in the army. "The Russian does not really know what he is fighting for," he wrote. "Nobody had ever told him what the war was about.... Now the Russians are leaving the trenches and the camps and wandering over the country trying to find their way back to their homes (most of them don't know how to get back home). They hear about peace, and they know that means they will not have to lie in the trenches this coming winter." Thompson believed Russia's generals could restore morale by ordering a new advance. "What Russia needs at the front is a leader, a Napoleon, someone who has the nerve to do things, no matter what the public says or how many mobs appear on the streets of Petrograd" (May 17).

Thompson returned to the United States in September 1917 as the Allies faced the prospect of Russia's withdrawal from the war and the collapse of the Eastern Front. The Allies feared that American troops would not arrive on the Western Front in time to stem a new German offensive. With the American press and public concerned by events in Russia, it was tempting to look for villains. The movie industry conveniently provided them in Thompson's feature-length film, *The German Curse in Russia* (also known as *Blood-Stained Russia*). It was released to enthusiastic reviews in December 1917, the same month that Russia withdrew from the war and the Germans occupied Ukraine. Its title summarized its theme—that the revolution was a giant conspiracy, fomented by German intrigue, and its leaders, Lenin and Trotsky, were spies and rabble-rousers, hired by the Germans to incite the people. According to *Motion Picture News*, "Every foot of the film helps to visualize for the American people the means that the Germans utilized in Russia to bring about food riots, street fighting and the final overthrow of the government which had been established for them upon a foundation of freedom and liberty."[35] Moviegoers were promised "the inside truth about Russia, showing how German intrigue, stopping at nothing, drove the

---

[35] "Pathé Shows Good War Films," *Motion Picture News*, December 29, 1917, 4535.

Russian people to revolt and put their armies out of the war."[36] *Moving Picture World* told theater managers that *The German Curse in Russia* would play on the patriotic fervor of their patrons, suggesting they hold free performances for schoolchildren and their teachers, and drape the lobby with American and Russian flags.[37] Thompson was treated as an expert witness, whose views on the situation in Russia should be taken seriously. According to *Picture-Play Magazine*, Thompson felt his mission was not only to observe but to warn. "He realized that he had been doing something more than merely taking war pictures. He saw that within his films lay concealed the pitiful story of how German intrigue had sapped a great nation. And he realized, too, that this story was needed in America as a timely warning."[38]

Did *The German Curse in Russia* live up to its claims? Was it, as its distributor Pathé claimed, "the greatest of all war pictures"? We may never know because the film has apparently been lost.[39] However, the themes of the film, as reported in the press, are similar to those outlined in *Donald Thompson in Russia* and in Thompson's still photographs. For nine months, from June 1917 to March 1918, *Leslie's Weekly* featured full-page or double-page spreads of Thompson's photographs, often with copy by Harper. The headlines played on anti-revolutionary sentiment in the United States—"Bolshevism—Talk, Poverty, Arson and Murder," "The Evil Reign of Russia Bolsheviki," "Bitter Lessons in Bolshevism," "No Peace for Struggling Russia." Some stills appeared in the motion picture trade press, in Thompson's and Harper's books, and in a book of his photographs.[40] As in Thompson's films, the images do not speak for themselves; it is the titles and captions that provide context and political perspective.

The claims by Thompson and others that German intrigue was the principal cause of the October Revolution were widely aired in the popular press of the United States, and supported by government officials and opinion leaders. In March 1918, Edgar Sisson, an American journalist serving as representative for the Committee on Public Information (CPI) in Petrograd, returned to the United States with documents purporting to show that the Bolshevik regime was a puppet government controlled by the German general staff. The head of the CPI, George Creel, told President Woodrow Wilson that the documents revealed an "amazing record of double dealing and corruption" that would constitute a coup for American propaganda. After

---

[36] *Canadian Moving Picture Digest*, February 9, 1918, 14.

[37] "Advertising Aids for Busy Managers," *Moving Picture World*, January 26, 1918.

[38] Louis Tenny, "Filming the Trail of the Serpent," *Picture-Play Magazine*, March 1918, 113–14.

[39] Sadly, no prints of the film appear to have survived, although some footage—apparently purchased from Thompson—was reused in Herman Axelbank's 1937 documentary compilation *From Tsar to Lenin*.

[40] *Blood-Stained Russia* (New York: Leslie-Judge Co., 1918).

a hurried and uncritical review, the government published them under the title, "The German-Bolshevik Conspiracy."[41] Although many of the documents were later shown to be forgeries, they made excellent propaganda, providing a suitably dastardly explanation for Russia's departure from the war. The simple conspiracy theory provided a convenient fiction to explain a series of events that Americans found confusing and threatening. Thompson's views were shared by many other Americans.

Thompson did not believe that this regime of revolutionaries and German spies could last long, and he expected a counterrevolution. "The thing that will conquer Lenin and his Bolsheviki," he said in March 1918, "is an army from outside Petrograd, an army that really represents Russia."[42] That army soon appeared, as counterrevolutionary White forces attacked Bolshevik forces in Siberia. The Allies sent an expeditionary force to support the White armies, and Thompson landed at Vladivostok ready to film the triumphal advance to Petrograd. It never happened. The White armies were too busy arguing among themselves to mount a concerted offensive, and the Allied force was unable to advance from Vladivostok. Thompson spent several frustrating months filming military parades and relief efforts for refugees. The Allied force was withdrawn in late 1919, but Thompson's experience only served to confirm his opinions; photographs of the Allied force and the White armies, published in *Leslie's Weekly*, provided what he judged to be further proof of German intrigue and the evils of Bolshevism.[43]

Details of Thompson's postwar career are sketchy. In 1920, he left for a year's tour of the Far East, with a commission from the magazine *Asia* to shoot stills and motion pictures of native life in fifteen countries, from Mongolia to Borneo.[44] He settled in Hollywood, and married for the third time. Throughout the 1920s and 1930s, he worked as a freelancer, selling topical films and travelogues. In 1927, he traveled to the Philippines and China, accompanied by his new wife, Maria. He dutifully recorded the usual travelogue scenes, such as the Great Wall and the Summer Palace in Peking, and then began work on a more controversial subject—the Chinese drug trade. The British authorities in Hong Kong, who quietly permitted the drug traffic, did not want a film exposé, and Thompson became an unwelcome visitor. They con-

---

[41] George Creel to Wilson, May 9, 1918, Box 2, Creel Papers, Library of Congress. See George T. Blakey, *Historians on the Homefront: American Propagandists for the Great War* (Lexington: University Press of Kentucky, 1970), 98–105.

[42] *Topeka State Journal*, March 6, 1918, 3.

[43] About seventy-five photographs are in the Red Cross Collection at the Library of Congress Prints and Photographs Division.

[44] *Topeka State Journal*, July 10, 1920, 7.

fiscated some of his film, but he held onto enough footage to produce a topical feature on the drug traffic and opium addiction.[45]

In the 1930s, Thompson filmed the Japanese invasion of China, the German occupation of Austria, the Italian campaign in Ethiopia, and the Spanish Civil War. Visiting St. Joseph, Missouri, in 1937, the "adventurer-correspondent" described meetings with Hitler and Mussolini, and offered a comparison of how they handled the foreign press. The "unsmiling fuehrer," said Thompson, seemed ill at ease, but Mussolini was "a born showman" who got on well with the correspondents.[46] Thompson said he was planning to leave for China to cover the Nationalist government's resistance to the Japanese. This may have been his last foreign adventure; his photographs of the Japanese attack on Shanghai have been preserved, but no film or stills shot after this time have been found. He seems to have retired before the beginning of World War II and died in Southern California in July 1947.[47]

Further Reading

Castellan, James W., Ron van Dopperen, and Cooper C. Graham, eds. *American Cinematographers in the Great War, 1914–1918.* Bloomington: Indiana University Press, 2015.

Mould, David H. *American Newsfilm, 1914–1919: The Underexposed War.* New York: Routledge, 2014.

Pipes, Richard. *A Concise History of the Russian Revolution.* New York: Knopf, 1995.

Rappaport, Helen. *Caught in the Revolution: Petrograd 1917.* London: Hutchinson, 2016.

---

[45] Interview with Thompson's relative, Lester William Burton, of Topeka, Kansas, April 1982. Some still photographs from the China trip are in the Donald Thompson file at the Kansas State Historical Society in Topeka.

[46] "Man Who Has Interviewed Dictators Gives Views Here," *St. Joseph* (MO) *Gazette*, April 7, 1937. See also *Wichita Eagle*, May 17, 1936.

[47] California Death Index, Los Angeles County, state file number 47-52543.

Editor's Note

In 1979, while doing research for my Master's thesis on American news film in World War I at the University of Kansas, I came across a reference in the movie trade press to "Donald Thompson—the daredevil war photographer from Topeka, Kansas." He sounded like a character with a story to tell, so I went through the local newspaper clippings, viewed his films, found a relative in Topeka who shared family photos, and devoted a thesis chapter to him.

Thompson has been a part of my research life ever since. I've found documents, film footage, and photos in archives in Washington, DC, Chicago, and Los Angeles. I've shown Thompson's films at public libraries and universities, and analyzed his work as a war photographer in journal articles and conference papers. Just when I think that our almost forty-year relationship is finally over, another opportunity arises. I was delighted to be invited to edit *Donald Thompson in Russia* for the *Americans in Revolutionary Russia* series.

Two people deserve credit for the fact that I am still writing about Thompson—my mentor, the late Charles Berg, Professor of Film at the University of Kansas, and film historian Ray Fielding, whose book, *The American Newsreel, 1911–1967*, inspired my research.

My thanks to Belen Marco Crespo for designing the maps for the book. You'll be thankful for the Petrograd 1917 map as you follow Thompson on his adventures.

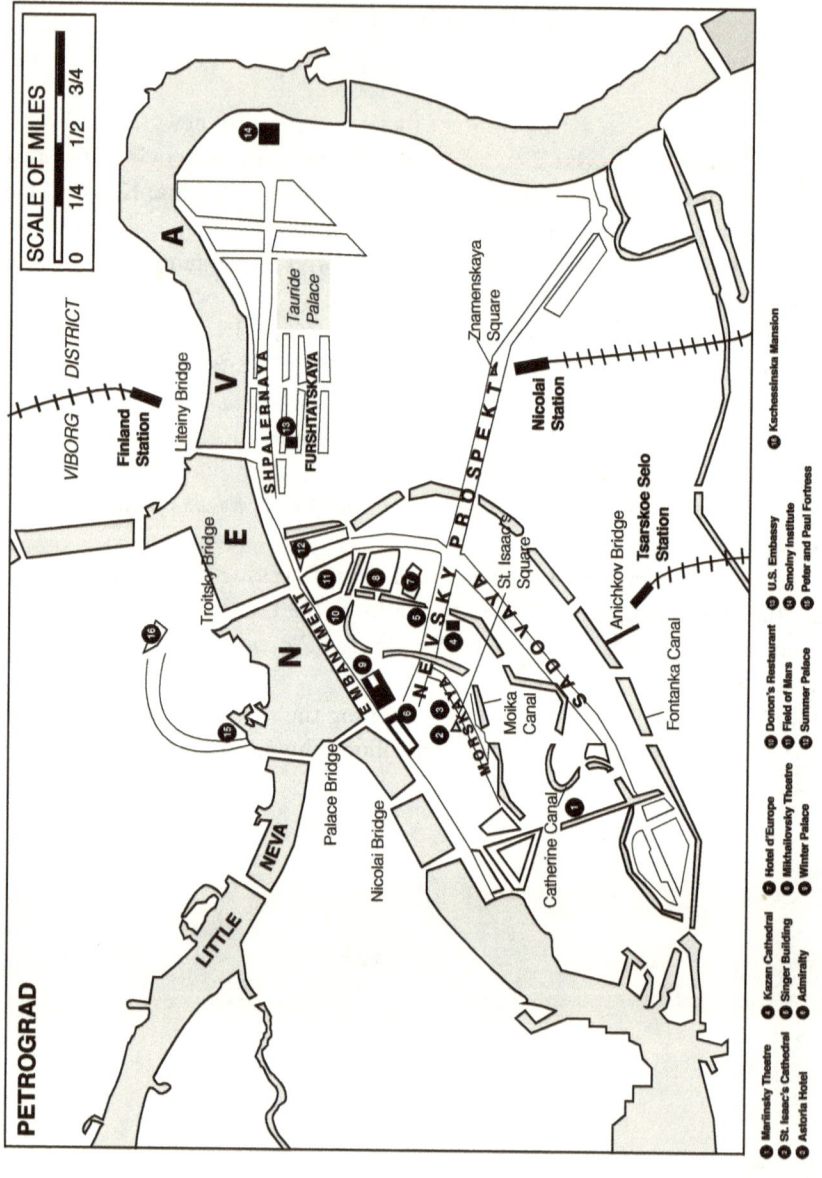

Figure 1. Petrograd, 1917. Map by Belén Marco Crespo.

DONALD THOMPSON IN RUSSIA

BY
DONALD C. THOMPSON

WITH NUMEROUS
PHOTOGRAPHS
BY THE AUTHOR

NEW YORK
THE CENTURY CO.
1918

TO DOT
**WHO COMES FROM THE
FINEST STATE IN
THE UNION
KANSAS**

Introduction

When Austria declared war on Serbia, July 28, 1914, I was working on a newspaper in Canada. My first impulse was to go to Europe, though I did not dream at that time what the war would mean. On August 1, when Germany declared war on Russia, and I heard that Luxembourg had been invaded, I knew that the war of nations, that we had read so much about but never dreamed would come true, had started. As a newspaper photographer, I knew it would be the greatest story in history, and I determined that I was going to cover it. I wired *Leslie's Weekly* in New York, but the wire was delayed. I didn't wait for the answer. I sold everything I had, pawned my watch, and bought a complete photographic outfit and my steamship ticket, which left me about fifteen dollars cash.[1]

Arriving at Liverpool I proceeded to London, took a taxi to the Savoy Hotel and asked for a room with bath, not knowing that that would take almost all my fifteen dollars for the first night. I made application to the British Foreign Office, presented my passport and credentials and was told that I would be allowed to go to the front as soon as the French gave permission. After a wait of two days I thought I would hurry matters along by going to Paris. I could not pay my hotel bill; I left my scanty baggage, except my cameras, as security.

Reaching Paris, I called on Mr. Myron T. Herrick, the American Ambassador, who gave me an introduction to the French War Office. There they told me that they would be only too glad to have me go to the front as soon as the English war office gave permission. I realized at once that no photographer was going to be permitted at the front if they could help it, so I pawned the last piece of jewelry I had and left Paris for the French front on my own responsibility.

I rode as far as I could on the train, and then walked at night until I caught up with the Second Army. I was arrested fourteen times before I actually reached the firing-line.[2] My first photographs were made with the English Fifth Royal Scots at the battle of Mons.

---

[1] For an account of Thompson's career as a photographer on the Western and Eastern Fronts and the Balkans from 1914 to 1917, see David H. Mould, *American Newsfilm 1914–1919: The Underexposed War* (New York: Routledge, 2014), 100–27.

[2] Thompson had a letter from the Canadian Ministry of Militia, giving him permission to film its troops in France and Belgium. He used this to bluff his way through checkpoints, claiming he was trying to catch up with the Canadian troops.

I then returned to London and went to Belgium for the *New York World* which, with the London *Daily Mail*, bought all my pictures at the highest price which at that time had ever been paid for war photographs. After this I took a steamer over from Folkestone to Ostend. There at the American Consulate I met Mr. Johnson, the Consul, who introduced me to E. Alexander Powell of the *New York World*, one of the first war correspondents to be given a permit to accompany the Belgian army. I noticed that Mr. Powell had a Belgian military car and that the soldiers jumped at his bidding. I thought that was the way I ought to travel. I told Mr. Powell that I wanted to get to Antwerp, and he wanted to know what for. I told him I would photograph the German atrocities that he was writing about. Powell replied that a photographer had as much chance of getting permission to photograph in Belgium as the Germans did of taking Paris. I told him I should go to Antwerp anyway, and he finally consented to give me a lift in his car to that point. We left Ostend the same afternoon after luncheon, arriving in Antwerp about seven o'clock.

While at dinner I heard Mr. Powell mention that King Albert lived a few doors down on the Place de Meir. Without waiting to finish my dinner, I excused myself, and walked up the street. Before the guard knew it I was past him. As I arrived in front of the door leading into the palace, it opened; and as it opened I stepped in. One of the servants began arguing with me, but as he spoke only French it fell against a stone wall so far as I was concerned. While he and I were arguing, he in French and I in English, M. Bassompierre, First Secretary to the Minister of Foreign Affairs, came down the stairs and asked in English, "What do you want?"

I replied that Mr. Powell, of the *New York World*, was telling the story of Belgium's sufferings at the hands of the Germans, of the atrocities the invaders were committing, and that I thought Belgium should have a record of these that could never be disputed, a photographic record that could be laid down at the peace table and would prove Belgium's case, no matter how strong the German denial might be.

M. Bassompierre asked me to step into a sort of library. After a ten hours' wait I was invited into another room. I noticed a tall gentleman sitting at a writing desk, a green lamp casting its reflection over him. Stepping up to the desk, I met his gaze. He asked me what I wanted. I replied that I wished to see King Albert of Belgium. "I am Albert, King of the Belgians," he said.

A few years before I had been husking corn in Kansas. For a few seconds I could not speak a word. The first thing that came into my mind was this: "King Albert," I said, "I have never met a king before in my life." (It was hard enough for me to hold a pair of jacks in a poker game.) "I do not know what to say except to tell you that I am here and what I want to do." I then explained that the world at large would believe the stories of Belgium's heroic fight against the Germans, but the stories of German atrocities were so awful that the people would doubt them. If he had photographs, however, the world could see what the German armies were doing in Belgium.[3]

The result was that I was given the famous *laissez passer* in Belgium. It was addressed to the armies of Belgium and to the civil authorities, commanding them to allow Donald C. Thompson to photograph, and to come and go as he pleased, and for them to assist him in every way possible. This was signed by King Albert and countersigned by General De Guys, Commander in Chief of the Belgian forces.

I followed the Belgians through thirty-two battles, remaining with them until the fall of Antwerp. Earlier I had been with the German armies, and when Antwerp was evacuated I remained with Mr. Powell in that city. What happened then I shall tell some day in another story. It is enough to say that I saw the German machine at work, probably as few others saw it. I saw German intrigue spread its foul net over Belgium. I was asked to become an agent, in other words a spy, for the Germans. My reward was to be money. I accepted their money, but their dastardly work I did not do. The money I spent in cafés in many a capital in Europe, afterward, and I am only sorry they didn't give me more.[4]

I was wounded later at Dixmude. When I recovered, Lord Northcliffe, of the London *Times*,[5] asked me to go into Germany. The Germans had found out that most of my photographs had been examined by the British military officials in search of information. As a result of this a reward had been posted for Mr. Powell and for me. I

---

[3] Allied propaganda in the United States in 1914 and 1915 claimed the German army had committed atrocities in Belgium. Most American correspondents who toured behind the German lines found no evidence for the claims. In a telegram to the Associated Press, a group of correspondents reported: "In spirit fairness we unite in declaring German atrocities groundless as far as we are able to. After spending two weeks with German army accompanying troops upward hundred miles we unable report single instance unprovoked reprisal. Also unable confirm rumors mistreatment prisoners or non-combatants ... Numerous investigated rumors proved groundless. [...] Discipline German soldiers excellent as observed. No drunkenness." At the time, Thompson agreed; in December 1915, he told his hometown newspaper, the *Topeka Daily Capital*, that he had seen no evidence of atrocities in Belgium. His assertion here that atrocities were committed was likely prompted by his experiences in 1917. Thompson found German spies and agitators wherever he looked—from Romania to China to Russia—and he consistently attributed street demonstrations and political turmoil in Petrograd to German intrigue and duplicity. Atrocity claims neatly fitted his conspiracy thesis.

[4] As a photographer from a neutral country, Thompson was able to work on both sides of the lines in Belgium in 1914. Reports and interviews with Thompson in newspapers and the motion picture trade press in 1915 and 1916 do not mention the offer to become a German agent, so this story may, like Thompson's assertion about German atrocities, simply be part of his post-1917 German intrigue narrative.

[5] By World War I, Alfred Harmsworth, 1st Viscount Northcliffe, was Britain's leading newspaper magnate. He was a pioneer in tabloid journalism, with the popular *Daily Mail, Daily Mirror,* and *Sunday Dispatch*. In 1905, he acquired the up-market but financially struggling *Observer* and in 1908 *The Times* and *The Sunday Times*.

paid no attention to this. When Lord Northcliffe asked me to go back into Germany, I accepted. First I went down to the *Daily Mail* office and had an interview with myself set up. In this I said that the English were a pack of liars and the Germans all gentlemen, that I had never seen an atrocity committed in Belgium, and that all the photographs of that nature that had appeared in American and English papers and, for that matter, in papers throughout the world with my name on them were fakes for which I was not responsible. I put an Abraham & Straus advertisement and some other camouflage on the back of the sheet; then I clipped out the interview, and the piece of paper looked as if it was a clipping from an enormously popular Brooklyn newspaper which doesn't exist, but which I called the *Daily Observer*.

The day I went back into Germany from London, I ran into Charlie Wheeler, of the *Chicago Tribune*, who was on his way to interview Cardinal Mercier.[6] As soon as we crossed the Holland border into Belgium, I was arrested by the Germans, beaten up and thrown into prison. Of course I was searched, and they found the clipping, which was sent to Antwerp. After it had been read by military and police officials, I was released and apologies were offered me. The great German Secret Service had been fooled by a fake newspaper clipping! I was reliably informed that not only Von der Goltz[7] but also Baron von Munn, who then called himself the head of the German Press Bureau in Berlin, but who was really the head of the German Secret Service, fell for it and didn't know the difference until a German spy, working in the *Daily Mail* office in London, got word to them. But I managed to escape from Berlin into Holland—which is still another story.

In January 1915, Robert R. McCormick, then war correspondent of the *Chicago Tribune*, now a Major on General Pershing's staff in France, received an invitation from the Russian government to visit the different fronts in Russia. Mr. McCormick invited me to make the trip with him. In February, we started for Russia by way of the Balkan States. To me it was one of the greatest trips I have ever had. Mr. McCormick had letters of introduction, passes to every country in Europe, and was received as no other war correspondent has ever been received during this war. Wherever he appeared the government officials went out of their way to assist him. In Russia, when we arrived, it was the same thing; nothing was too good for Mr. McCormick, and as

---

[6] Désiré-Félicien-François-Joseph Mercier (1851–1926) was a Belgian cardinal of the Roman Catholic Church, noted for his staunch resistance to the German occupation. He distributed a strong pastoral letter to be read in all his churches, urging the Belgian people to keep up their spirits.

[7] Wilhelm Leopold Colmar, Baron von der Goltz (1843–1916), a field marshal in the German army, served as military governor of Belgium.

I was in his party the same kindness was shown me. Mr. McCormick secured permission for me to accompany him on his trip and to photograph the Russian armies.[8]

When I arrived at the front and saw the great masses of men, I expected to follow the armies into Berlin a few weeks later. In talking to officers I was surprised to find that a great many of them spoke English. They told me that I would not see much fighting. This I could not understand. In Belgium I had seen only a small army advancing against that German machine and biting it and putting dents into it, but here in Russia, wherever I went, it seemed that there were millions of men; I could not understand why they did not push the German army aside and go where they pleased.[9]

I remember one evening in the Carpathians at Hill 1102, while I was rolled up in my blanket, talking to the officer of a Cossack regiment, of which I was a guest, I asked him why the Russian army didn't take Berlin. He said that Russia when she went to war had failed to lock up the Germans and that she was now paying the price. Their generals were bought, their ammunition was going astray, and they were losing thousands of men in fruitless battles as a consequence. In Petrograd the excuse was made that the Germans had lived there a long time and had become citizens of Russia. I was also told there something I didn't know before, that a German might take out naturalization papers in another country without losing his citizenship in Germany. I was told that German citizens in Petrograd worked as they pleased, that they were supplied with a great deal of money and were permitted to buy any one they could. They caused thousands to die in hospitals, for while millions had been appropriated for field hospitals, German intrigue had diverted that money into other channels.

Later I saw lying in front of field hospitals hundreds of poor Russian wounded, dying because of the German intrigue that was working throughout Russia. When ammunition was received on one sector it would be found that the shells would not fit the guns there, the proper shells for that front having been sent elsewhere to supply

---

[8] McCormick and Thompson traveled via Greece, Bulgaria, and Romania to Petrograd, arriving in early April 1915. After an audience with Tsar Nicholas II at Tsarskoe Selo, the pair traveled to the Galician front where Thompson filmed members of the Russian General Staff, military parades and drills, artillery in action in the Carpathian Mountains, field hospitals, refugees, and scenes on the front line. The *Chicago Tribune* released *With the Russians at the Front* in August 1915, a week before *The German Side of the War*. McCormick wrote an extensive account of the trip and his meetings with military staff, politicians, and diplomats in *With the Russian Army, Being the Experiences of a National Guardsman* (New York: MacMillan, 1915).

[9] The war had begun disastrously for the Russians. At the end of August, the Second Army, which had advanced into Prussia, was surrounded and defeated at the Battle of Tannenberg, where the Germans took 92,000 prisoners. However, to the south in Galicia, the Russians routed the Austro-Hungarian armies and besieged the fortress of Przemysl, which eventually surrendered in March 1915. The victory was short-lived. By the time McCormick and Thompson arrived at the front, a combined German-Austrian offensive had ended with victory at the Battle of Gorlice-Tarnow in May. Nevertheless, McCormick and Thompson offered positive assessments of the competence of the General Staff and the fighting spirit of the soldiers.

guns that could not use them.[10] I saw the Russian soldier fight, and he seemed to me as brave as any soldier in Europe. I had seen the Prussian Guard charge, I had seen the Uhlans make a dash in a village in Belgium, but when I saw the Russian soldiers in the Carpathians climb into the firing-line trenches with only wooden clubs in their hands, I realized that they were men with fighting blood in them. Those Russian soldiers would wait until other Russian soldiers had been killed or wounded and then take up their guns. I visited the various Russian fronts, and everywhere I found the same fear that German intrigue would undo in one day what it was taking months of hard fighting to accomplish.

I left Russia for Romania, arriving at Bucharest the day that war was declared on Italy by Austria. The streets were crowded with cheering thousands. The Italian Embassy was next door to the German Embassy, and while the Italian Ambassador was delivering a speech to the Romanian people, the minions of the German Ambassador from the roof of the embassy threw eggs down at him; most of the eggs that did not hit me, hit him. I was making pictures at the time, and it seemed to me that every egg in the world hit me or my camera. I remember that afterward someone told me that several eggs had struck the Italian Ambassador. "They must have glanced off me," I said.

I was told by the chief of police of Bucharest, with whom I had luncheon the following day, that Germany had thousands of spies on her pay-roll in that city alone. The spies were employed as chambermaids, street-cleaners, clerks, and cabmen; in fact, they were found in every walk of life, even to government officials themselves, and all were liberally paid.

From Romania, I traveled into Bulgaria, where I was arrested and held for a week at Sofia. At the end of a week I was released from prison and placed on a train. When I asked why I had been arrested no reason was given me; to this day I don't know what the reason was. I finally got to Nish, in Serbia. There I spent a day before going down to Constantinople and on to the Gallipoli front, where I spent a couple of weeks with the Turkish army. While in Serbia I met Dr. Richard P. Strong of the Harvard Medical School, who was just finishing his wonderful campaign against typhus.[11] German

---

[10] As Richard Pipes notes, Russia's state-controlled munitions factories "lacked the capacity to meet the demands of a modern war." At the end of 1914, with mobilization complete, Russia had 6.5 million men under arms but only 4.6 million rifles. Factories could produce a maximum of 9,000 artillery shells per month, and within months many batteries ran out of shells and could not reply to enemy fire. Movement of men and supplies was hampered by an inadequate railroad system, most of it single-track. Of the warring powers, Russia had only 1.1 kilometers of railroad track per 100 square kilometers, compared to Germany's 10.6 and Austria-Hungary's 6.4. Transportation problems, primarily the congested railroad system, led to the food shortages that contributed to popular unrest in Petrograd in 1917. See Richard Pipes, *A Concise History of the Russian Revolution* (New York: Knopf, 1995), 59–60.

[11] Richard Pearson Strong did significant work on plague, cholera, bacillary dysentery, and other diseases. He was the first professor of tropical medicine at Harvard, and his department was eventually incorporated into the Harvard School of Public Health, founded in 1922.

intrigue started to work shortly after and it was not long before Serbia was crushed, principally by force of overwhelming armies, but partly by the devious methods that Germans love and excel in. Later in Rome I saw the same methods at work. After that in Greece I saw German influence undermining the national spirit.

In Rome, I was told by an Italian officer that although Italy had a wonderful army it would be thrown back some day, because there were too many Germans running loose in the country, doing the dirty work of the Kaiser. In short, every country that I visited that is now at war with Germany, and had not locked up its Germans, has since felt the disastrous effect of the Teutonic spy system.

In July, 1916, I was once more on the French front, where I was wounded by a fragment of shell. I returned to the United States as soon as I was able. On November 14, 1916, my family physician told me that my fractured skull from my last wound had healed, and that I could go to work again. On November 15, I called on John Sleicher, publisher of *Leslie's Weekly*,[12] to discuss my next assignment. "The Chief" told me that he wanted a series of pictures from the Romanian front and that I had better start immediately, making my headquarters at Bucharest, for the papers were then full of Romania's great advance. I told "The Chief" that I doubted very much if I could get to Romania in time to get any pictures. He naturally wanted to know why, when things seemed to be going so well with the Romanian armies. I told him that when I was in Romania in 1915, Bucharest was infested with thousands and thousands of German spies, and that although Romania had started to advance, her army was threatened by intrigue in the rear. He seemed incredulous, but I insisted that the German agents in Bucharest would undo in one week what Romania had accomplished in months. "The Chief" smiled, however, and told me to do my best.

Florence Harper,[13] one of Leslie's correspondents, was going to Petrograd, so it was arranged that we should sail on the same steamer. I thereupon set out to buy a new photographic outfit. People used to tell me that German cameras made the best pictures, but I have used graflex cameras,[14] made by the Eastman Company, on every front in Europe and have never lost a picture through the fault of the camera. I have seen other people use German cameras and fail to equal the results that I have

---

[12] *Frank Leslie's Illustrated Newspaper*, later renamed *Leslie's Weekly*, was an American illustrated literary and news magazine founded in 1852. The weekly developed a reputation for its enterprising war coverage, from the Civil War to World War II, with reports, illustrations and photographs.

[13] Florence MacLeod Harper was apparently the first American female journalist to arrive in Petrograd in 1917. She and Thompson worked as a team during most of their time in Russia. Harper published an account of her experiences in *Runaway Russia* (New York: Century, 1918).

[14] From 1912, the Eastman Kodak company produced large- and medium-format Graflex press cameras. Their quality and rugged design made them a popular choice for photojournalists for half a century.

obtained with the American made goods. I also use American lenses. I have never used a German lens and never will.

On November 20, a banquet was given me by *Leslie's Weekly*, and I left the following day for the West, sailing November 30 on the steamer *Empress of Russia*. I promised my wife that I would write her daily letters while I was away, and this book is made up of letters written by me throughout my seven months' trip. They were not written for publication and, indeed, at the time they were penned the idea of writing a book had never entered my head. These letters tell a story that I know a great many people may doubt. Fortunately, the details are largely substantiated by the motion-picture film I have shown in this country,[15] supplemented by thousands of photographs which have appeared in *Leslie's Weekly* and in newspapers throughout the world.

When I came back from Russia, after one of the most exciting trips of my life, I was glad that I could show the whole world the proofs that German intrigue was the cause of Russia's downfall. German intrigue, working among the unthinking masses, has brought Russia to her present woeful condition. As these pages are being written the situation looks very dark, but I hope that a change for the better is not far off. The one man who, in my judgment, could bring order out of chaos and stand the nation on its feet, is the Grand Duke Nicholas, the biggest man in all Russia, the man that German intrigue never could buy, the man who was deposed as commander in chief of the Russian armies and sent to the Caucasus because the German armies could not whip him.[16] Every true friend of Russia should pray for the day when he shall start his march from the Caucasus toward the capital, for millions of loyal Russians will flock to his standard, and the Bolsheviks, the Socialists, and the anarchists will be crushed under the Russian steam-roller with Grand Duke Nicholas at the throttle.

Let me add, too, that every true friend of the United States should pray that our own beloved country shall not suffer from the same policy that has brought Russia to national shame and impotence—the unrestricted liberty allowed to myriads of rabid German residents who put Kaiserism above every holy instinct of humanity and democracy.

---

[15] *The German Curse in Russia*, also called *Blood-Stained Russia*, was released in December 1917, the same month that Russia withdrew from the war and the Germans occupied Ukraine.

[16] Grand Duke Nikolai Nikolaevich Romanov of Russia (1856–1929) was a grandson of Tsar Nicholas I of Russia, and a cousin of Tsar Nicholas II. He served as commander in chief of the Russian armies in the first year of the war, including the catastrophic defeat in East Prussia where the Russians lost a quarter of a million men. He oversaw the strategic retreat from Poland in spring 1915, and was later a successful commander in chief on the Caucasus Front.

I. Yokohama, Japan, December 12, 1916

Dear Dot:

The steamer docked this afternoon after a very rough passage. Captain Robinson, the ship's commander, said it was the roughest passage he had ever made. One evening, the fourth day out, we had waves thirty feet high and I guess the missionaries who were on the boat thought that their end had come, for they started an all-night prayer meeting. I did not attend, as I had a date in the smoking room with Bill Church, Ed Throckmorton, and Kelly, a tobacco man of New York. A crap game was started. Just when you would start to reach for the money, after seeing "7" or "11" on the dice, the boat would give another roll and "craps" would appear. As it was, I came out ahead.

In the smoking room, I met Sam Blythe of the *Saturday Evening Post,* and Tom Millard, the editor of one of the American papers in China. I hope to see Millard again when I pass through Shanghai.

I will not go to Bucharest, now that the Germans have captured it. I met a Russian army officer here who gave me the story of Romania. We had met in Russia in 1915, and when he saw me, he came up and recalled himself to my memory. He said that Romania had paid the price of German intrigue at court, and especially in Petrograd. Assistance promised by Russia had not been sent [to] Romania. Trainloads of the ammunition that had been delivered to the Romania front was purposely of the wrong caliber, with the result that the Romanians had to fall back and abandon their capital. He said, too, that they had left the Dobrudja border unprotected, after they had made a great advance and had invaded the Hungarian province of Transylvania. German agents found ways to have the border left unguarded, so that German and Bulgarian armies under Field Marshal von Mackensen easily compelled the Romanian armies to withdraw from Transylvania. When that army had given way, General von Falkenhayn attacked what was left, broke through the passes and swept across southern Romania. Bucharest, I learned, had fallen on December 6. Generals von Mackensen and von Falkenhayn then joined forces and occupied all of Wallachia and the Dobrudja.

I think I shall go to Jassy[1] anyway, as it is now the capital, and I do not think it is possible for the Fritzes to advance that far before I get there. I am going to take a little longer than I planned, and stop in Manila for about a week.

---

[1] Jassy, today Iași, a city in northeastern Romania, and former capital of the Principality of Moldavia.

I am writing this at my desk near a window which overlooks the harbor at Yokohama. It does not look like the Japan of old. In every direction are factories. It is now one o'clock at night and they are as brilliantly lighted as they were early in the evening. I am told that dock-yards and factories are working twenty-four hours a day. For the life of me I cannot understand why Japan does not do something. Japan has been in this war over two years, and beyond capturing a little island from the Germans she has done nothing at all. My Russian officer claims that his country is receiving very little ammunition from Japan. I asked him what Japan was doing with all the ammunition she manufactured. He replied, "She is making it for herself." He said that Japan had offered to send troops to France if England would give, or rather sell, her all of her battleships of the Queen Elizabeth type after the war. I fear Japan is getting ready for another war against some other nation than Germany. Will write you as soon as I get to Manila.

Don

II. Manila, January 5, 1917

Dear Dot:

I have been intending to write you every day, but have been so busy that this letter must cover a long interval. I found your letters and cables awaiting me here. I met General Liggett and had a long talk with him; also, visited Fort S— and gave a little talk on the war there.

Dr. Thomson, who has charge of Bilibid Prison,[2] told me that I could make a film of the prison, and I have just finished a remarkable story of what our government has done to this old Spanish jail. I was never so surprised at anything as I was with the change that has been made in it; I venture to say it is now the most modern institution of the kind in the world, and one of the best managed.

Wednesday of this week I went out to Cavite,[3] the naval base here, with Throckmorton and Church (tennis players who are contesting here for the Far Eastern Championship) and we were invited to make a trip in one of the submarines of the B type. When we were down in the submarine, one of the officers commanding it played a joke on us. After we had submerged and were down about forty feet, they allowed us apparently to run the boat. I had to keep it balanced and Church and Throckmorton each had a wheel they were supposed to watch. While we were intent on our "duties" the lights went out. The officer gave an order to turn on the storage lights. A sailor

---

[2] The Old Bilibid Prison, known as Carcel y Presidio Correccional (Correctional Jail and Military Prison) in the center of Manila, was established by the Spanish colonial government in 1865.

[3] Control over the port of Cavite was turned over to the United States by Spain after the Treaty of Paris of 1898. It became the main base for U.S. naval forces in the Philippines.

bawled out that they would not work. Then we got orders to rise at once. I glanced at the dial in front of me and it looked, to me, as though we were going down fast. Then I felt a splash of water. The first thought I had was that someone had left one of the hatches open and that we were being drowned like rats in a trap. Then lights were turned on, and it took Church, Throckmorton and me about five minutes to pull ourselves together. A telltale bucket in the hands of one of the officers put us wise to what had happened. Bill Church claimed he wasn't afraid, but Eddie Throckmorton and I told the truth when we said we were never more frightened in all our lives.

After I had been in Manila a few days, a weekly paper published here came out with a long story which read something like this: "By the SS *Empress of Russia*, there arrived two people, one by the name of Donald C. Thompson, who calls himself staff photographer of *Leslie's Weekly*, and Florence Harper, staff correspondent of *Leslie's Weekly*. Both are registered at the Manila Hotel." The editor then went on to say that he had read *Leslie's* for years and had never heard of Thompson or Florence Harper, and wound up with the insinuation that they were a couple of fakers, out for a good time.

This editor, I am told, receives money from the Germans for publishing such statements. His policy has been to attack anyone who shows sympathy for the Allies. I swore out a warrant for his arrest at the request of the Prosecuting Attorney of the Philippine government, who informed me that it would not be necessary for me to remain in Manila to prosecute, but that they would secure all the evidence necessary. So this editor may spend several years in Bilibid Prison. His wife and little child have begged me several times to withdraw the charge. I would do it, but I am told that he has libeled so many people that he is overdue at the jail. And really, Dot, he is a dangerous man to be left outside of a prison, especially in the Philippines. This again shows how German propaganda is working throughout the world. I wonder how long it will be before America wakes up to its dangers![4]

I am leaving tomorrow on the SS *Shinyo Maru* for Hong Kong, from which place I will write you.

Don

---

[4] After a lower court ruled in September 1917 that the article was libelous, the editor of the *Philippine Weekly*, Daniel O'Connell, appealed to the Supreme Court of the Philippines. In a unanimous decision, the justices upheld the verdict. "Mr. O'Connell," they wrote, "intended to charge Mrs. Harper and Mr. Thompson with having told falsehoods, intended to ridicule them as war correspondents by terming them 'comedians' and 'bunko artists,' and finally intended the public to think of them as travelling together under circumstances which were highly immoral." O'Connell was ordered to pay a fine of 500 pesos. G.R. No. L-13173, The United States vs. Daniel O'Connell, March 11, 1918 (Philippine Law and Jurisprudence Databank).

III. Shanghai, January 22, 1917

My dear Girl:

Arrived in Shanghai at nine p.m. after a pleasant trip from Hong Kong. I am leaving in a few days for Pekin. Then I start for Harbin and on from there by the Trans-Siberian Railroad to Petrograd. I have given up my plan to visit Jassy.

I paid a visit to the big gambling-house here, which is located just outside the European concession in Chinese territory, and found it full of Europeans playing roulette. The playing here has increased a great deal in the last few years, and the sky is the limit. I had something like $120 loose but luck was with me. After I had played about four hours I walked out with $8,000 gold. That will buy a nice lot of presents for you.

Exchange here is a funny thing. I took over to a bank my American Express letter of credit and told them I wanted $1,000 Mex. The Chinese cashier took his little bead-board, ran up and down it for about eight or nine minutes and then handed me a bunch of Chinese bank-notes. After counting the money, I asked him if he hadn't made a mistake. He counted it again, handed it back and said, no. I got mad and asked for the manager. After waiting about five minutes I was ushered into his office. I told him that the bank had robbed me. He asked me to explain. I did. Then he told me where I got off. You see, first you must change dollars into taels[5] and then the taels into Mexican dollars, and they lop off some of your money each time. He told me that the Mexican dollar is still going up, and that by next year it would be worth as much as a gold dollar. When I was in China a few years ago it was worth only forty-eight cents.

I concluded to wait until I got to Pekin to cash my check, as I had enough money to keep me going. I told the cashier that I wanted my letter of credit back, and turned in the roll he had short-changed me with. He got out his bead-machine, did some more figuring, this time doing it in about five minutes; then he told me I owed him thirty-five dollars Mex. That was the exchange on turning my letter of credit into taels and then turning the taels back into my letter of credit. Back to the office of the manager I went again. He saw the point, and gave me back my letter of credit and called it square. But the other fellow was out to make a dividend for the bank on that bead-machine of his.

Shanghai is full of Germans who are busy night and day. It is a regular pest-hole for German spies. I found a man in my room night before last going through my baggage. When I asked him what he was doing, he told me that he had been hired by my valet to look after me for the day, and he was just arranging my things. That was good for a laugh, as you know I never had a valet in my life. I called the manager of the

---

[5] A Chinese unit of weight that, when applied to silver, was long used as a unit of currency. Most taels were equivalent to 1.3 ounces of silver.

hotel, to whom he told the same story. The manager had him searched but nothing of mine was found on him, so he was allowed to go. Coarse work, I call it, but it has taught me I must be very careful of my passports, credentials, etc.

Don

IV. Pekin, February 14

Dear Dot:

I had a very interesting visit in Pekin. The Chinese government officials sent invitations for me to visit different points of interest. I had several long talks with members of the cabinet. I find them, in a way, in sympathy with the Allies. Some of them, though, I am doubtful of.

The two managers of the — hotel are Swiss. That is, they have Swiss passports. They were very nice until I found one of them going through my baggage with the aid of a couple of coolies. I saw my Russian credentials laid on the table with other papers that they had already taken out of my bag. I immediately slammed him one in the jaw, grabbed my papers and kicked him out of the room. I went down to the office and met the other manager, who asked me what I meant by such conduct. I asked him what his partner meant. He then accused me of stealing towels. Later, when I was leaving the hotel, they tried to gang me with a lot of coolies, but a Mr. Sulzberger and his brother from New York came to my assistance, and the coolies were afraid to start anything.

I also had a great deal of trouble in getting my baggage checked to Harbin on the Chinese government railroad. When I got to the station they told me I was only allowed one trunk which could weigh only a limited number of pounds. Well, as I was carrying three trunks packed with motion-picture films and photographic supplies, my baggage weighed almost a ton. I had to buy ten extra railroad tickets with sleeping-car accommodations for each ticket. Florence Harper, on account of her extra baggage, had to buy six extra railroad tickets. This was a hold-up. There were only nine passengers on the whole train from Pekin to Mukden. I was the only passenger in my sleeping-car, but I had paid for most of the state-rooms.

The Chinese railroad officials told me that people had been sending so many goods into Russia as personal belongings, by paying excess baggage, that they had to use this means to keep the trains from being swamped with trunks.

This train is pretty good. The dining-car service is not bad. At Mukden I transfer to the Japanese railroad, changing again a few hours out from Harbin to the Russian line. I am due at Harbin some time Friday.

Don

V. Harbin, February 18, 1917

Dear Dot:

I arrived at Harbin[6] this afternoon at 4:30. There was a report current that our train was to be stopped and that the Russians are going to close the Manchurian border and not allow any one in or out of Russia. Why this is, I don't know.

The city here is covered with about two feet of snow, and the thermometer is sometimes about twenty-two degrees below zero. Harbin has many Chinese, but almost every nationality in the world can be seen here. It is an international city, in other ways: You can get anything you want to drink here. The Russians have only the right to run their railroad through here, their territory being a strip some ten miles wide.

The station at Harbin is stacked with mail from the floor to the roof, all parcels post. Outside you find more mail covered over with canvas. I asked an Englishman here what it was; he told me that leather and other articles are so scarce and command such high prices in Russia that the people are using the parcels post as the quickest way to ship things into Russia. He said that this was a small stack compared with what they generally had in the station.

I am writing this letter at a little café in Harbin. At 11:30 tonight our train arrives here from Vladivostok, remains an hour, and then goes on its way. I will write you daily letters, if I can, on the train. Will cable you when I arrive in Petrograd, before I leave for the front.

Don

V. Saturday, February 17, 1917[7]

Dear Dot:

I am sitting out in the aisle of the International Sleeping Car in which my compartment is, using a book as a writing desk. The car has no heat to speak of, and there are no English-speaking people on board. Most of the passengers are Russians. The electric light does not work, so they gave us a candle to burn. There is only one blanket and one sheet for each bed. I lay in bed and almost froze. Finally, I got up and dressed, put on my fur coat and threw myself in bed again. My feet were next to the window, and they are cold yet. There is a stove on the platform that is supposed to

---

[6] Harbin was a major railroad junction city in Manchuria. To reduce travel time to the Far East, Russia had obtained a concession to build and administer the Chinese Eastern Railway as a southeastern branch of the Trans-Siberian Railway. It ran from Chita to Vladivostok across Manchuria. At Harbin, it linked with the main line running north from Peking and the port of Dalian.

[7] This may be an error because it is one day before the date of the previous letter when Thompson says he arrived in Harbin.

heat this car, but no heat from it seems to get back to my stateroom. The dining-car is eight cars ahead of us and we are given a coupon for first or second sitting. The food is not bad, but I do not care for the crowd on this train. It is too cold for long letters, so goodbye for the present.

Don

VI. En Route, February 24, 1917

Dear Dot:

About this time tomorrow I will be in Petrograd if the train stays on the track. As it is, the train is one day late now. I have, in a way, had a good time on this trip. Have met two or three English-speaking Russians who have given me a great deal of information. They have also told me something that I expect is going to cause a lot of trouble. They say there is a shortage of food in Petrograd, although I see there is plenty of food in every town we have passed through.[8] People on the train have bought halves of pigs, young suckling pigs, tubs of batter, etc., until the train looks like a meat shop. They hang this meat up in the vestibules of the cars. When I inquired the reason for this one of the Russian gentlemen told me about the shortage in Petrograd. I asked him how this happened, and he replied that it seemed to him to be the work of the Germans. I couldn't see how the Germans would get any benefit from that, but he said that the working people in Petrograd were very dissatisfied on account of the high prices and scarcity of food, and that I could expect trouble if the government did not take some means to bring food into Petrograd and to force the prices down.

He also told me that Russia would make a big spring advance, and that there is more ammunition in Russia now than there ever was before.

I also met a young man who was born in Romania. His mother is a Russian and his father an Englishman, but he has always lived in Russia, with the exception of a few years in Romania. He told me that I would have trouble in getting a room, but I assured him that I had cabled from New York and telegraphed from Pekin to the Astoria and would be taken care of when I arrived. He seems to be doubtful, though, and has sent a couple of wires along the line for himself. He has also volunteered to help me at the station in getting my baggage down to the hotel.

---

[8] By the end of 1916, Petrograd was facing a severe food shortage, which was to intensify because of the harsh winter. Historian Helen Rappaport notes that although output had been affected by the conscription of peasants into the army, "many of the shortages were artificial, caused by profiteering and the breakdown in the national railway system. At depots and supply centres in the food-producing south, flour and other food supplies lay stranded and rotting, for lack of rolling stock to bring them by rail to Russia's hungry cities in the north.... By now stories were rife in Petrograd about the deliberate stockpiling of flour, meat and sugar by speculators in order to push the prices ever higher," (Rappaport, *Caught in the Revolution: Petrograd 1917* [London: Hutchinson, 2016], 16–17).

But this Petrograd news has got me worried. Russia's action throughout this war has been the most dramatic of any of the nations fighting. She was one of the first to enter the war and has several times been on the point of quitting, but she always comes back.

I also heard that Romania had lost one of her important grain cities, where vast stores of wheat fell into Germany's hands. Russian officers at the front are of the opinion that if Russia can get away with this spring drive the war soon will be over, but they tell me that the German agents are working [with] more boldness than ever before.

I have also just heard that the monk Rasputin has been killed.[9] You will remember the pictures I had made of this man in 1915 and that I told you I thought he was a friend of the Germans. This has been confirmed by some of the officers on the train, who say he had been into Germany two or three times since the war started. I will try to get the complete story when I reach Petrograd, and will write you more about it.

Don

VII. Petrograd, February 26, 1917

Dear Dot:

Here I am in Petrograd at last. Reached here yesterday at 1:10 a.m. The thermometer was below zero when we arrived, and Florence Harper and I had a great deal of trouble in getting a droshky[10] to take us to the hotel. Our Russian-English-speaking friend volunteered to go to the hotel to act as interpreter for us, as he said the porter at the Astoria spoke only Russian. We were an hour and a half getting out of the railroad station and securing a droshky for our hand baggage.

When I arrived at the Astoria Hotel,[11] Mister English-speaking Russian did the talking. He said that they had a room for Florence Harper and a room for him, but

---

[9] The political establishment resented Rasputin's influence at court, particularly over the Empress Alexandra. While Tsar Nicholas was away at the front, Rasputin had virtual control over ministerial appointments. "From August 1915 on," writes Pipes, "it was impossible either to stay in office or obtain office without his consent." Some monarchists concluded that to be rid of the Empress, "it was only necessary to remove Rasputin, whom she allegedly needed to preserve her emotional equilibrium." After an attempt to bribe him to leave Petrograd failed, Prince Felix Iusupov hatched a plot in which he implicated Grand Duke Dmitrii, the Tsar's nephew, and Duma deputy Vladimir Purishkevich. On the night of December 16–17, Iusupov lured Rasputin to his palace where he and Purishkevich shot him. They weighed the body down with chains and threw it into a canal. It was discovered a few days later (Pipes, *A Concise History of the Russian Revolution*, 68–70, 73).

[10] A two or four-wheeled horse-drawn carriage.

[11] The Hotel Astoria on St. Isaac's Square was built in 1912 to cater to tourists coming to the city for the Romanov Tercentenary, a celebration of 300 years of imperial rule, in May 1913. It

none for me. This was after Florence Harper had gone up to her room. I argued and argued and argued. I asked him to tell the porter to let me sleep downstairs and I understood the porter to say "dada," which means yes. I waited until he had been shown to his room, and I then asked the porter, in the few words of Russian I know, where I was to sleep. All he said was "niet." "Niet" in Russian means no. Finally, I concluded that I was not going to be allowed even to sleep on a chair in the hotel office. Perhaps that is against the law; almost everything here is.

Well, I got mad and left. I thought I would go back to the railroad station and sleep there until the next day when I could straighten things out. Outside the hotel I found there wasn't a droshky to be had. I walked up the Morskaia to the Nevsky Prospekt,[12] and still did not see a droshky that was not in service. I walked to the Nikolai Station[13] in a blizzard. I was lucky in having left my baggage at the hotel. I arrived at the Nikolai Station about three o'clock in the morning, and started to walk in the front door. There I was stopped by a Russian soldier, who spoke only one word that I could understand, and that was "niet." I tried to see an officer, but found it impossible. I walked down the Nevsky Prospekt, looking for a doorway where I could stand and keep warm. I was never so tired in all my life and never so cold. Every time I stood in a doorway a policeman would come along and push me out. At last I had an inspiration: I spoke to a young woman, one of the number that were out on the street that late. She answered in Russian and I said "dada," yes. She took me by the arm and in about five minutes I found myself in what I took to be a second or third class Petrograd hotel. I made them understand that I wanted someone who understood English. After fifteen or twenty minutes a waiter, partly dressed, appeared on the scene. He asked me, in a sort of English, what was the trouble. I told him there

---

was named by its Russo-Swedish architect, Fredrik Lidvall, in honor of the Astor brothers, the New York hoteliers. With 350 rooms, telephone lines, a banqueting hall, and a French restaurant, it quickly became the most popular hotel in the city for foreign visitors, including diplomats, businessmen, and journalists. By 1917, it had become known as the "Military Hotel." "Every room," writes Helen Rappaport, "was crammed with either Allied officers—French, Romanian, Serbian, British and Italian—or Russian officers on leave from the front, many of whom had their wives, mothers and children with them" (*Caught in the Revolution*, 15–16, 109).

[12] Nevsky Prospekt, the main thoroughfare in Petrograd, was named for Alexander Nevsky, the thirteenth-century prince whose military victories repelled German and Swedish invaders. Planned by Peter the Great as the beginning of the road to Novgorod and Moscow, the avenue runs from the Admiralty on the bank of the Neva to the Nikolai (now Moscow) Railway Station and, after making a turn at Znamenskaya (Vosstaniya) Square, back to the river at the Alexander Nevsky Lavra (monastery). Most of the major street demonstrations in Petrograd in 1917 either began on or passed along the Nevsky.

[13] The Moscow-Petrograd line, opened in 1851, was at the time was the longest double-track railway in the world. Nikolai Station on the south bank of the Neva was the departure point for most destinations in Russia; the Finland Station on the north bank handled northern destinations, including Helsinki.

wasn't any trouble, that I was only an Americansky who wanted a place to sleep and that the girl needn't wait. I gave him a few rubles for her and got to bed a little after four in the morning.

I reported this afternoon to the Foreign Office and was sent over to the General Staff, and will leave tonight for the front where I will report to the commander-in-chief, and will start to work at once making pictures.

I find plenty of food at the hotels but I notice bread-lines in front of bakeries and, in fact, at every place where food is sold.

Don

VIII. Russian General Headquarters, February 28

This letter, Dot, will be very short, as it is impossible for me to write about things of a military nature. I asked the censor here today how far I could go, and he said I could tell how well prepared Russia is now. I find the Russian troops much better equipped now than in 1915, and ammunition is plentiful, artillery ammunition especially. Shells are stacked up wherever you go.[14] One of the officers whom I met in 1915 is at General Headquarters, and he, too, talks confidently of the coming spring drive. He promises me lots of opportunities to get good pictures.

I am in the best of health and am getting more than enough to eat. In the villages near here every one seems to have plenty of food. Famine in Petrograd, I am afraid, means trouble. When you ask an officer why it is that Petrograd is starving while this district has food, he shrugs his shoulders and says, "Germans." The general impression is that hostile influences are at work to cut down transportation facilities. All indications lead me to think that I should hurry back to the capital. Send my mail to the American Embassy; do not send it to the Hotel Astoria, although I expect to keep my room there.

Dot

IX. Petrograd, March 5, 1917

Dear Dot:

This is the day of all days when you and I should be together. But here I am in Russia and you are out in Kansas. Well, better luck when our wedding anniversary comes around next year.

---

[14] Special war councils consisting of government officials, elected representatives, and private businessmen were established in 1915 to improve munitions production and the transportation of food and fuel. Ending the state monopoly on munitions manufacture led to significant production increases. In 1915, artillery shell production increased nine times to almost a million a year, in 1916 to 1.8 million. "On the eve of the February Revolution," writes Pipes, "shell shortages were a thing of the past" (*A Concise History of the Russian Revolution*, 66).

The reason that I am back in Petrograd is that they expect trouble here. I am sending this letter out by a friend of mine so I can tell you about things which I could not do in an open letter.

The Germans, I think, have gotten wise to Russia's preparation for a big offensive and are working through some of the ministers here to cause internal disorders in Petrograd and try to bring about riots like they had in 1905. Most of the factories of the government are closed down, that is, with the exception of the factories which are controlled by English people. So far they are still working. No food is coming into Petrograd at all and it has reached such a stage now that with the factories closed and the price of food going up and only a small lot left, something serious is going to happen. My Russian acquaintances all tell me to wait until next week and I will see something.

I went out to the Embassy today and found a lot of letters but did not think of asking them if they knew anything of the trouble that was expected until an American just arrived from Moscow said that serious disturbances were expected before the week was over.

Today I called on an old friend of mine on the Nevsky Prospekt, and he told me that the government had placed four machine-guns on top of his building and that several police were quartered in his house. He said that guns had been mounted on a great many houses along the Nevsky Prospekt. When I asked him about how many he thought were on the street, he replied "about 180 machine-guns." If his statement is true it means hell some day on this street. One of my servants at the hotel said that the working people were going to march next week to the Palace and demand food and work and that a notice, or article, had been published in the paper telling people that they must not make any demonstration, that the food situation would be relieved in a few days.

I find that Boris, the Russian boy who was working at the American embassy in 1915, and who was drafted into the army when he came of age, has been in the hospital here for over a month and a half. He was twice wounded on the Romanian front. I am going to call at the hospital tomorrow and see him. I made a request at the General Staff for him to be assigned to me as interpreter when he is able to leave the hospital, and they have given me the order. This will make it much easier for me in traveling around the Russian fronts as he is very well educated and speaks English fluently. He has been to America, in fact he went to school in Brooklyn for a couple of years, for after the riots in 1905[15] his people went to America and were there for three or four years. He is only a kid and I can never imagine him as a Russian soldier. I am told that he has been decorated with the St. George Cross for bravery. After I see him

---

[15] The strikes and riots led to the establishment of a constitutional monarchy with a legislative body, the Duma, and guarantees (at least in principle) of civil liberties.

I shall tell you all about his experiences in Romania. He will probably be able to give me the inside story of what really happened there.

Don

X. Tuesday evening, March 6

Dear Dot:

This morning's papers are full of articles and proclamations are posted in the streets imploring the people not to make any demonstrations or cause disorders that might halt the manufacture of munitions or paralyze the industries of the city. I was told this morning that a general strike by the workingmen had been planned and that they were going to march to the Duma, but the street notices and articles in the paper by some of Petrograd's popular men had averted it. Rumor has it that the former prime minister, Stürmer,[16] is in the pay of Germany and has been caught with the goods on him, and that Protopopov[17] is playing the same game and would betray Russia into their hands. I do not know what to believe. I met Protopopov the other day and although personally, I did not like his face, I doubt if it is true that he would try to make a separate peace with Germany. The Liberal leaders in the Duma are also against any demonstrations. So far as a revolution is concerned, I do not think it is

---

[16] Boris Vladimirovich Stürmer (1848–1917), a former master of ceremonies at the Imperial Court, was appointed prime minister on February 2, 1916, while Tsar Nicholas II was at the front, primarily because of his association with the Empress Alexandra and Rasputin. "A dyed-in-the-wool monarchist bureaucrat," Stürmer was "hardly qualified to direct Russia's government at a time of crisis," writes Pipes. Critics in the Duma and press accused him of being a German sympathizer, but no evidence supports these claims; he became a target because of his German name. Under pressure from the Duma, Nicholas dismissed him on November 8, 1916. Placed under arrest by the Provisional Government, he died in prison (Pipes, *A Concise History of the Russian Revolution*, 71–73).

[17] Like Stürmer, Alexander Protopopov (1866–1918), a landowner, industrialist, and member of the liberal Progressive Bloc in the Duma, was appointed minister of the interior in September 1916 on the recommendation of the Empress Alexandra, under the influence of Rasputin. The Duma initially welcomed the appointment but reacted angrily when it became clear that Protopopov was "little more than a royal steward." Lacking administrative experience, he seriously underestimated the threat of revolution and failed to deal with food and fuel shortages and street demonstrations in Petrograd in February 1917. Instead, he assured Nicholas that the situation was under control. On February 23, the day after the Tsar left for the front, violent street protests began, and four days later units of the Petrograd military garrison mutinied. Although politicians and military commanders warned the Tsar that the situation was now out of control, Protopopov continued to reassure him. After the Duma and Petrograd Soviet agreed on the formation of a Provisional Government, Tsarist officials, including Protopopov, were rounded up and imprisoned in the Peter and Paul Fortress. Protopopov was executed by the Cheka (the political police) in Moscow during the Red Terror in September 1918 (Pipes, *A Concise History of the Russian Revolution*, 70, 74–77, 86, 224).

possible. Still, when you talk this way to Russians they say, "you do not know the Russian." If Protopopov tries any trickery with the people, they will drive him out of office.

We may not have any bread in a few days. The black bread that we now get is something awful. I had eaten black bread in Russia before and I preferred it to white bread. But the black bread that one gets now in Petrograd is one of the major horrors of war. I cannot describe it. I have tried several times to eat it, but I never get very far.

As you know, Dot, I could almost live on bread and coffee. If I do not have coffee and toast in the morning I am out of sorts. Well, I get coffee, but it's coffee only in name and the bread is not bread at all. So, I am beginning to feel the pangs of hunger even in the Astoria Hotel. I wonder how the poor people live.

The Minister of Agriculture issued statements in the form of posters and the people tore them down the minute they were posted and spat on them. That is a bad sign. Also, I notice a great many working people appearing on the streets. I never saw so many before. Formerly you seldom saw a man of this type on the Nevsky Prospekt. Today I find hundreds of them walking up and down and they have a very serious look on their faces. Bread shops are besieged by hungry people. Last night I did not retire until nearly 2:30 and I could look out from the back of the hotel from my window and see the people lined up in front of a bakery. In the morning when I got up some of those same people were still standing there. In some districts, they have to stand for four or five hours before they can get their little pittance of bread. If the government does not do something to relieve this situation, I am afraid that they will regret it. If this is the work of Germans they are intriguing with someone in power, some of the highest officials.

I will not mail this letter in the regular way but will give it to someone who is leaving Russia. I doubt if this would ever get by the censor.

Will write you daily, and if trouble starts will cable you.

Don

P. S. Just heard another piece of news. The government has brought 14,000 Cossacks into Petrograd to increase the number of troops in the city. I am also told that there are several reserve regiments here and that other troops are either in the city or near it and more are coming. I have just seen a regiment of Cossacks crossing the Neva.

One of the shops on the Morskaia was nailing up big boards on the window as I came in just now. They say that means that rumors of serious trouble are in circulation.

I am going out as soon as I seal this letter. I shall have Boris come down and stay with me. I have sent a note to Florence Harper's room telling her this news. If there's a revolution coming, as I think there is, I am in luck again. I have my police permits to photograph any place in Petrograd, also my army passes, so that I ought to be able to get some remarkable photographs if then is any trouble.

Don

XI. Petrograd, March 7

Dear Dot:

I met Fleurot[18] of the *New York World* today and he does not know what to think of the situation, although he fears serious trouble is at hand. I think he knows a lot that he is keeping to himself. I heard that he had an interview with Paul Miliukov[19] and got a wonderful story. I am going to try and see Miliukov this week and get a picture of him.

I went to the hospital and got Boris released. He was called into the army in 1916 and after a few months' training was sent to Romania. He claims that they did not have sufficient ammunition; that each soldier was given only twenty-five rounds and that the artillery never seemed to be able to support them and orders were given that their officers could not obey. They lost about 40 percent of the men during the first week of the fighting and Boris was wounded twice. He said that they almost

---

[18] Arno Dosch-Fleurot (1879–1951) was a Harvard-trained lawyer who turned to journalism before the war. In November 1916, he arrived in Petrograd as correspondent for the *New York World*. During the war, he adopted his French mother's surname, Fleurot, to avoid problems when reporting on the Western Front. After leaving Russia, he spent the rest of his career as a newspaper correspondent in Europe, and later published a memoir on his experiences in Russia and the Eastern Front—*Through War to Revolution* (London: John Lane, 1931). See Rappaport, *Caught in the Revolution*, 27–30, 329.

[19] Pavel Nikolayevich Miliukov (1859–1943) was a prominent historian, founder and leader of the liberal Constitutional-Democratic Party (known as the Kadets), and editor of its newspaper. He was a leading member of the Progressive Bloc in the Duma—an alliance of liberal and conservative deputies who called for parliamentary government and supported Russia's continued role in the war. In a speech to the Duma in November 1916, he accused the government, headed by Prime Minister Stürmer, of numerous failures, and hinted at collusion with the Germans. He ended each attack with the rhetorical question, "Is it stupidity or is it treason?" Although newspapers were forbidden by the censors from reporting the speech, copies were reproduced and sent around the country and to the front. "The passions unleashed by Miliukov," writes Pipes, "played a major role in instigating the February Revolution, in which anger over alleged government treason was, at first, a dominant motive." Miliukov led the Duma delegation that met with the Petrograd Soviet on March 1–2 to set the policy guidelines for the Provisional Government that was to serve until a Constituent Assembly was convened. Miliukov, as minister of foreign affairs, and Alexander Kerensky, the minister of justice, were the most prominent members of the Provisional Government, overshadowing the figurehead and ineffective prime minister, Prince Lvov. Miliukov favored retaining the monarchy, fearing anarchy if the Tsar was removed (Pipes, *A Concise History of the Russian Revolution*, 72, 83, 85, 119). On April 20, the government sent a note to Britain and France (which became known as the Miliukov note) proclaiming that Russia would fulfill its obligation towards the Allies and wage the war as long as it was necessary. The note was condemned by other ministers, and street protesters called for the removal of "bourgeois ministers," for an end to the war, and for the appointment of a new revolutionary government. Miliukov resigned in early May but remained a leader of the Kadets. He opposed the Bolsheviks and supported the White Army in the Civil War. He lived in France from 1921, and remained active in Russian émigré circles.

starved, having to live off the country on their retreat. For about fifteen days or so they retreated all the time. Sometimes they would only be asleep an hour along the road when they would have to get up and run for their very lives.

Boris says a revolution is coming and he has heard that Protopopov has sold Russia to Germany, that he is going to make peace and that there will be lots of food in a few days. I asked him where he got this information and be said he couldn't tell me but that I would hear it from other people.

I have had Boris get himself a new pair of boots and am going up to the Jewish market with him tomorrow to buy him an overcoat. He has no coat. I will also get him a new uniform now that he is going to be with me. Poor boy! He is nothing but a kid, and it is hard to believe that he has gone through what he has.

All day Cossacks have been riding through different sections of the city. One of the bread shops near the hotel had to call for police protection today as the people smashed in the windows to get bread. It is very pitiful to look at the long bread lines and to see the women with small babies in their arms in this severe cold weather, waiting hour after hour. The milk shop close to the hotel has a sign out which Boris translated for me. It says, "No more milk."

If this is the work of Germans, God grant that they will suffer for it. It is all right for them to fight in the field if they play the game square, but when they begin to do the things they are doing here, that's another matter. But this is the way Germany fights. If you could see these bread lines and see the looks upon the faces of these people as you pass, you would hardly believe that this is the twentieth century. I am wearing a heavy fur coat and am ashamed when I pass them, for when they look at me I wonder what they think. Many of them are almost in rags, and they stand in the freezing cold for hours to get a bit of that awful black bread. Boris says the people will not stand for it any longer and that the government most do something at once.

I understand that more factories were closed on account of the working people striking today. I am sending Boris out tonight to find out what he can. He belongs to one of the Anarchist societies and they will probably know something of what they are going to do.

All of these letters I am sending out through the Norway mail-bag. One of the couriers has promised to take my letters out for me any time I want him to do so.

Don

XII. Thursday, March 8

Dear Dot:

I am writing this letter with some doubt as to whether you'll receive it, for we are going to have a revolution in Russia. Boris has just come in with a lot of news. The government has agitators out trying to excite the people to blood-madness. I saw dozens of machine-guns placed on tops of buildings this morning. The mills and factories are closed, not because of strikes, but because the government ordered them shut down. This I have proof of. They are trying to make these poor devils start a demonstration. Then there is going to be such a massacre as the world has never yet seen. I fear that when it is over we shall find that Russia has made peace with Germany overnight. All of the big munition factories, with the exception of one or two, are now closed. From what I have heard, Protopopov is selling out Russia. I went over to the cable-office today and tried to send you a message. The old lady in charge, whom I had known for some time, told me not to waste my money—that nothing was allowed to go out. Quite a number of bread-shops have been broken into, and I heard that there had been several small clashes between the people and the police in front of the shops. This happened mostly in the factory districts, across the Neva, where the arsenal is. Down along what they call the Little Neva, where the old arsenal is situated, a policeman was found with his head cut off, lying in front of a bread shop where there had been fighting. I know two of the secret police, one of whom has lived in England, and the other in France for a good many years. They are both pro-Ally, and give me a great deal of information. They have promised to tell me when it is not safe for me to be on the streets. That will give me time to get some photographs.

This morning, about eleven o'clock, Florence Harper and I were walking to the American Consulate to see the vice-consul, Mr. Lee,[20] whom Florence met a few years ago in Bordeaux. Mr. Lee is from Colorado, and knows several of my friends there. Lee is skeptical about any trouble. We stayed in the consulate until noon, and coming out of the Singer Building,[21] we met a large crowd being pushed on to the sidewalks by police and Cossacks. The Cossacks were riding up and down the streets and seemed to be very good-natured. They are fine-looking fellows and do not seem to be anxious for trouble. We managed to get into a restaurant, making our way through the crowd, and after luncheon Florence Harper wanted to go to the British Embassy,[22] and I accompanied her. When we arrived at the bridge, leading into the

---

[20] Frank Charles Lee (1891–1963) served as U.S. vice consul in Bordeaux, France, and in Petrograd from 1916. In February 1918, with peace negotiations stalled and the German army within 100 miles of Petrograd, the Bolsheviks transferred the government to Moscow. Many members of the diplomatic community, including the U.S. ambassador, David Francis, were evacuated to Vologda, 350 miles south (Rappaport, *Caught in the Revolution*, 325–26). Lee and a skeleton staff provided consular services in Moscow.

[21] The Singer Building on Nevsky Prospekt opposite the Kazan Cathedral was a Petrograd landmark. The Art Nouveau Building, crowned with a glass tower, was designed by architect Pavel Suzor for the Russian branch of the Singer Sewing Machine Company. During World War I, it also housed the U.S. consulate, the Petrograd branches of American banks, and other commercial enterprises. After the revolution, it became the city's largest bookstore and was later renamed "The House of Books."

[22] On the Palace Embankment of the Neva, close to the Summer Palace and the Field of Mars.

Place de Mars,[23] we found it guarded by police. When we turned into the entrance of the big parade ground, we saw some groups of women. Florence then asked a Russian officer, who spoke French, what the trouble was. He said that these women were from the Peterhof side, old Petrograd so-called, across the Neva. Their cry was, "There is no bread; our husbands have no work." All the factories across the river were closed. A few minutes later about four or five hundred workmen marched along the sidewalk joining the women, and then almost as if by magic hundreds and hundreds of students came into view. Several men and women were held up on the shoulders of other people, and our Russian friend told us that they were crying, "Let's stop talking and act." The crowds increased rapidly, and orators began to make speeches. A street car came along, and in a minute the mob had stopped it, pulled down the trolley, and forced the people to get out. The crowd soon numbered at least 2,000. A few more cars came along and they were stopped and the passengers were forced to get out. Suddenly, a voice started to sing the Marseillaise, and the crowd took up the song and began to move slowly toward the Sadovaia. Whenever they came to street cars they stopped them and made the people get out. I noticed that the cars were not damaged. One car came along loaded with wounded soldiers in the care of nurses. This car, too, was stopped! One of the Russian nurses tried to deliver an address, with so much vehemence that I thought she would fall in a fit. The women laughed, and finally the soldiers, who were convalescent, left the car and joined in the singing, which grew in volume as the crowd turned into the Neva. I was walking along at the head of the column when a man tied a red flag, about eight inches long and three inches wide, on a cane and held it in the air. The minute I saw that rag, and noticed our position in front of this mob, I realized that it was no place for an innocent boy from Kansas. I said to Florence, "You are British and I am American. These are Russians. What the game is here, I don't know. Bullets have a way of hitting the innocent bystanders, so let's beat it, while the going is good." So we left the mob.

I noticed that when people saw the red flag, they rushed into doorways or any shelter they could find. It looked to me as though they were playing "safety first." Men, and especially students, began to leave the mob, so that when it had marched a few blocks along the Neva most of the men were on the sidewalk. The women, however, kept ahead down the center of the street with their red flags waving. The man who had first displayed the flag of the revolution turned it over to a woman.

The singing by this time had become a deep roar, terrifying, but at the same time fascinating. At the corner of the Nevsky and the Catherine Canal,[24] the police

---

[23] The Field of Mars, the large military parade ground near the bank of the Neva, facing the Summer Palace.

[24] The three-mile canal was constructed in 1739, enlarging an existing river. In the latter half of the eighteenth century, during the reign of Catherine the Great, it was deepened, and the banks reinforced and covered with granite. It starts from the Moika River near the Field of Mars and flows into the Fontanka Canal.

were waiting. They were mounted police, and a good many of the mob dropped out when they saw this. Their intention was to get through the police lines and form lower down. While this was happening, two or three companies of Cossacks came up at a gallop behind them and scattered the women, but they only formed again. The women cheered the Cossacks each time they charged, and it was a wonder that some of them were not thrown down. I saw one woman fall when the Cossacks came along. I expected to see her trampled to death by the horses, but when two of the Cossacks came up to where she was lying they jumped their horses over her body. The people cheered. The mob kept surging back and forth until six o'clock, but there was no real trouble. People I talked to laughed and said, "Well, you saw what has happened today, there will be no further trouble." But I knew better. This mob had walked down the street carrying a red flag and had not been fired upon.

I told some officers about this when I got back to the hotel and they looked serious and said, "Red flags, and not fired on? Impossible!" I asked them if they would have fired if they had been in charge of the troops. One of them said it would have depended upon his orders and another said that he would not have waited for orders but would have given them a taste that they would have remembered, as that is the only way to deal with the lower classes.

So far, Dot, I have guessed this war to a T. The people can say what they please, but I smell trouble. And thank God I am here to get the photographs of it! If there is a revolution I hope it comes now, for although I should hate to see bloodshed, if it has to be it might as well come while I am on the ground with plenty of film.

Tonight, I am taking Boris and going into the factory districts to see how things are there.

Don

XIII. Friday, March 9

Dear Dot:

Well, this has been one day of days for me. I tried to send you a cable but was turned down as usual.

Last night after dinner I went over to the old Petrograd side, back of the Peter and Paul Fortress,[25] around the old arsenal. When I started across the Troitsky bridge I was stopped by the police, but after presenting my American passport and my military pass I was allowed to proceed. Florence Harper went with me, also Boris. We

---

[25] The Peter and Paul Fortress, established by Peter the Great, was built from 1706 to 1740 on a small island near the north bank of the Neva. Built to defend the city from a Swedish attack, the fortress served as a base for the military garrison and a prison for high-ranking and political prisoners. During the February Revolution, it was attacked by mutinous soldiers of the Pavlovsky Regiment and the prisoners were freed. Under the Provisional Government, hundreds of Tsarist officials were held in the fortress.

found the street in some localities jammed with excited men and women. Boris talked to several of them and they told him that they could not get bread. We kept walking around until eleven o'clock when I noticed that Florence Harper attracted too much attention with her seal coat. The people looked at her, and Boris said it would be best for us to leave this district as he had heard some of the women remark that she ought to have her face cut to pieces. "Look how she is dressed! Yes, she gets bread but we get nothing," were some of the remarks that Boris translated for us. He said that they might cut her face with a sharp knife, thinking that she was a Russian aristocrat.

We arrived at the hotel at twelve o'clock and on our way back we noticed that a great many troops were patrolling the city. Very few people were out, however. We were stopped several times and had to show our papers.

Early this morning, I had breakfast at eight, and by nine I called Florence on the phone and asked her to go with us up the street. When we arrived on the Nevsky, we found the crowd larger than yesterday. From the Catherine Canal to the Nikolai Station the Nevsky was crowded with thousands of people. Many soldiers were slowly riding up and down trying to keep the crowds on the move, but when they cleared one block and left it and started back to clear another, the mobs immediately formed again. Finally, the Cossacks charged the mobs. Several people fell and were trampled on, but the soldiers did not use their sabers and their guns were slung on their backs. I saw a Secret Police officer trying to take a picture of a man who was standing on a fire plug addressing the people. This man said something to the crowd around him and they immediately attacked the officer, smashed his camera, and were killing him when he was rescued by a mounted policeman.

I was using my small camera, but was careful not to attract attention. A few windows were smashed today and I hear that blows have been exchanged in some places between the working people and the troops. The Cossacks are very quiet but the police and the people are getting ugly. Many of the police are dressed as Cossacks and are striking the people with lances when they don't move quickly enough.

From one o'clock till three, Frank Lee,[26] Florence Harper and I trailed the mobs and at times had to run for our lives when the Cossacks charged. All the afternoon we were pushed up and down the Nevsky. Sometimes we ran and slid and sometimes lay flat along the edge of the buildings as the other people did. There is plenty of snow on the pavement, and when running you slip and slide. Still, after many a narrow escape we went back into it again. At four, Lee left and returned to the consulate. We then started toward the railroad station with another mob. Cossacks charged us from front and rear. We dodged into the doorways, but were routed out by a Cossack who was just a kid about nineteen years old. First he gave me a poke with his lance and then he gave Florence a slap across the back and a good push, but he smiled and laughed

---

[26] The U.S. Vice Consul. See n. 20.

when he did it. We told him we were foreigners but he pushed us along just the same, though gently.

Boris picked up the report that several of the regiments have had letters from the working people asking if they would shoot on them if they appeared on the streets, and that the soldiers have sent word back that they wouldn't. In Boris's regiment, one of the soldiers asked the colonel what assistance his regiment was going to give to the working people who were crying for bread. The colonel pulled his gun and shot him dead. Boris thinks that this will eventually start trouble as this man was very popular with his comrades.

In the demonstrations today, I noticed a better class of people than in those of yesterday. There seemed to be lots of people springing up and inciting others to do things, but when the troops charged they stepped aside, only speaking when the mob came in their direction.

By seven in the evening, the mob, so far as the Nevsky was concerned, had given up and dispersed. When I left the Nevsky, it was very quiet. We had dinner at the Donon Restaurant.[27] Our waiter told us that there had been riots in different sections of the city.

After I finish this letter I am going with two or three officers who are friends of mine to the outlying districts. We are to wear civilian clothes so as not to be too noticeable. My two Secret Service Police friends have not appeared at the hotel all day.

Don

XIV. Saturday, March 10

Dear Dot:

Well, this has been a great day for me. I was up until three this morning. Boris, Florence Harper and I walked out to the Tauride Palace[28] where the Duma meets and found nothing exciting there, not even people standing around talking. We then went down by the Preobragenski Barracks, where many soldiers were standing guard but nothing was going on. From there we turned into the Nevsky Prospekt and went

---

[27] A fashionable restaurant on the Moika River embankment near the Winter Palace, popular with writers, artists, businessmen, diplomats, journalists, and wealthy Russians.

[28] The former residence of Catherine the Great's lover, Prince Grigory Potemkin, the Tauride Palace, built in the 1780s, was "a graceful Palladian building of white colonnades, grand reception rooms and columned galleries" (Rappaport, *Caught in the Revolution*, 100). Since 1906, it had served as the meeting place for the Duma. After the February Revolution, crowds descended on the palace to observe or participate in the long and raucous deliberations between members of the Duma and the Petrograd Soviet that resulted in the formation of the Provisional Government on March 2. The short-lived Russian Constituent Assembly met at the palace in January 1918.

down as far as the Kazan Cathedral without seeing anything in the way of excitement. In front of the cathedral we found about twenty people, who seemed to be mostly business folk. From there we went towards the British Embassy and tried to cross the Troitsky Bridge, which faces the Peter and Paul Fortress, but as the guards turned us back we went over to the Alexandra Bridge. On our way, we passed the artillery depot and I noticed a great many troops going in. On the other side of the Neva we began to meet knots of people, mostly workmen and their wives. No one said anything to us, or paid any attention to us.

Today the first killing occurred. Mobs began to gather early on the Neva and to show evidences of bad temper. The situation has rapidly assumed an alarming aspect. The crowds were driven back and forth by the Cossacks and mounted police. The Cossacks so far have not drawn their weapons, but the police are using the flats of their swords. Machine guns have been placed on some of the bridges across the canal.

Florence Harper, Boris, and I were out on the Nevsky at eight o'clock. It is very, very cold and we kept walking up and down the Nevsky mingling with the crowds. At times, we had to do some sprinting to escape being ridden down by the Cossacks. The idea is to get to a corner and beat it down a side street when the Cossacks charge. They do not follow down the side streets, as they seem to be satisfied to keep the Nevsky clear. The trams started to run this morning, but soon gave up the attempt as the mob pulled the trolleys down and stole the controllers.

Near the Nikolai Station at about eleven o'clock this morning I noticed machine guns being posted by the police on a balcony of a house.

At noon when we started for the restaurant near the Kazan Cathedral where we lunch the Nevsky was one mass of people from the Sadovaia to the Nikolai Station. The people cheered the Cossacks, who seemed to hold their horses back a bit when they reached the mob, and I saw only a few people trampled. The police, however, got quite nasty and I saw many people that had received ugly, though not serious wounds from police sabers.

We came out of the restaurant after lunch just in time to see four wounded police being carried into the courtyard of the building where the restaurant is located. They were bleeding pretty badly and Boris said that they had been attacked in front of the American consulate. When we walked towards the Sadovaia we noticed more police and Cossacks driving the mob to the Fontanka Canal Bridge[29] where they allowed them to remain until about two o'clock after which they tried to drive them further up. They succeeded in clearing the street as far as the Nikolai Station square. Further it was impossible to move them. Crowds continued to collect down on the Nevsky, but were quickly dispersed. Almost every person in front of the Nikolai Station had his hat off. This, in Russia, is a sign of peace. All they shouted was "give us bread and we will go back and work." I thought that if the government had had some responsible

---

[29] The Fontanka is a branch of the Neva which flows through central Petrograd.

minister address this crowd things would have quieted down, but Boris said no. The only thing that would satisfy these people was food.

About two o'clock a man richly dressed in furs came up to the square in a sleigh and ordered his driver to go through the crowd, which by this time was in a very ugly mood, although it seemed to be inclined to make way for him. He was impatient and probably cold and started an argument. All Russians must have their argument. Well, he misjudged this crowd and also misjudged the conditions in Petrograd. I was within 150 feet of this scene. He was dragged out of his sleigh and beaten. He took refuge in a stalled street car where he was followed by the workingmen. One of them took a small iron bar and beat his head to a pulp. This seemed to give the mob a taste for blood. Immediately I was pushed along in front of the crowd which surged down the Nevsky and began smashing windows and creating general disorder. Many of the men carried red flags on sticks. The shops along the Nevsky, or most of them, are protected by heavy iron shutters. Those that were not had their windows smashed. I noticed about this time that ambulances were coming and going on the side streets. There were usually three or four people lying in each one.

Now the people who smashed these windows and threw things at the soldiers were not the working people, but the police. I saw a Secret Service man who lived at the hotel dressed as a workingman, and he was deliberately smashing windows. To watch him trying to push soldiers off the walk you would have thought he was an anarchist of the worst type. This is just a clever plan to start serious trouble. I told Boris about it and he said that he had heard from a great many people that the Secret Police are mingling with the mob and trying to make it appear that the mob wants to fight the soldiers.

At about four o'clock I was startled by a heavy explosion. From the top of the Nikolai Station someone had thrown a bomb into the midst of a squad of Cossack soldiers. Luckily, I am told, none of the soldiers were killed, though several were wounded. Five horses were left dead in the street. The mob then put on their hats and began to stand against the charging Cossacks and police. From the top of the hotel another bomb was thrown. The Cossacks then drew up at attention on one side of the square and the police kept driving through the crowd. About an hour after the second explosion, a police officer came up to the Cossacks and ordered them to fire on the mob. They refused and the mob started to cheer. Everyone had seen the act. This officer wore the uniform of a colonel. He drew his revolver and fired into the mob. He was saved from the mob by a Cossack who quickly drove his lance through his chest. Boris began to cry. I said to him, "What in hell are you crying about?" He then began to talk so fast that I could not understand him. I shook him roughly and ordered him to speak slowly. He then told me the "day of days" had come, for, said he, "The Cossacks are with the people." This is the first time in the history of Russia that a Cossack has disobeyed orders.

The people continued to cheer and shout to the Cossacks, "We only want bread; we do not want to fight you." The Cossacks would reply, "We will not fire upon you, brothers." One of the proofs that went home to the Cossacks, I think, was that when the first bomb was thrown from the roof of the Nikolai Station, the whole mob, by some instinct, held their hands in the air. This was to indicate that none of them had bombs and that they were unarmed. Several people started to make speeches, and the cry went up, "On to the palace! On to the palace!" Other speakers got up and said, "No, to our homes, to our homes!" After that the mob started down the Nevsky. At the corner of Mihailovsky Street and the Nevsky, the mob stopped and stormed a café which is located in the Europe Hotel[30] building. They completely wrecked this place. Five people who were sitting in the cafe were killed. The mob had become very ugly.

Boris said the reason that they attacked this cafe was that it was full of German agents and food controllers who met there and decided each day what they would charge for food.

The police came up the side street from the Kazan Cathedral in strong force and drove the mob back to the Nevsky. I followed to the station, where I found students, anarchists and socialists making speeches. The police were also out here in force and were trying to break up the mob and drive the people away, but they might as well have tried to drive the ocean. All this time we were on the edge of the main mob close to a side street. From the ugly looks on the faces of both the people and the police, I expected firing to start any minute.

At about six o'clock another bomb was thrown exploding with tremendous force. I saw the smoke rising from the very center of the crowd. Florence Harper and I then decided on Boris's advice, to move down the street. Boris said that the police might bring up reinforcements and surround the whole square and that in this case those at the edge would be the first hit. As we neared the corner of the Sadovaia and the Nevsky, a crowd of several hundred detached themselves from the main mob and started past us almost at a trot. They were singing and carrying red flags. We turned and trailed them. I might mention, however, that we kept well in the rear. Several times we were forced to turn and run from the police who kept charging this mob, which only re-formed on the sidewalks and started on again.

So far the police had left the side streets open, and with the exception of some bruises we had no other marks to show for our day. But the mob we had been trailing was in earnest. Just before it reached the Singer Building the police charged, using the edges of their sabers. This mob, however, was entirely different from any that I had thus far seen. It seemed to be composed of the worst elements of the city. Every individual in it looked tough and brutal and capable of any crime. During this last charge, we were lucky enough to fall flat in a big doorway leading into a court, where it was

---

[30] The Hotel d'Europe was on the Nevsky near the Singer Building. With its roof garden and glass-domed restaurant, it competed with the Astoria for wealthy and foreign customers.

impossible for us to be hurt. The police went by the street. When they had passed and we had got up, we noticed a great many people bleeding from cuts. As we neared the American Consulate I noticed across the street Mr. Winship, the consul-general,[31] and Mr. Lee, the vice-consul, coming out of the doorway. I was trying to get over to them when I noticed several students rushing by me. The police had dismounted down by the Catherine Canal and were stretching slowly across the street with the mob marching toward them carrying their red flags. Boris gave a shout of warning and the three of us fell flat. This was in the park in front of the Kazan Cathedral. A few seconds later came the crash of rifles. Three volleys rang out, followed quickly by another. Then the Nevsky was filled with a screaming, howling mob of people, everyone fighting for a place to hide. As the last volley died out, the three of us jumped up and started to run through the park to the steps of the Kazan Cathedral. We mounted them and hurriedly got behind one of the big pillars of that beautiful building. A few minutes later we made a detour up to the Sadovaia and then back to the Nevsky. As we came down the street, we found no mobs in that district, but toward the Nikolai Station square, we could hear them roaring. There was something about it that made me tremble.

As we neared the Catherine Canal bridge I noticed about a dozen bodies lying in the snow. Around most of them you could see a tell-tale blotch of blood. Two soldiers who talked later to Boris told him that they must have fired a good many blanks, so few people having been killed. The crowd was so dense that every bullet fired into it must have found a mark. I am told that the first volley was of blanks, the last three lead. I do not know whether it was the mounted police or the cavalry that did the shooting.

At eight o'clock Florence Harper and a friend of hers went to the French Theater. As it was impossible for me to stay indoors, I got Boris and went out to see what was happening. When we got up to the Nevsky Prospekt we found the surrounding streets were almost deserted except for Cossack patrols. In the working districts, however, I found things more exciting.

I am finishing this letter at one o'clock. I have been back in the hotel for an hour. I dropped in at the French Theater but grew tired of it after a few minutes and left. One of the things that pleased me more than anything in the theater was the decorations. These were of orange. I believe that if the theater had been decorated in red I would have screamed for today has been a hard day for me, one that I never will forget. I have seen enough red today. The red flags and those red blotches in front of the Kazan Cathedral are still before me.

While I was walking around, I kept wondering and wondering what was really going to happen. That the situation is very serious I know. Now that the Cossacks will

---

[31] North Winship (1885–1968), a career Foreign Service officer, served as U.S. consul in Petrograd from 1914 to 1917.

not fire upon the people, I wonder what the people will do—those from the factory districts, especially. I wonder too what the army thinks—those poor devils at the front who are lying in the trenches suffering all kinds of hardships. What will they do when they realize that every war material factory in Petrograd has suspended work!

Tomorrow is Sunday and Florence Harper, Boris and I are going to the services at St. Isaac's Cathedral. I will write you a note in the afternoon. By then I shall probably have heard more news of what has happened outside Petrograd.

Don

XV. Petrograd, March 11

Dear Dot:

Well, I did not go to church today after all. Late last night, Boris came in and said there was rioting in the streets. I dressed and went out with him. At two o'clock or a little later while we were over on the old Petrograd side, we met a mob of about sixty people who had taken two heads and jammed them on poles and were carrying them down the middle of the street. On inquiry Boris found that they were the heads of policemen. I told Boris I had had enough and would go back to the hotel. On the way back in front of the Bourse, we saw three bodies lying in the street, wearing uniforms. We did not stop to investigate but hurriedly crossed the bridge and went on to the hotel. Passing the Admiralty, we noticed a great many troops being marched into it. I heard from officers today that the mobs paraded the city here all night and that a great many policemen were killed or seriously wounded; also that several regiments had mutinied. This rumor, however, was said to be false later in the day when I called at the War Department. The officer there who told me that no regiments had mutinied also warned me to keep off the street today. Boris's father told me that all of the police had been put in soldiers' uniforms and that the soldiers themselves have found this out and are in a very ugly frame of mind. Last night the soldiers were ordered several times to fire upon the people, and refused.

Today was a beautiful day. The Nevsky was filled even as early as ten o'clock this morning with a real Sunday crowd and it seemed to me that all the children in Petrograd were out. We started for lunch at twelve o'clock, as the little French restaurant close to the Kazan Cathedral where we dine has only a limited amount of bread and the early bird gets it. Mr. Lee, the American vice-consul, and Mr. Grant, an Englishman connected with the British Mission here accompanied us today. After lunch I persuaded Florence to walk as far as the Fontanka Canal. I put my camera into a bag and my battery underneath my coat. By raising the flap I have cut in the end of the grip, I can get pictures with this gyroscopic camera of mine without anyone knowing what I am doing. We went as far as the bridge.

The military commander of Petrograd has posted notices everywhere warning people not to congregate any more, and threatening to disperse them by force. As we started up the Nevsky towards the Fontanka Canal Bridge, and just before we reached the Anitchkoff Palace[32] we noticed a mob form on the Fontanka Canal Bridge. We stopped across the street from the palace and watched about fifty mounted police dressed as soldiers charge this mob and drive them down along the side streets near the canal. Presently, to our surprise, we saw a new mob forming. A student got up on one of the big pedestals at the end of this bridge and raising a red flag began to make a speech. While he was talking thousands began to run toward him. Two or three of the people who passed us were holding something underneath their coats. I then noticed that down by the Sadovaia the police had stretched themselves flat on the pavement and others were pulling out a machine-gun into the middle of the car-tracks. That worried me. I called out, "Let's hurry to the end of the bridge and turn to the left and go down towards the skating rink." As we turned to do this, the mob started down the street, with red flags flying and hats in their hands, singing the Marseillaise. We backed up against the window of a little glove shop. I thought it would be better to let the mob pass us than to be pushed on ahead. As soon as the mob, or the main part of it, had passed us, we walked out to the edge of the curb. I wanted to get a picture. I ran out into the middle of the ear tracks and stood behind one of the poles that holds the wires. As we reached the middle of the street I heard the snarl of that deadly machine-gun and the spit of rifles. I watched that mob. It did not stop, but moved slowly forward. I knew what was happening to those in front.

Did you ever break off the crust of a pie and still hold the center in your hand? That is what the police were doing to that mob. They were eating the crust of it, and eating it quickly. It seemed hours to me, but it was only a few seconds later when the people began to prostrate themselves. In a moment, where we had seen thousands, no one was standing upright, everyone hugging the pavement. I had shouted to Florence to lie flat when I heard the first shots, either she failed to understand me or did not hear me, for she remained standing. I immediately struck her in the face and knocked her flat, falling myself. As we lay there, it seemed as if hell itself had broken loose on the Nevsky. I looked back over my shoulder. From the top of one of the buildings rifle and machine-gun fire was belching down. I have been in many an engagement at the fronts during this war, but never have I heard the roar of a battle like this afternoon's. It was terrifying and the noise seemed louder than anything I had ever heard, probably because it was amongst buildings.

I managed to make quite a number of pictures during that time and after a half hour of constant firing by the troops and police from the tops of the buildings, the shooting gradually subsided, although anyone who got up and started to run for a side street was fired upon. The police at the comer of the Sadovaia then slowly started up the street. I noticed that they were firing at the people lying down. That frightened me. I thought they were going to make a clean job of everyone in the street. I told

---

[32] The former imperial palace, at the intersection of the Nevsky and the Fontanka Canal.

Florence what was happening. She did not get frightened to my surprise, but began making rude remarks about the police. I told her we would make a run to the window of the glove shop and smash the windows in with our backs, and that we could then crawl into the store and be safe. I gave the word for her to get up, expecting that I would have to help her. Instead, she almost had to help me. I found my knees were weaker than they had ever been in my life; but after a couple of shots had been fired especially at us, we gained speed—got to the window in a few seconds, turned our backs to it, and pushed. There was a crash and we climbed into the window. Others seeing what we had done, also began to run for this window. In a moment ten or fifteen people were trying to get in. They cut themselves on the jagged glass and screamed and groaned. At the same instant the police at the Anitchkoff Palace got the range of the window and the caretaker of the shop opened up with a revolver from the inside. The only thing we could do was to get out. A Russian with a general's shoulder-straps had crumpled into a heap in the window, slowly his light blue coat began to turn red in the back. He had been hit while trying to get in.

We then rushed to the edge of the curb and lay flat again. A little girl about sixty feet away from us got up and started to run in our direction. When she was about ten feet away she was hit in the throat by a bullet that almost severed her little head. A woman near us jumped up. Whether in the hope of saving this little girl or not I do not know; but she let out a scream and fell to the street. She pulled her dress up and I could see that she had had her knee-cap shattered. I have never heard a woman scream as that woman did; and I can still see that little girl with her face toward me slowly bleeding to death. From where I was lying I counted twelve soldiers with officers' straps on their shoulders lying on the ground. One was groaning, others were very still. I could see blood on the white snow around those nearest to me.

After we had been lying in the snow about an hour and a quarter, a number of ambulances appeared and began to pick up the people. I told Florence to pretend she was wounded, having noticed that when the ambulance started to back up the people who tried to run away under cover of them were immediately fired on. Three fell and were picked up, but before that I had been picked up first and put in one of the ambulances, while Florence was still lying in the street. After ten minutes she was also picked up, as I learned later. I arrived at the hospital after a half hour's ride. When they ran up the curtain in the back, I slipped down. The people who were pulling out the stretchers seemed to be surprised. I shouted "Amerikansky," and while I was trying to explain what the trouble was, and that I was not hurt, a doctor, wearing a Russian army uniform, came up and asked me in English what I had done. He was an Englishman in the Russian Red Cross. I told him I had resorted to this plan in order to escape from the Nevsky, and asked him how to reach my hotel. He suggested that we have tea in his room in the hospital, saying I could go to the hotel later when, perhaps, it would be quieter. We had tea and I set out. When I arrived at the Nevsky the police would not let me cross. On the side streets and in fact everywhere I went afterwards, I found knots of people of all classes. The story of what had happened had begun to spread. I made a detour around the Nikolai Station, gradually circling towards the Liteiny. While I was near the Morskaia, coming in by way of the Admiralty arch, which the Morskaia runs into, I saw the American Ambassador, David Francis,[33] riding in his carriage towards the Nevsky. I tried to reach him, but I saw he was being advised to stop anyway. I do not believe he had heard what had happened. I have tried to get the Embassy by phone but have so far failed.

I got back to the hotel about seven o'clock. Florence Harper was already in her room. She had been taken to a hospital and afterwards sent home accompanied by a couple of Russian soldiers who volunteered to see her safely through.

The crowds are gradually being reinforced by people from the outlying districts. Boris says they are very incensed about the Saturday massacre and that when they learn what has happened today the government will not be able to control them. They say at the hotel that the Tsar has telegraphed for the Duma to be dissolved and that the Duma has refused.

I am going to attend an anarchist meeting to-night with Boris. He says the police are putting heavy guards on all the bridges that cross the Neva and that in several localities the soldiers have refused to obey orders and fire on the people. General Khabalov,[34] who is commanding the district now, has issued another order which is posted in front of the hotel. It says that any crowds gathering will be fired upon without warning. The Cossacks have been almost entirely withdrawn for some reason

---

[33] As Rappaport points out, David Rowland Francis (1850–1927), "a genial Democrat from Kentucky," had no previous foreign service experience before taking the post of ambassador to Russia in April 1916. He was "a self-made millionaire who had made his money in St. Louis from grain-dealing and railroads," had served as governor of Missouri (1889–93), and lobbied for St. Louis to stage the 1904 World's Fair. He was selected, writes Rappaport, because of his business experience, to promote trade with Russia and the sale of U.S. grain, cotton, and armaments. Although some fellow diplomats in Petrograd (and members of his own staff) disparaged his lack of diplomatic experience and knowledge of Russian politics and society, his open, relaxed personal style—so different from that of other diplomats—endeared him to many Russians, foreign business owners, and members of the expatriate community. "He made no bones about his enjoyment of the finest Kentucky bourbon and fat cigars," writes Rappaport. In February 1918, with the German army advancing towards the city, Francis and other diplomats left Petrograd for Vologda, 350 miles south of Moscow. In October, he fell ill with a gall bladder infection and had to be evacuated by a U.S. cruiser from Murmansk (Rappaport, *Caught in the Revolution*, 8–15, 325–26). Francis later published a book about his experiences, *Russia from the American Embassy, April 1916–November 1918* (New York: Charles Scribner's Sons, 1921).

[34] General Sergey Khabalov, commandant of the Petrograd garrison. Under orders from the Tsar, he had resolved to suppress the street demonstrations with force. On his orders, machine guns were placed in attics, towers, and rooftops along the Nevsky. In police stations around the city, he stockpiled rifles, revolvers, and ammunition, and had infantry and machine gunners in reserve (Rappaport, *Caught in the Revolution*, 58, 71).

or other. On the Nevsky Prospekt between the Sadovaia and the Fontanka Canal there is a constant fire of machine-guns. Since one o'clock today it has been a bloody Sunday for Russia.

About two hours ago I was on the Nevsky and found it in control of the police. I went to the French Theater, which was fairly full of people. I saw Arno Dosch-Fleurot of the *New York World*, and a couple of other newspaper men. It is now about half-past three. I have been out of the hotel four or five times until I would get so cold that I had to come back and warm up. Wherever I went I found ugly looking mobs and Boris tells me that mobs have been attacked several times in the heart of the city.

About 2:30 a.m., while I was standing at the corner of the Morskaia and the Nevsky, a heavy fire started from the Catherine Canal bridge. After about twenty minutes it ceased. All bridges over the Neva have been closed in order to prevent the workingmen from reaching the Nevsky. A soldier friend of Boris says that the soldiers are fighting each other near one of the bridges in the Viborg district. This district is out near the Duma in the same neighborhood as the American Embassy. I think the Embassy is safe though, for in that district there are a great many barracks full of troops.

There was a meeting in the Field of Mars this evening by the Pavlovsky regiment.[35] They have been joined by thousands of others. The commanding officer of this Pavlovsky regiment forbade the regiment to take part and had his arm struck off by a soldier's saber. This regiment was gathered close to the Field of Mars at the corner near the canal. As soon as this happened, troops seized the barracks and from there they went to the Field of Mars. While they were meeting another regiment tried to disperse them. I think this regiment was the Keksgolmsky. Ten of the Pavlovsky regiment were arrested and taken to the Peter and Paul Fortress. If this spreads to other regiments, Russia will be a republic in a few more hours.

I am very tired and I will bring this letter to a close. I am going to hide my letters as I write them each evening until this thing is decided one way or the other. I am afraid if I mail them now I will get into serious trouble. I am going to have Boris hide them down in the basement of the hotel. I am afraid to have anything in my room.

---

[35] On February 26, a company of the Pavlovsky regiment of the Imperial Guard fired on a crowd in Znamensky Square that failed to disperse. There were forty civilian casualties. When other soldiers from the regiment learned of the massacre, they grabbed guns and set out for the square but turned back after an exchange of fire with mounted police. The ringleaders were arrested and imprisoned. The following night, members of the Pavlovsky Regiment held rallies where they voted to disobey orders to fire on civilians. Other Imperial Guard regiments joined the mutiny; in some units, officers were assaulted and killed (Pipes, *A Concise History of the Russian Revolution*, 77–79). The Russian Imperial Guard, officially known as the Leib Guard (Life Guards), were military units founded by Peter the Great to serve as personal guards of the emperor. The Imperial Guard subsequently increased in size and diversity to become an elite corps of the Imperial Army rather than household troops. Most regiments of the Imperial Guard were stationed in and around Petrograd.

I wish you would send me some sugar, and have some flour put up in small packages and sent to me by registered mail, first class. I also need some quinine and aspirin tablets.

Don

XVI. Petrograd, March 18

Dear Dot:

I haven't written you since Sunday. In the last three days, as you probably know by this time, Russia has become a republic, and I, with my usual good luck, was able to get the best pictures of my life. Russia has at last realized its fondest hopes. All are free and equal now, and the story which Florence Harper told in a cable Tuesday, and which I hope got through, has already informed you of what really happened these last few days. I am going to write a long letter and tell you what I have seen myself and what I have done, so you will understand how lucky I am. I wouldn't go through it again, but I would hate to have missed any of it. Just imagine if someone had had the French Revolution in motion pictures! Well, I have thousands of feet of film of the Russian Revolution. I have worked every day and have followed the mobs day and night. I went seventy-two hours without any sleep at all to speak of, with the exception of perhaps one or two hours, but I got my film and hundreds of still pictures. Florence Harper has been with me almost the whole time. She is dead game. We have worked in some devilish positions and have seen hundreds killed before our very eyes but I haven't had a scratch. This whole revolution might have been staged by an opera company.

Although Russia is a republic now, different factions are fighting for control. If they keep it up the republic will go under. But I hope the right men will come forward. Just think, Dot, what it means to have Russia a republic! From the east to the west boundaries of Russia the distance is greater than from New York to the center of China. Over 300,000,000 acres of land are devoted to farming and over half of this is of the best ground in the world; it is even better than the best of the Kaw River valley land in Kansas. Three quarters of this land is devoted to the raising of grain, in which Russia leads the world. And the revolution and the republic itself were brought about by lack of bread in Petrograd!

Today we have plenty of bread in Petrograd, also plenty of fish. A few days ago we had neither. The national dish of the poorer people in Russia, next to bread, is salt fish. The reason for this, I have been told, is the number of fast days prescribed by the Church. We are also beginning to get plenty of wood again in Petrograd. A few days ago wood was almost impossible to obtain.

I am lying in bed writing this letter and I will now get out my diary and a few notes I have made the last few days and tell you the story from Monday morning on.

The first real outbreak of the troops against the government occurred at one a.m. on Monday when the Volynsky Regiment[36] revolted and killed their officers. They had been ordered to fire on the mob in one of the factory districts. Another regiment was immediately ordered out to fire on the Volynsky regiment. They refused and joined forces. This news spread rapidly to other barracks and before eleven a.m. the next day six more regiments had joined them.

I set out for the American Embassy on foot, as all the trams had stopped running and there were no droshkys to be seen. On the Nevsky Prospekt some of the shops were open as usual and the people were going along attending to their business. I doubt if they knew just what had happened during the early hours of the morning. As I approached the Field of Mars I heard shots, and when I finally came out in the square I found a scene beyond description. Soldiers were firing volleys into the air with their rifles, others coming behind them said the best thing I could do was to keep on my way. I got in among these soldiers. Instead of treating me as an enemy, several of them threw their arms about me and kissed me. I stood around for half an hour or so till I met one of the clerks of the English Magazine, a man who speaks Russian and English. The English Magazine is one of the big department stores of Petrograd.[37] This man said the troops had first mutinied upon receiving the news that eight regiments had joined the people, and that the revolution was on. I asked him to go with me and carry one of my cameras. He consented. I began taking photographs. The soldiers all wanted to pose for me. My new friend told me that one of the soldiers had just made a speech and told his comrades they must organize and prepare for the fight to come. In a few minutes they formed in lines and began moving off across the Field of Mars. They started toward the Troitsky Bridge, where they were met with rifle and machine-gun fire from the Peter and Paul Fortress and the troops guarding the approach to the bridge. The latter were overwhelmed, threw down their guns and joined the revolutionary forces. Other troops started to advance slowly across the bridge, made a sudden rush, and then fell flat. The firing became so heavy by this time that I fell back to a side street.

At 11 or 11:30 I heard people shouting that the fortress had fallen and that the revolutionists were now in possession of it. I talked to the soldiers who were standing around, my friend interpreting for me. They said the reason they had joined the

---

[36] The Volynsky Regiment was an Imperial Guard infantry regiment created in 1817. On Sunday, March 11, the regiment was ordered to fire on unarmed demonstrators. The soldiers fired into the air. The next day the regiment mutinied and was quickly followed by the Semonovsky, the Izmaylovsky, the Litovsky regiments, and even the legendary Preobrazhensky Regiment, the oldest and staunchest regiment, founded by Peter the Great.

[37] Better known by its French name, "Magasin Anglais," it was one of several retail stores in the city catering to expatriates and rich Russians. "You could buy the best Harris tweeds and English soap and enjoy the store's 'demure English provincialism,'" writes Rappaport (*Caught in the Revolution*, 2).

revolutionists was that they were hungry, that their families were hungry and that they would not fire on working people who only wanted bread. Many soldiers were carrying extra rifles which they were offering to people, and I noticed a great number of civilians carrying guns and joining the soldiers.

I left the main mob, started across the Field of Mars, and stopped to make pictures of a group of twenty-two officers who had been killed when some regiment had mutinied early in the morning. No one paid any attention to me at all. On my way to the Embassy I passed the police barracks located in that neighborhood. Just as I arrived at the door, a truck dashed up filled with police, who rushed inside. I thought I had better ask if my police pass was good for the district where I was. Walking into the courtyard, I stopped a gendarme, but he couldn't understand me and there was no one in the office who spoke English. I then walked up the Liteiny to the American Embassy on Furshtatskaya Street.[38] There I found business going on as usual. The Ambassador, busy as he was, granted me a few minutes' interview. I told him about Sunday and what I had seen. He didn't commit himself in any way and was very cool and collected.

At the embassy I heard they were having a big fight on the Liteiny. I walked down there again. I found a mob of about a million people, it seemed to me; and this mob was out for blood. The police were still on the streets and were cutting and slashing in all directions. They used those short police whips with which they can tear a piece out of you if they hit you. I saw a woman lying at one corner of the street who had had her eye and a part of her face picked out by one of these whips. A great many people were banged up and the mob was armed with every weapon you can think of. I started to take pictures with my small camera, but I had to be very careful not to be taken for a police spy. I saw Memes of the London *Daily Mirror*[39] working also, and just by luck I ran into Boris with a revolver and his pockets full of ammunition. Well, we fell on each other's necks like two small children for I was as glad to see him as he was to see me. He said he had seen Memes hit in the back a few minutes before and knocked down by a Cossack whip, but that he had got up and ran down a side street There was also one French newspaper photographer working. I didn't run across him, however.

At 4:30 the Liteiny was in an uproar, as were the side streets. Women were running around with their hair hanging down their backs and Boris said the people were continually shouting, "Kill the police! Kill the police!" At five o'clock more police

---

[38] The embassy, writes Rappaport, was "very well positioned ... in a well-to-do district in the center of the city populated by Russian civil servants and other foreign diplomats." It was a short walk to the Duma at the Tauride Palace and government offices. However, the two-story building, rented from a Russian aristocrat, was modest, poorly furnished and in need of decoration; the ambassador, Francis, thought it looked like a warehouse (Rappaport, *Caught in the Revolution*, 11).

[39] Probably George Mewes, the only official British photographer assigned to the Russian army at the front (Rappaport, *Caught in the Revolution*, 88).

came from two directions and began cutting and slashing. A great many of the Secret Police working in the mobs made arrests. Finally I was arrested and taken to the police station. The man who arrested me was in civilian clothes. Boris went along with me of his own accord. At the police station I showed my pass and Boris told them I was an American newspaper man. But no attention was being paid to passes. They said I was in the mob and that a great many police had been killed by that mob, and that I would have to be investigated. We were taken into the cells and locked up with about nineteen or twenty women and three or four men, packed in so closely that it was almost suffocating. All the cells we saw were packed this way. Boris got bossy and ordered the people to make room for the "Americansky," as he always called me. The people began cheering and kept it up until the police ordered them to be quiet. By this time we could hear the roar of the mob in the prison and the constant rifle and machine-gun fire. Some people in a cell either beside or behind us, I couldn't tell which, were singing the Marseillaise. Ten or fifteen revolver shots rang out and there was no more singing.

At about eight o'clock the firing grew nearer and louder; then there was a roar such as I never heard before in my life. There was something about it that made your blood run cold and hot by turns. The cells were filled with the roar of rifle shots. You could hear the bite of the revolvers and the snarl of machine-guns, mingled with sounds like bombs or heavy artillery, and then voices of men and women screaming, and all the time the shouts of thousands of people in the mob and the smashing of doors and the crashing of glass. The firing inside the building soon stopped. A few minutes later the lock on our door was smashed open and the first thing I knew the people were throwing their arms around Boris and me and kissing us, saying that we were free. The mob had liberated us. In the office or lobby, I found a sight beyond description. Women were down on their knees hacking the bodies of the police to pieces. I saw one woman trying to tear somebody's face with her bare fingers.

In the court outside the jail we found the main mob. Cheers were given as we came out. The red flag was everywhere. As we got into the street, four or five big trucks loaded with rifles and munitions came up, followed by touring cars literally jammed with revolutionists. Boris said, "Get a revolver and some ammunition." I did. Then I noticed a man tearing off a piece of red cloth from a bolt he had under his arm. I tied a strip around my arm and then we went over to the Liteiny.

The mob we were with now was composed of men, women and children and many soldiers. When it halted I noticed back of us the flare of fire. We stood to one side and waited for an hour, watching the mob going down the Liteiny toward the Nevsky. Several "delicatessen" shops had been wrecked. Boris got some cheese and sweet crackers from one. A wine shop located in this neighborhood had been wrecked also and the liquor poured into the street so that the people would not get drunk. The Court of Justice had been set on fire and the blaze lighted up the whole district. I asked Boris to go to the American Embassy, but soldiers were stretched across the street who had not yet joined the people and they were firing on any one who came that way. I went with Boris to the Law Courts, which were burning fiercely. People were carrying out piles of papers which, I was told, were police and court records, and burning them. We then walked back toward the police station and found the mob trying to burn that too. They were having a hard time of it. They carried in a lot of wood but it wouldn't burn. Boris told me that yesterday over 200 people were killed by troops in one factory district. We stayed around the Liteiny until about twelve o'clock, when Boris told me that some of the mob were going to attack the Astoria. That interested me as all my film and clothes were there. By this time the police had given up and fled. The only policemen I saw after I was liberated were some captured by the mob and some lying dead in the streets.

The real turning-point of the revolution in favor of the people came at about the time I was arrested. Before that, for a couple of hours, two regiments had opposed each other on the Liteiny in almost complete silence. I found out later that the members of the regiment holding with the people went over and got the others to join their side a few at a time. The revolution was won by the action of these regiments facing each other, for the result was that the revolutionists' troops were finally joined by all the others. This would probably have been impossible had not the government failed to give definite orders to the officers, so that the latter were in doubt what to do. In a great many cases they ordered the men to go over to the revolution.

All this time along the side streets constant firing was kept up by small bodies of working people, anarchists, and mutinous soldiers who were fighting other soldiers that still remained true to the old government. But I think everything depended on the regiments who were stretched across the Liteiny near the Alexander bridge. These men faced each other with machine-guns, and at first exchanged a few volleys. When the loyal troops marched over and joined the revolutionists' forces the word swept along throughout the city and this scene was immediately duplicated through Petrograd. To the revolutionists, who had no plans arranged, but had acted on the impulse of the moment, this spelled success.

At one o'clock I went to the Duma. This section of the city was in the hands of the revolutionists. As I neared the building, hundreds of automobiles passed me with excited soldiers and civilians cheering and waving guns. The red flag appeared everywhere and in the cars I noticed a great many students. Pamphlets were thrown from the cars and Boris, who translated them, said that they called on the people to act at once, to take arms and go into the streets and help Russia; for Russia was at the turning-point and they must help at once or it would be too late.

I was unable to get into the Duma on account of the jam. Boris and I asked some soldiers if we could go with them. They consented and laughed, patting us on the back. Boris told them I was an "Americansky" revolutionist. All this time soldiers were arriving on the streets leading to the Duma. They were cheered by other troops who had revolted ahead of them.

By the time I arrived on the Nevsky Prospekt, leaving the Duma about two in the morning, I found, with the exception of the Morskaia corner, which runs toward the War Department, Winter Palace, and Admiralty buildings, in control of the revolutionists. Nevertheless, there was a constant roar of musketry over the city. The square in front of the Winter Palace was dark. A search light had been put on the tower of the Admiralty building and it played across the square every few minutes. At about three the corner of the Morskaia and the Nevsky were captured. No matter where I went, I met, as it seemed to me, hundreds of automobile trucks and automobiles filled with soldiers, working people, and civilians armed with all sorts of guns, knives, etc., cheering, but not interfering with anyone who did not interfere with them. You were perfectly safe unless caught between the cross fire of two factions fighting each other. During the fight, while the wide thoroughfares were being cleared, thousands of working people swarmed in the side streets. In the same mob were thousands of civilians in heavy fur coats and polished boots, and a large number of officers whose shoulder straps in many cases indicated that they were above the rank of Colonel. There were students with their green uniforms on, sailors with their typical garb, and soldiers of many different regiments. Rifles were being distributed to the civilians, the arsenal having been captured early on Monday. The only positions the police continued to hold were those about my hotel, St. Isaac's Cathedral, the Admiralty, the Winter Palace and the Foreign Office. The rest of the city was in complete control of the mob.

One of the barracks down behind the Post Office, called Calvary Barracks, was being used by the Minister of Marine for sailors. It held out until about four in the morning. I was with the mob when they attacked this place. I was afraid to approach my hotel, thinking I would be fired on if I did so, the neighborhood being held by loyal troops. After a great deal of firing, with very few killed at this point, the sailors, or marines, finally came over to the people, shouting as they ran, "On to the Post Office! Burn it to the ground!" The secret service headquarters was already a roaring mass of flames.

Every prison in Petrograd had been opened and every one had been liberated. While I was in this mob a woman who had just escaped from one of the prisons took a notion that she wanted to go with me. She was the ugliest woman I ever saw in Russia. She worried me because she insisted on talking with me and attracted attention to me. Boris called to me to come away, but she followed and kept on talking. Finally I decided it would be wiser to humor her. We walked along the Moika Canal,[40] crossed a little bridge and got away from the howling mob. I then gave her a shove that pushed her off her feet and, turning to Boris, said, "Let's run back." We made a detour and got on the other side of the mob by the cathedral. By this time it began to be daylight.

---

[40] The Moika River encircles the central portion of Petrograd, effectively making it an island. It flows from the Fontanka near the Summer Garden past the Field of Mars and crosses the Nevsky before entering the Neva River delta.

At six o'clock we were down by the Tutschkov Bridge, where we met thousands of people, streaming across to join the forces in Petrograd proper, all heavily armed and having artillery with them.

At eight o'clock a committee was appointed to go over to my hotel, the Astoria, and ask the officers there to join the revolutionists. The Astoria is a military hotel, having been taken over by the government, and it was occupied by the Russian staff officers and the English, French, Romanian, and Italian military missions.[41] Word was brought back by the committee that no shots would be fired from this building and that the officers had agreed to all conditions.

I then went to the Astoria to lie down and rest, but I had not been there fifteen minutes when I heard firing at the front of the hotel. I put my camera up on the window ledge, pulled the curtains across, broke out a window pane and began to photograph the mob rushing across the square. Soldiers had advanced from all directions and were firing on the hotel. Boris was lying flat on the floor behind me. Suddenly the door opened and a Russian lady ran in screaming, telling us that the police were firing from the roof with machine-guns. That meant trouble. I warned her to keep away from the window. Instead, she pulled aside the curtain to look out. She was shot through the throat. I carried her back to the bathroom, where she died about fifteen minutes later. I lost a lot of my film, thanks to this woman's damn foolishness.

Then I began to hear shots inside the hotel. I threw my camera into my trunk and pinned my American flag on my room door, leaving it half open. Pretty soon a student entered the room. Boris told him who I was, and said that we had been with the mob and had been arrested and freed. Then we shook hands all around. The student gave orders for the soldiers to stand guard at my door.

Half an hour later word was sent around that we must leave the hotel at once, as it was going to be burned. I didn't believe it, so I carried the film I had made during the last two days back to my room, and started some coffee boiling in the electric percolator. I was joined by some revolutionist soldiers and two sailors who told me about their fight. The police by this time were on the roofs, and were fighting like rats in a trap. The mobs were now in complete control of the city, with the exception of the Admiralty building, and the Winter Palace, where the loyal troops still held out.

By eleven o'clock Tuesday, the Astoria Hotel square was blocked with troops of all grades, artillery, armored car divisions and thousands and thousands of civilians all armed and hunting for the police.

Tuesday was a day of intense fighting. The police would sneak along on the rooftops and fire on the people with machine-guns. By Wednesday afternoon they realized that there was no escape for them, firing having become general from the tops of buildings throughout the city. The worst sniping was done around our neighborhood.

---

[41] The Astoria was often referred to as the "Military Hotel." See n. 11.

Signs are being posted now throughout the city quoting the prices which should be charged for food. Butter has been selling for $2 or $3 a pound; it is now only thirty cents. The revolutionists have found hundreds of places stocked with food that was being held by the government.

I got no sleep till Thursday at midnight.

The behavior of the mobs has been absolutely unbelievably straight. Although a great deal of looting has been done and lots of houses robbed, it has been almost entirely the work of criminals who have been freed from the prisons. The revolutionists opened the prisons and gave liberty to all, and a great many criminals of the very lowest type have been set free. It is they who have done the killing and robbing.

On Tuesday troops from Siberia arrived at the Nikolai Station and joined the mobs. British and French officers are going around together and are cheered wherever they go.

On the evening of March 12, the only section remaining in control of the old government was the War Office, the Admiralty building, and St. Isaac's Cathedral. The police had taken refuge in the cathedral and kept comparatively quiet, only firing a few shots every now and then. For five or six hours the mobs were at a loss to know where the shots were coming from. The priests said there were no police in the cathedral and at first the mobs believed them, but they soon found that all the shots came from that direction. Word was sent to the Duma. The Cossacks came, made a rush on the cathedral, forced an entrance and killed forty police in the basement.

Before the end of Wednesday, a great many of the cabinet ministers were arrested and taken to the Duma, and I understand were later imprisoned in the Peter and Paul Fortress.

For a few hours the fiercest battle of the day took place around the War Office and the Admiralty. I knew that all the troops had gone over when I saw a regiment pass with a band playing the Marseillaise. Upon inquiring, Boris and I found out that they were the troops who had been holding out with the last of the ministers.

On Thursday, the red flag was raised over the Winter Palace. A paper came out yesterday, printed in Russian and issued by the Duma, I think, which gave the first official news of what had happened.

I will write you now fully just what is taking place. These letters I wish you would save until I return home. I will not write any more today, as I am tired, but I have more to tell you and I'll begin again tomorrow. From now on I will write you daily letters of what is happening in the new republic of Russia.

Don

XVII. Petrograd, March 19

Dear Dot:

Well, after a week of revolution, things are beginning to settle down today. I see things changing for the better. The government has posted notices throughout the city and has placed advertisements in the papers asking the workmen to resume work, and many men have gone back to the factories. The manager of one of the English factories making munitions here feels quite encouraged and reports that 70 percent of his people have returned to work. He also told me that one of their managers, an Englishman, was killed last week. During the height of the trouble he went up into one of the towers of the factory and was standing on the balcony, watching a fire. He was probably mistaken for one of the police who were in hiding, and was shot through the head and instantly killed. His body will be sent back to England.

Last night firing was resumed in different parts of the city by people operating from automobiles. These people are probably members of the old government or police. They are firing on the military police force, that is, the police force organized to take the place of the old police. They have accounted for a great many people. On one corner they drove into a crowd, opened fire with machine guns and killed twenty or thirty, and then managed to escape. This will be stopped in a few days, as the government is now issuing numbers to all automobiles and cars without numbers will be stopped and the occupants will have to give an account of themselves.

On Saturday the streets were quiet, principally on account of one of the worst blizzards ever experienced in Russia, which took the anger out of the mob.

The banks and shops have reopened and food is being distributed with lavish hands. The city's militia has already started to disarm criminals and hooligans by the hundreds. I hear that most of the criminals have been arrested and placed under lock and key again.

The acts of these criminals are most horrible. I went into the home of a physician who lived in a big apartment house near the old Austrian Embassy, and he took me across the hall to an apartment where a Russian family had lived and showed me a sight I shall never forget. Criminals, dressed as soldiers, had come into the apartment and said they had orders to search for police whom they thought were hiding there. They were invited into the apartment. When once inside they closed the door and, while one of them stood guard, the others attacked the wife of the man and his three daughters, one of the daughters being only ten years of age. They remained until the early hours of the morning, then packed up all the silver of value and left. This dastardly crime was discovered by a friend of the family who called the next day about noon. This is only one of hundreds of instances I have been told about although it is the only one I actually saw the evidence of. These criminals are being rounded up, as I say, just as fast as possible; but I expect to hear of a great many more outrages before they are all caught.

The story of the last day of the revolution, which I call March 13, is very interesting. The President of the Duma, on March 12, issued an appeal at three a.m., calling on the people to spare life and property. This was done at the command of an executive committee which was composed of the following: Mih. Vlad. Rodzianko, A. F. Kerensky, N. C. Cheidze, V. N. Shulgin, P. N. Miliukov, M. A. Karaulov, A. I. Konovalov, L. L. Dmitriukov, V. A. Rjevsky, S. I. Shidlovsky, N. V. Nekrasov, V. N. Lvov, Colonel Englehardt.

The other order they issued at the same time and had thrown from automobiles to the mobs was a message from the temporary committee and members of the national Duma, wherein they said that, on account of internal disorders brought about by the old regime, they found themselves forced to take into their own hands the reestablishment of national and public order. They appealed to the people to help them, and asked the support of the army at the same time to aid them in creating a new government which would meet with the wishes of the people of Russia.

The Duma is located in the Tauride Palace. It is filled with prisoners, the police and other members of the old government who have been arrested. I saw I. G. Shcheglovitov,[42] who was arrested on February 12, brought in by the soldiers. They did not treat him roughly. Except for a few words spoken to him in a quiet tone there was nothing to indicate that he was in the hands of a committee representing the new Russia.

B. V. Stürmer, the former president of the Council of Ministers, has also been arrested, and Protopopov, who, I am told, was the real cause of the Russian trouble, came himself to the Duma and was in the building before anyone realized he was there. At that time the cry was on all lips, "Kill Protopopov!" How he was able to get to the Duma without being arrested is beyond me. He appeared in the hall and asked a student where the committee representing the people was located. They told him where the room was, and another student volunteered the information that no one could see the committee. He then told them he was Protopopov. Although I am told be said it in a low voice, it seemed as if all in the building heard it. The word flashed over the city, "Protopopov is arrested." He was then brought before the committee and, I understand, has been taken to the Peter and Paul Fortress.

The Chief of Police of Petrograd, Major General Balk, has also been arrested, as have Admiral Giers and Vice-Admiral Kartzev. These are only a few of several thousand. Some of them have been taken from their homes by force, and others have given themselves up. They are brought before the Duma, where they are all held a short time, questioned, and then told that they must stand trial before the courts of free Russia, which are being established.

---

[42] Ivan Shcheglovitov (1861–1918), president of the Imperial Council and a former minister of justice. He was imprisoned in the Peter and Paul Fortress and, together with other monarchists, executed by the Bolsheviks during the Red Terror.

The Peter and Paul Fortress is now the home of many a member of the old regime and the royal family. Here is one story. The Duma last week sent a dozen soldiers to the home of a Russian officer of rank. When they knocked the door was opened by one of the servants, who asked them to step in quickly. This home faces the Neva and is on the same street as the Winter Palace. They stepped in and said they had come with an order for the arrest of so-and-so, by order of the Duma. The servant went upstairs. They remained standing below. To their surprise, they were fired upon and five of them were killed. People told me more were killed, but I was near the place where this happened and went into the house afterwards while the mob was looting the place. I saw five bodies in the hallway. Another story is that they were actually killed by their comrades while fighting over the loot. The other soldiers thereupon rushed upstairs and wounded the officer and his servant. Then the mob dragged them out into the street and were taking them to the Duma when some other soldiers came along and asked who the prisoners were. They were told what the prisoners had done, which infuriated them so much that one of them put a gun to the officer's head directly behind the left ear and let go, blowing his head off his body. Both bodies were thrown onto the ice of the Neva. The servant, who had assisted his master and was badly wounded, kicked around on the ice in agony, much to the amusement of the crowd. His sufferings were stopped by the mob taking potshots at him.

The militia is being organized by a man named Kujjynovsky who, I understand, was a professor in one of the colleges or schools in Petrograd. He is drawing most of his recruits from the students.

All the telephones are working again and the former employees of the station, with a few exceptions, have returned to work. Telephone communication is forbidden with any person connected with the old government. The president of the Duma, Rodzianko,[43] granted an interview to Florence Harper on Thursday and also permitted me to make photographs of the executive committee meeting. I have been given a

---

[43] Mikhail Rodzianko (1859–1924), a deputy in the Duma since 1907, served as chairman of the Fourth Duma from November 1912 until its dissolution in October 1917. He opposed Rasputin and the Empress Alexandra's meddling in state affairs and urged the Tsar to promulgate reforms and appoint a government that had the support of the people. On March 1, he exchanged telegrams with General Ruzsky, the commander of the northern front in Pskov, where the Tsar's train had been stopped on its way back to Petrograd. Rodzianko reported that the situation in the city had deteriorated so badly that the only option to restore order was for the Tsar to abdicate. After consulting with his army and navy commanders, the Tsar stepped down in favor of his son Alexey, but because of the boy's health (he suffered from hemophilia) then appointed his brother, Grand Duke Michael, to succeed. After meetings with Duma members, including Rodzianko, Michael declined the crown. Rodzianko led the Duma delegation that negotiated with the Petrograd Soviet over the establishment of the Provisional Government, and served as prime minister for a few days before being succeeded by Prince Lvov. After the October Revolution, he left Petrograd. When it became clear the White Army had lost the Civil War, he emigrated to Serbia in 1920.

pass to photograph everything I wish and another to go wherever I wish on the front. I asked the executive committee to give me a copy of the telegram which was sent to the Tsar on March 13. This telegram was sent by the so-called Imperial Council, and reads as follows:

> Your Imperial Highness, we, the undersigned members of the Imperial Council, by election, in recognition of the threatening danger approaching the country, appeal to you in order to fulfill the duty of conscience toward you and toward Russia.
>
> In consequence of the complete disorganization of transportation and the absence of necessary materials, the factories and mills have stopped. The enforced idleness and extreme acuteness of the provision crisis, caused by, the said disorganization of transportation, has brought the masses to the limits of desperation. This feeling has been made still worse by the hatred of the government and the grave suspicion of the authorities which have taken such deep root in the soul of the people.
>
> All this has taken the form of popular disorders of great strength, and the troops are now beginning to join this movement. The government, which has never enjoyed the confidence of Russia, has been definitely discredited and is entirely helpless to cope with the threatening position.
>
> Sire, the remaining of the present government in power will mean the complete wreck of the legitimate order and lead to inevitable defeat in the war, the fall of the dynasty and great misfortunes for Russia.
>
> We consider the final and only means to be the decisive change by Your Imperial Majesty of the course of the internal policy, in accordance with the frequently expressed wishes of the representatives of the people, the classes and the public organizations—the immediate convocation of the legislative bodies, the retirement of the present staff of the Council of Ministers and the entrusting to a person deserving of the national confidence to present to you, Gospodar, for confirmation the list of a new cabinet capable of managing the country, in complete accord with the representatives of the people. Every hour is precious. Further delay and hesitation threaten incalculable misfortunes.
>
> Your Imperial Majesty's faithful subjects, members of the Imperial Council: Vasiliev, Vernadsky, Vainstein, Glebov, Grimm, Guchkov, Prince Drutskoi-Sokolinsky, Dyakov, Subashev, Komsin Laptev, Marin, Meller-Zakomelsky, Oldenburg, Stakhev, Savitzky, Stakhovich, Count Tolstoi, Prince Troubetzkoi, Shmurlo, Shumakher, and Iumashev.

It is amusing to me how things are working along. The old government had hardly been overthrown before the politicians of Russia began to work. The Socialists have already formed their party and on the 12th, a council of workmen's deputies was constituted from representatives of factories and mills and from the different regiments who had helped to overthrow the old government, also from the Democratic Socialist party. In fact they have allowed representatives from all parties to sit in this council. Their cry is organization, that the people must be organized and show their strength and make laws which will protect them before the capitalists have a chance. They have appointed their own officers to establish authority in the city here. They have also had notices posted asking the people here to rally around them, promising that everyone will be satisfied. They wound this up with a statement that they are sending deputies throughout Russia with the message of what they will give. They say that everyone is to be equal. Well, this is all very well to say. I think I know Russia better than I did a few weeks ago, and when it comes to all Russians being free and equal, nothing doing! It will never work, and personally I think they are starting out wrong. The members of this Council are the orneriest bunch of devils I have ever met. I will bet $1,000 to a cent that 90 percent of them cannot read or write, but they are being led by some pretty smart people. They are handing out proclamations every five minutes to appeal to the rabble they represent. One of their most popular proclamations is, that the old government, when you asked for bread, gave you lead. They are trying to take all of the credit for the revolution. They said: "We seized the military depots, we did it all, and now Russia is free." Well, they are mistaken. Russia is going to have trouble for the next ten years if this is the beginning of the new government.

As I see it, we have two Councils here, the Council of the Executive Committee, members of the old Duma, and this Council of Soldiers' and Workmen's Deputies. One of the first orders issued by the Executive Committee was that all men in the army were equal, and soldiers did not have to salute their officers any more.[44] If this order has reached the front it has wrecked the Russian army. Russia is short of officers as it is and from what I have seen in the last few days here in Petrograd, I shudder to think of what might happen at the front. They also announced that each company at the front shall have a committee, that this committee shall send representatives to sit in this council of theirs and that no orders are to be issued until the committee of the regiment votes on them. It is silly. I am almost afraid that German intrigue has started to work again. Still, you don't know what to think.

The Duma is trying to establish some kind of order and better relations between the officers and privates, but at present the soldiers are overdoing it. Some of them who have personal grudges against the officers in their companies are making it hard for the officers. A great many of the officers have been thrown out of their regiments and had their places taken by soldiers who have been promoted from the ranks. These soldiers are uneducated, as a rule. In spite of this, however, the officers have held a

---

[44] The famous Order No. 1, issued by the Executive Committee of the Petrograd Soviet (Ispolkom) (Pipes, *A Concise History of the Russian Revolution*, 86, 88).

meeting and almost to a man have marched to the Duma and offered their services in any capacity, taking an oath of allegiance to the Russian republic. They are doing everything in their power to help. I have seen 2,000 of them in one crowd marching to the Duma.

There has been very little drinking among the soldiers. An incident occurred during the sacking of the Astoria which impressed me very much. The mob made a break for the wine cellars, but to their surprise they found that most of the bottles and barrels had been broken open and were flooding the cellars two or three feet deep. I found out that this had been done by some British officers who were living at the hotel, and that they had done it to protect the people. Some of the bottles that remained unbroken were found by the soldiers and mob. But when they carried them out to the streets the bottles were taken away by others in the mob and broken and the liquor allowed to run away. This happened in a great many instances. What drinking there was was done mostly by the criminals and hoodlums. All wine cellars and liquor ware-houses are now being guarded by the new government.

A general in charge of the Artillery Academy the other day brought his whole command to the Duma building, drew them up to attention, and requested that they be allowed to swear their oath of allegiance to the new government. Rodzianko, the President of the Duma, came out and said that the new government would need the support of all Russia and that everyone should now lend every effort he could to carry on the war to a successful finish and not to be led astray, since their brothers by the thousands were at the front and needed support and encouragement. He wound up his address by calling upon everyone to give a welcome to this general and his troops. His last words were, "Remember Russia will have critical times, rough roads will have to be gone over and we have just started the fight." While addressing this crowd he was surrounded by a great many members of the executive committee. Another member of the executive committee briefly addressed another regiment which had just come up, saying, "Let us not lose time in talking, brothers; we must join the army and co-operate with each other; officers and soldiers must be friends, and everyone must obey the orders of the temporary committee of the Duma. This will be our only means to conquest." There were fully 75,000 people packed in the square in front of the Duma at this time. The speaker then shouted, "If we don't do this today, tomorrow may be too late." Then a roar went up from the crowd, "We will do it."

I will write you a longer letter this evening. I am going out to get some more information.

Don

XVII. Petrograd, March 20

Dear Dot:

Last night I intended to write you another letter but was too tired when I got back to the hotel. So I am writing you now, while waiting for Boris to bring me some breakfast.

I hear that very little trouble has occurred at Moscow, only one policeman being killed there. We had reports last week for a few days that it was simply hell in Moscow and other cities, but reports are coming in at headquarters that prove all these stories were lies.

Kronstadt[45] had a lot of trouble, though. Kronstadt, I might add, is the big fortress that protects Petrograd (see figure 2). At Kronstadt the admiral in charge was killed along with 380 naval officers. From the information I get at the General Staff, it seems that these officers were called out and shot one by one in front of the cathedral. I asked how many of the revolutionists had been killed there and they told me only four or five. A naval officer told me today that the officers killed at Kronstadt were experts and that the Russian navy is almost useless now that these men are dead.

The soldiers are getting nasty with their officers. Whoever allowed the order to be issued that soldiers were to be treated as equals is going to be responsible for a lot of disorder. The soldiers are now drunk with their new-born freedom, and are overdoing it. They seem to think that every time they meet an officer they ought to insult him. I have, in the last few days, seen hardly more than five soldiers salute their officers, but I have seen old generals pushed off the walk by soldiers.

I went to the opera the other night, and such a change! It was the Imperial Opera House and they have taken down the royal purple curtain and have hung in its place one of bright red. The boxes were filled with soldiers and sailors and workingmen and their wives and sweethearts. I wish I could have made a picture of it. I was more amused and laughed more at these people than I did at the show. The show was some kind of an opera which I could not understand, but I could understand the people. Most of them had never been to a theater in their lives, and think of it, they were now attending the Imperial Opera. The boxes were jammed with people of this class and about every five minutes the orchestra would be requested to play the Russian Marseillaise, which is a version of the French, and everyone would stand. It almost

---

[45] The naval base of Kronstadt on Kotlin Island, on the Neva River near the head of the Gulf of Finland, was established by Peter the Great in 1704. Its fortifications guarded the sea approaches to the city, and it was the main base for Russia's Baltic Fleet with 30,000 sailors. During the February Revolution, they rose up, killed their officers, seized the arsenal and ships in dock, and voted in their own Soviet. Even after the Kronstadt leaders agreed to the authority of the Petrograd Soviet in May, the island remained a "hotbed of revolutionary militancy, stockpiled with weapons ... and ripe for Bolshevik exploitation" (Rappaport, *Caught in the Revolution*, 207). During the Civil War, the sailors supported the Bolsheviks. In 1921, they rebelled against harsh Bolshevik rule, but the uprising was suppressed by the army and Cheka.

reached the point where you stood through the whole performance. A great many of the soldiers and workingmen brought their guns with them to the opera. It was a sight I shall never forget.

Out in front of the opera was another scream. It looked as if all the droshkys in Petrograd had driven up there. Before the revolution it was against the law for a droshky to stop in front of the door. Now they had it their own way and were doing a land office business, while the automobiles of the rich were forced to stand aside as the people of the new republic took the droshkys and drove home. These droshky drivers are lucky. If I had my way they would all have been killed during the revolution. They are outlaws. Before the revolution these men were making so much money that they could afford to buy bread and feed it to their horses. Now they are even more independent and charge more exorbitant prices than ever, and there is no way to get back at them. They are also now getting plenty of feed for the horses.

The royal stables have been taken over by the revolutionary committees and the carriages, sleighs and automobiles are being used by the Soldiers' and Workmen's Deputies. The warehouses where the government had kept great quantities of food stored are being emptied and distributed throughout Petrograd, but the first thing they will have to do is to start getting food in here, as they will soon run out.

A great many regiments have arrived in Petrograd from the outlying districts. On reaching the city they march to the Duma, where they swear their allegiance and take an oath to the new government. They are cheered all along the line of march.

The new Minister of Foreign Affairs, Miliukov, I met in Chicago[46] a few years ago. He speaks English perfectly and was connected with the Chicago University. I had a talk with him today. He promised to assist me in every way possible and also asked me to send out as many pictures as I could and to see that the story of Russia reached the outside world. He likes America and I think he is one of the best men in this new national cabinet. The Minister of War and Navy, Guchkov,[47] is a very good

---

[46] Because of his political activities, Miliukov lost his Moscow University position in 1894 and spent several years lecturing outside Russia. He visited the United States in 1903 to give public lectures on Russian history and politics at the University of Chicago and the Lowell Institute in Boston.

[47] Alexander Guchkov (1862–1936) led the Octobrist party in the Third Duma, convened in November 1907. The Octobrists were a moderate party prepared to cooperate with the monarchy. In 1915, Guchkov was among the founders of the Progressive Bloc, and was appointed minister of war and navy in the Provisional Government. A close ally of Miliukov, Guchkov wanted to retain the monarchy to preserve social stability; he was one of two Duma deputies who traveled to Pskov to advise the Tsar to abdicate. Guchkov was forced to resign on April 29 in the uproar over Miliukov's Note (see n. 19). He continued to support the Duma and Provisional Government in its struggle against the Petrograd Soviet, and after the October Revolution provided financial support to the White Army. When it became clear the Bolsheviks would win the Civil War, he emigrated to Germany and later France.

man, and was formerly President of the Duma. Prince George Lvov[48] is also a good man. The Minister of Justice is one of the youngest members of the council. His name is Kerensky. He is a socialist and a lawyer and was formerly a Russian journalist. Kerensky is one of the greatest orators I have heard. Every day at the Duma there has been a demonstration of workingmen, soldiers, and socialists. Boris told me they want all the old regime ministers killed at once. Kerensky got up on the steps and delivered a stirring address. At least, it sounded all right to me, and Boris told me afterwards what he had said. In a way he is doing a lot of good. One of the most important things that he is asking of the soldiers is to obey their officers. He also says that no one will be executed without trial in open court. One of the strongest appeals that he makes is that the soldiers should listen to their officers and not to outsiders, as he says that the agents of the old regime are working night and day to bring about another revolution. Kerensky always starts his addresses with the word "comrades," and he gives a talk that appeals to the uneducated classes. He seems to me a very clever politician. I believe he is playing something higher.

For the last few days the soldiers and mobs have been busy knocking off the royal coat of arms wherever it appeared in Petrograd. At the Winter Palace where the crown rested on the eagle's head they have knocked off the crown on the big gates, but in most places they have knocked the whole bird off. Why, I do not know. It seems foolish to me, but someone issued the order and everyone is removing this crest. I noticed on Morskaia that a shop that used to display pictures of the royal family has taken them down.

They are now taking up a collection for the relief of the families of the people killed during the revolution, for the Red Cross and for about a thousand other things, including the relief of the prisoners that they are going to bring back from Siberia. One bank alone subscribed about a quarter of a million dollars to this fund. This same bank, however, is in the insurance business. It writes burglary insurance. After this Siberian mob has been back a short time it ought to do a land office business in burglary policies.

The government has posted soldiers around the different places where art treasures are stored to protect them from being stolen. They have also abolished the censor's office. There is no more censorship on anything except military affairs at the front.

---

[48] Prince Georgy Yevgenyevich Lvov (1861–1925), an aristocrat and former civil servant, joined the Constitutional Democrat Party (Kadets) in 1905, was elected to the Duma and became the first prime minister in the Provisional Government. Pipes describes him as "an innocuous and indolent civic activist," chosen because he lacked strong opinions or authority. Lvov served as a figurehead, the leadership in the new government taken by Miliukov, the minister of foreign affairs, and Kerensky, the minister of justice (Pipes, *A Concise History of the Russian Revolution*, 84–85). Lvov resigned as prime minister after the failed Bolshevik coup in July, and Kerensky succeeded him. He was arrested during the October Revolution but escaped and eventually settled in France.

Thousands upon thousands of tons of food of all kinds are being discovered in every conceivable place in and around Petrograd. This is being seized as fast as it is found and notices are being published that people hoarding food will be tried for treason and shown little mercy. This law pleased me very much, as I am getting hardly anything to eat at all. The food they have had here I cannot digest properly. At the present time I am just about all in on account of this poor food. I wish you would hurry up and send the food I cabled you about.

The foreign minister, Miliukov, gave a reception to the ambassadors of the Allies Sunday afternoon. He also made an announcement that the Emperor Nicholas had renounced the throne for himself and his son in favor of Grand Duke Michael Alexandrovich. This was done at a town called Pskov, where the Emperor's train was met by a committee representing the Duma. The Grand Duke announced that he would not take the throne unless the people by vote wished it. The story, as I got it, of the abdication of the Tsar is as follows:

The Tsar signed the document on the train at Pskov. He was on his way here but had been halted early in the week. From officers I understand that he was on his way back to Petrograd when he first heard of the trouble. I believe that if he could have been in the city Monday and had driven down the main street of Petrograd, the Nevsky Prospekt, and stood up in the back of his automobile with his hat off and talked, as Teddy Roosevelt would have done, he would still be the Tsar of Russia. He could have had the people with him and all that he would have had to do would have been to grant what the people wanted, to see to it that bread was brought into Petrograd, and to appoint new ministers. I believe, as others do whom I have talked with, that no one would have touched him. As it was, he did nothing; why, I do not know. Probably because royalty doesn't do things that way.

He was notified at Pskov that the Duma was sending a committee to him there. This is true, for a member of the Duma committee and one of the ministers of the new cabinet went to this place and had an interview with him before General Ruzsky,[49] who was a member of the Council of the Empire and of the Military Council. Count Frederiks,[50] one of the ministers of the court, and several others told the Emperor the

---

[49] General Nikolai Ruzsky (1854–1918), commander of the Northern Front with headquarters at Pskov, where the Tsar's train was halted on March 1. The next morning, Ruzsky showed the Tsar the messages he had exchanged with Rodzianko about the deteriorating situation in Petrograd, and the call by Duma deputies for the Tsar to abdicate. Following the February Revolution of 1917 he resigned his command and went south to the Caucasus, where he joined other Tsarist generals. Captured by the Bolsheviks on September 11, 1918, he was executed along with the other officers.

[50] Count Vladimir Borisovich Frederiks (1838–1927) served as imperial household minister from 1897 to 1917. He was responsible for the administration of the imperial family's personal affairs and living arrangements, as well as the awarding of imperial honors and medals. A staunch conservative, he described the deputies of the First Duma as "a gang of criminals who are only waiting for the signal to throw themselves upon the ministers and cut their throats."

story of what had happened in Petrograd and how many different regiments had gone over to the revolutionists, among the first to revolt being his own Imperial Guard. I am told that when he heard that his favorite troops had gone against him he was greatly shaken. They also told him that troops were going over to the new government as fast as they could, and that wires were being received from all over Russia reporting that such and such regiments had sworn the oath of allegiance to the new government. The Emperor then asked what he should do and what they wanted, and I am told that one of the ministers from the Duma said they wanted his throne. The Emperor then retired to his own car to think it over. After a while he issued an order appointing the Grand Duke Nicholas Commander-in-Chief of all the Russian armies and Prince Lvov Prime Minister. Later he went back to the committee and said that he did not want to be separated from his son and that he was going to abdicate in favor of a brother, as he could not live without his boy. The Emperor was then handed a paper which had been made out in advance, but I understand before he signed it several changes were made. A Russian general advised him not to sign away the throne, but to open the Dvinsk front[51] and let the Germans through, saying that they would keep him on the throne. I am told that no one ever saw him as angry as he was at that suggestion. In a voice trembling with rage he said: "I am no traitor to Russia." I used to think that the royal family was pro-German, but that statement proved to me, and I think to all Russians, that Nicholas was not a traitor, but was loyal to his country.

I am told that the Tsar was trying to escape and get to the Grand Headquarters, but that the revolutionary agents arranged it so that he could not. I also understand that most of the telegrams that were sent him by officials in Petrograd were held up and that he never really knew the true conditions. After he had abdicated we had a report that he was being sent to Petrograd; also that his son had been killed and that the Tsarina had committed suicide. Two of the children are sick at the Palace with measles.

I was talking with a Russian Jew today and am surprised that the Jews do not hold a big celebration. I asked him if they were making arrangements to, and he asked, why. I said: "You have been made free." He answered: "By whom?" I said: "By the soldiers and workmen who say that everyone is equal." He told me that he was more afraid of them than he was of the Cossacks under the old regime. When I have time someday I am going to write you a story of the Jew in Russia.

During the February Revolution, his private mansion was pillaged and set on fire. Frederiks lived in Petrograd until 1925, when he was allowed to leave for Finland.

[51] Dvinsk (today Daugavpils) was a strategic fortress town in Latvia, on the front line after Russia's retreat from Poland and Galicia in 1915 (see figure 3).

They found an old man in a cell at Schüsselburg[52] who had been there twenty years. He was at the head of a band of anarchists before he was cast into this prison. They tell me his hair reached to his knees. Boris says that his name is Lopatine, but as he is doubtful of the spelling, I do not know whether that is correct.

The Duma is the center of attraction here now. The Duma has given one room over to the newspaper men, but I think that everyone in Petrograd is using the room for business. I have never yet been able to find a place there to sit down. The Duma is just one seething mass of people, and about every other person you meet is making a speech.

The train service is now as regular as it formerly was. Even during the height of the revolution, trains arrived and departed from the station.

The old general whose name, I think, is Sukhomlinov,[53] former Minister of War, made a good piece of copy for several of the newspaper men who saw him brought into the Duma. The soldiers seemed to have it in for him, for I am told he was arrested by a committee from the Duma and was brought there and that the soldiers demanded that they be allowed to kill him. They tore most of his clothing off his body in the hallway of the Duma trying to get at him. The general, I am told, never said a word, but stood with his arms folded as his decorations were ripped off his breast and his clothes literally torn from his body.

The newspapers are beginning to come out now. Before, we depended on news issued by different committees, which had their work organized in a fairly orderly manner. They had automobiles that distributed at a certain hour at certain street corners proclamations and news of the situation in Russia, printed on pieces of paper about the size of a page of the *Saturday Evening Post*. This was all the news we got.

The American Consulate has been ordered to keep open until twelve o'clock each night. With the exception of the Englishman I told you about being shot, I have heard of no foreigners being killed or molested during the revolution. Russians tell me, though, that I will see plenty of trouble in the near future. They say that the factions struggling for power are going to clash, and predict that the first serious trouble will be between the Duma and the Soldiers' and Workmen's Deputies. I hope this doesn't come to pass, but I can almost feel it in the air, when I look at that committee calling themselves the Soldiers' and Workmen's Council. It is very interesting to sit and watch them from the balcony, to study their individual actions. I made a

---

[52] The Tsarist government used the fortress at Schlüsselburg, at the head of the Neva River on Lake Ladoga, 22 miles east of Petrograd, as a political prison.

[53] Vladimir Aleksandrovich Sukhomlinov (1848–1926) served as the chief of the General Staff in 1908–09 and minister of war until 1915. With the Russian army in retreat from Poland, he was dismissed, accused of failing to provide necessary armaments and munitions. He was arrested during the February Revolution but released in May 1918. He moved to Finland and later Germany.

photograph of them the other day which I hope comes out all right. I haven't developed it yet, but I will in a few days.

The pictures I have developed so far, made during the first days of the revolution are fine. I have already sent copies to *Leslie's* and to France and England, which I hope get through all right.

I learned over at the General Staff that the reason Brusilov's[54] great advance was stopped was that his supplies were shut down, though there were enough supplies in Russia. German intrigue in Petrograd saw to it that they never left the bases. Warsaw, they say, would have never fallen if ammunition had reached the troops when it was needed.

A general, or a colonel, I do not know which rank he is, has promised me a great deal of information from the records of his department. He has just taken over this office and says it is astonishing how boldly the Germans were working and what dastardly things they were able to accomplish and how easy it was for them in a few hours in Petrograd to undo what the army had accomplished at the front through months of hard work.

While the revolution was at its height and the mobs were hunting the police from their holes and hiding places, they were also systematically running down all classes of people in the employ of Germany, or who were Germans by birth and were suspected of German intrigue. They also went after hundreds of people who had German titles and names.

The mob on Wednesday went down to old Count Frederiks' house, below the Post Office, and wrecked it in a few minutes, and then put a match to it. One of his female relatives, a cripple, had no harm done to her, and was given every tender care when she was assisted out of the house. I am told that she is a daughter, but I am not sure. Anyway, the mob which I thought was going to deal hardly with her showed her a great deal of consideration.

---

[54] Aleksei Alekseevich Brusilov (1853–1926) was the most successful Russian general of World War I. In July 1914, his 8th Army in Galicia crushed the Austro-Hungarian forces, rapidly advancing almost 100 miles; however, the defeat of the Russian armies in Prussia led to a general retreat. In early 1915, Brusilov again advanced in the Carpathian Mountains. In March 1916, he was given command of the Southwest Front. Instead of mounting a conventional offensive by concentrating artillery and men at one point on the front, he distributed his forces the length of the front, looking for weak points. The new tactic, the so-called Brusilov Breakthrough, resulted in rapid gains and the capture of 400,000 Austro-Hungarian prisoners, but Brusilov was forced to retreat when an offensive to the north did not materialize and the Germans moved seventeen divisions from France to stop the advance. In May 1917, Brusilov was appointed commander in chief of the Russian army. Although Brusilov supported the revolution, his first concern was to win the war; he was concerned about the breakdown of discipline in the army and asked the Provisional Government to take firm action to stop soldiers deserting or disobeying orders. This stand made him unpopular, and in July 1917 he was replaced by his former deputy, Lavr Kornilov. After the October Revolution, Brusilov, unlike other Russian generals, supported the Bolsheviks and urged former officers to join the Red Army.

Boris tells me that the police are to be sent to the front where they will have to fight. A Russian policeman never had to go to the front; that was his reward for being an agent of the government. The gendarmes, who are mounted police, were also exempt from military service. These men will now have to go into the trenches. This has been ordered for all districts in Russia where there is a police or gendarme force.

Don

XVIII. Petrograd, March 21

Dear Dot:

Well, the anarchists are still celebrating the abdication of the Tsar. But some people in Petrograd still doubt that he really has abdicated. I understand that a whole regiment marched to the Duma and asked to be told officially if it was true. Although he was hated by a great many people, I find that as a rule the soldiers have nothing against him; it is only the anarchists who hiss his name. But I find that all denounce the Empress.

The revolution isn't two weeks old yet and already they are fighting amongst themselves. They talk about their brilliant future, but I can't see from the look of things that it is very promising. As things stand now, all are in favor of the republican form of government, such as we have in the United States. I hear through Boris that this is the sentiment in all the large cities.

The Duma has ordered Mr. Romanov and his wife, former rulers of this country, to be imprisoned in Tsarskoe Selo palace (see figure 2).[55] Miliukov, the Foreign Minister, notified the American Ambassador today that Russia is now ready to make a commercial treaty with the United States. I can imagine that in New York and throughout the United States the Jews are holding pow-wows all night long now that they have been granted free and equal rights in Russia.

We had this story in the papers today from the front. Germans at one point stuck up a board with a notice pasted on it, "Your ministers have been arrested." The Russians immediately put up a notice, "Not our ministers, your ministers." One of the newspapers near the corner of the Sadovaia and the Nevsky had the story posted in the window and it attracted a great deal of attention.

The former Tsarina is getting it hot and heavy in the papers. We were told today by the committee of safety that only 3,000 people have been killed. I placed the loss

---

[55] Tsarskoe Selo (usually translated as "Tsar's Village") was an estate fifteen miles south of Petrograd, developed by Catherine the Great in the eighteenth century as a royal country residence with houses for other members of the nobility and guests. Tsar Nicholas II and his family lived in the Alexander Palace, built in neoclassical style in the 1790s. The estate had a garrison to guard the imperial family and a private railroad line to Petrograd. The Tsar and his family were placed under house arrest at Tsarskoe Selo on March 9 after his abdication and return from Pskov.

of life at 5,000, or a little more. We also hear that Nicholas wanted to throw Stürmer and Protopopov and the other crooked ministers out, but his wife wouldn't let him. Poor man, at heart he was a real Russian and even now I believe that if he were asked, he would go to the front and fight for Russia. The general staff has been re-organized to a great extent and is carrying on the work as of old. The real danger today is that the extremists will get control of things and the Duma will be powerless to act. The Duma at present has some very able members who can be supplemented from time to time by other men as they come forward. I doubt, however, if they will take advantage of things now while they have a chance.

Kerensky let me make a picture of him today and told me I could visit the Winter Palace. It is rumored that the Emperor will be brought there, and I hope to make pictures it he does come. Kerensky told me I could have the inside story from his records of how old Rasputin was killed. He told me the pall-bearers of Rasputin were members of the royal family and ministers and other officers and that Protopopov himself was among the pallbearers, and that the Empress put on deep mourning.

The servants are beginning to get stuck up with this new-born freedom. You have to call them "comrade" or "friend." The servant in my room notified me today that from now on I will have to shine my own shoes. The servants are going to hold a meeting tonight in some big hall where they will arrange their plans for the future. The servants at the hotel demanded the same rooms for their use as the guests have and gave notice that the rooms should be designated at once.

The munition factory workers are holding meetings now and asking those who are not at work to return at once. Most of them have marched in demonstrations carrying banners saying that they will do their utmost now that they are free. Guchkov has asked the people to be patient until he can organize the War Department. He promises to remove all the incompetents and have only experts around him, and says that the war will not lose a day by the revolution. He also says that he will order hundreds of officers to the front who have always been able to stay in soft jobs because they were favorites. He says no graft will be tolerated, and that all commissions will be reissued.

Guchkov is very popular. He was the head of a committee of the Duma, that made inquiry into the conduct of General Sukhomlinov, former Minister of War.

Ambassador Francis is a frequent visitor to the Duma, accompanied by Captain McCully,[56] one of the navy attachés here. Francis has done more than anyone else here to create friendly relations between the new government and America. At the height of the revolution, the embassy was cut off entirely and he saw the hottest

---

[56] Newton McCully (1867–1951) had served as a military observer with the Russian army during the Russo-Japanese War in 1904. In 1914, he returned to Russia as a naval attaché. In 1918, as a rear admiral, he was placed in command of U.S. Navy forces in northern Russia, and in 1919 was sent to south Russia on an intelligence mission, to join the Whites and report on the strength of the Bolsheviks and their potential threat.

fighting from his window. As late as Wednesday night of revolution week there was constant firing from house-tops in his neighborhood. While the Duma was in a hurrah over the ministers who had been arrested Francis was granted permission to enter and go round as he pleased.

My stomach is bothering me a great deal. I have tried several times to get a doctor, but have failed so far. Still there is no use hollering.

Don

XIX. Petrograd, March 22

Dear Dot:

I did not intend to write you at all today for I am in such pain I cannot move. It is now getting so serious that I think I shall have to have the embassy notified and see if they can get some doctor to come and see what is the matter with me. Boris has done all in his power for me. I have taken about thirty different kinds of pills on his recommendation. Nothing has given me any relief.

My bed has not been changed. When I asked the servant to do it she only sneered at me. If I ever get up out of this bed, I will take a punch at one of them.

Boris tells me that the papers have a story out that America has recognized Russia as a republic, that the American Ambassador, accompanied by his whole force, went into the Mariinsky Palace,[57] and that they are now arranging a big demonstration in some district of Petrograd, to march to the embassy and have the Ambassador address them. Boris says that everyone is tickled to death that America was the first to recognize them as a republic. I asked him if France or England or Italy or any of the other Allies had recognized the new government yet, and he said, "No." He also told me that Nicholas had arrived at Tsarskoe Selo Palace today and was in the custody of the members of the Duma and that his arrival did not cause any excitement. According to Boris the commander of the guard was put in charge of him and an order had been given for him and his wife to be watched closely. The papers announce that permission has been given to him to walk around the yard and attend church, which Boris says was all he ever did while he was Emperor.

Florence Harper has just come in and tells me that I must lie down flat on my back and not write any more. This morning she told Boris to take my clothes and lock them in the trunk and give the key to her. Her excuse was that she was going to keep me from getting up if any excitement started, and that I was under arrest. I told her

---

[57] Mariinsky Palace, also known as Marie Palace, on the south side of St. Isaac's Square, was the last neoclassical imperial palace to be constructed in Petrograd between 1839 and 1844. From 1905, the upper house of the Duma, the Council of Ministers, most of whom supported the old regime, met at the palace. It was attacked and damaged by crowds during the February Revolution. After the October Revolution, the palace housed various Soviet ministries and academies.

that I was willing to abdicate at once and get rid of this pain with her help. She hurried out saying that she would not come back until she could bring a doctor with her.

Don

XX. Hospital, somewhere in Petrograd, Monday, March 26

Dear Dot:

I guess you wonder why I haven't written to you the last few days. Well, it is a long story. Florence Harper found a doctor, all right, and he gave me some medicine and I immediately became worse. He promised to come back the next day, but didn't, and we finally got another doctor at two in the morning. He is a Russian who speaks English and has been in England and America. He said that I had appendicitis and that I should be taken to a hospital immediately, but he didn't know where I could go as all the hospitals were full of the wounded from the revolution. He and Florence finally, with a great deal of trouble, found the hospital where I am now. Where it is or what they call it, I don't know. I have a room all to myself and two nurses to take care of me. I was taken out of the hotel on a stretcher. They told me a little while ago that I would pull through but that it would be a week or so before I would be up, if not longer.

Yesterday, I noticed a priest coming in the room. Where in the devil he came from and where they got the idea that I had changed my religion from a Presbyterian to a Catholic is beyond me. I noticed he was spreading a table and setting up a couple of candles. I asked the nurse what the idea was and she began to cry. Just then another sister came into the room and said that I should make my peace with God. I then got wise that they thought I was dying. Well, I got mad. If they had tried it some other way I might have died, but the idea of shoving me off before I was ready did not suit me and I threatened to get up and walk back to the hotel in my shirt, if they didn't cut it out. The doctor came in about that time and said I was getting better. The Ambassador has sent word if there is anything he can do to let him know.

Mr. Winship, consul-general, and Mr. Lee, vice-consul, have been splendid. Winship calls every afternoon. I have told Nemo—a nickname I gave him here in Petrograd—not to come each day for it means an expense to him of ten rubles for a droshky, and I can't bear the thought of him spending his money to see me so often with such a small salary.

The doctor lets me write now as long as I don't exert myself too much, so I will get Boris to round up some of the Russians who promised to tell me inside stories. I can listen while it is not possible to take pictures. Florence Harper tells me they are going to bury the dead revolutionists in front of the Winter Palace, where a great grave is now being dug. Some day they will put up a wonderful statue over the spot.

Boris tells me that the Allies have all recognized Russia as a republic and that all the papers have been full of proclamations since I came here, which when translated will give a complete story of what has been going on in Russia this week. But I cannot write any more now.

Don

XXI. Hospital, somewhere in Petrograd, March 30

Dear Dot:

I am still being fed through my legs and chest and I think that there is not a fresh place left in which to give me a meal. They jab the needle into me every two hours and keep me packed in ice. Boris goes out during the day, visiting the Duma, Foreign Office and War Department and a few of the cafés and gets all the papers and proclamations and brings them back and reads to me for hours.

The papers are full of stories that the socialists in Germany should throw out the Kaiser and join their brothers the Russians. They declare that if the Germans do not do this they will fight to their last drop of blood.

A cabinet member named Chkheidze[58] of the Soldiers' and Workmen's Delegates made a motion which was adopted by the members sitting, that an order be issued confiscating all the Tsar's lands. The Minister of Agriculture, Shingarev,[59] has demanded that the government buy up all the grain, forming a monopoly, so that speculation cannot be made in food.

A statement of what it costs to keep the royal family has also been published, which I consider very low. It only cost them a million a year for court ceremonies, another million for one of the palaces where the Tsar lived and 600,000 for automobiles. The automobile item is very low. The royal family saved money for if they had used droshkys it would have cost them 100 times as much. I have spent that much on droshkys myself. That is, I have had to pay 100 times more than anyone else. Each time I step into a droshky the driver begins to figure on another ten rubles, whereas the fare should be thirty kopecks. Under the old government, if you were overcharged you could call a policeman and have the driver arrested. Now if you even protest he gets up on his seat and shouts to the people passing, "Here is one of the old aristocracy who is trying to beat me, a poor droshky driver, out of an honest living." Before I leave Russia I am going to beat one of them up. And if there should be another revolution,

---

[58] Nicholas Chkheidze (1864–1926) was a Georgian Social Democrat. From February to October 1917, he served as the Menshevik president of the Executive Committee of the Petrograd Soviet.

[59] Andrei Ivanovich Shingarev (1869–1918) served as a Duma deputy and one of the leaders of the Constitutional Democratic party (Kadets). After the February Revolution, he led the food committee; in the first Provisional Government, he was minister of agriculture, and later minister of finance. He was arrested by the Bolsheviks in November 1917, and imprisoned in the Peter and Paul Fortress. After falling ill in January 1918, he was transferred to a Petrograd hospital, where he was murdered by Kronstadt sailors who broke into the building.

I am going to do a little shooting at some of these droshky outlaws myself. There is a long article in the paper, supplemented by documents and letters, showing that Stürmer, the former Prime Minister, now in the Peter and Paul Fortress, had been given $9,000,000 to make a separate peace with Germany. In the paper it says that this was only a small advance on the millions he was to get.

Rodzianko has handed out a statement that the front is perfectly satisfied with conditions and the government in Petrograd. We have also heard that the soldiers on the Riga front have vowed to hold the line there, no matter what happens. The Soldiers' and Workmen's Deputies have sent a regiment of soldiers to the palace where the Tsar is, the Tsarskoe Selo, to see that he does not leave the country. There was a report that he was getting ready to run away.

We hear that the Germans are concentrating troops on the Northern front, which looks like a threat to Petrograd.

Guchkov, Minister of War, is at Riga now and I understand was received very heartily there. The Volynsky guards, one of the first regiments to join the revolutionists, are marching over the city carrying banners asking the other soldiers not to be traitors to their comrades in the trenches and exhorting the citizens to make shells, save food and get to work. The pacifists are also getting busy now, but every time they try to hold a public meeting on the street they are hooted at and shoved aside.

Boris has picked up a wild story that the grave where Rasputin was buried in the palace grounds has been opened and that his body was burned and then thrown into the month of a cannon, which was discharged into the air, blowing the ashes of Rasputin to the clouds.

The officers are forming unions for mutual protection and they announce that they will meet the soldiers' committees to make plans for the better conduct of the war. The greatest worry is how the army is going to be re-organized so that the officers and men will be able to work together. If the Russians were attacked now, I doubt if they could fight at all, on account of the feeling between the officers and men. There is also a cry that the national assembly should be called at once.

Now they are talking about counter-revolutions. It is just as I thought—the trouble has only started. The new cabinet has pledged itself to suppress any attempts to restore the old regime. The working people seem to favor a republic such as we have in America, but the Council of Workmen have formed so many committees which are all demanding things that it is impossible to find out just what they really do want. The situation is growing more serious every hour as agents of the old regime are trying to cause dissatisfaction.

The workmen have agreed to give up their eight-hour working day on account of an appeal made by the different committees stating that munitions must be turned out in double the former quantity. As soon as they have a certain amount of munitions on hand and at the front they will go back to their eight-hour day.

Every day at least one procession goes by the hospital and Boris tells me it is the same in all parts of the city. He adds that most of them don't know what they're marching for.

A commission has been appointed to investigate the charges against the former ministers and Kerensky has promised that they will be brought to trial immediately. The socialist papers are demanding that the ex-Tsar should be put into prison, a palace being considered too good for him.

General Kornilov,[60] Commander of the Petrograd district, was the one who placed the ex-Empress under arrest. He went out to the Palace with the order, was shown into her apartment and told her that he had been sent by the Council of Ministers to inform her that the Provisional Government had ordered her arrest. She rose with dignity and said, "I am ready to hear you." General Kornilov then read her the warrant which he told her deprived her of all her liberty. He ordered a new guard established at the Palace, all the old guards being removed. The Empress made only a few requests, most of them about certain servants whom she wanted to remain with her.

We hear that prisoners from Siberia have started on special trains to Petrograd.

As I am tired out, and have no more paper anyway, I guess it is time to close.

Don

---

[60] Lavr Georgiyevich Kornilov (1870–1918), the son of a Siberian Cossack and a former intelligence officer and military attaché to China, became a divisional commander in World War I. Captured by the Austrians at Przemysl in March 1915, he escaped the next year and was placed in command of an army corps. After the February Revolution, he was made commander of the Petrograd military district but faced resistance to his attempts to restore order and discipline in the army. In April, when the Provisional Government refused to allow him to suppress street demonstrations by force, he resigned in disgust and returned to the front, where he took part in the abortive June offensive in Galicia. After the failed Bolshevik coup in July, Kerensky appointed him as commander in chief to replace Brusilov. As Pipes points out, Kornilov "knew little and cared less about politics"; his priority was to restore order and discipline in the army, and he insisted on reducing the power of the soldiers' committees, restoring the authority of officers, and reintroducing the death penalty for desertion. Kerensky reluctantly agreed to most of Kornilov's demands but was not in a position to meet them because Order No. 1 had been promulgated by the Petrograd Soviet, not by the government. As liberal and conservative politicians threw their support behind Kornilov as the country's savior, Kerensky came to regard him as a rival for power. At the end of August, Kerensky tricked Kornilov into sending troops towards Petrograd to counter a rumored Bolshevik uprising. Kerensky then interpreted the deployment as an attempted coup d'état and dismissed Kornilov. The troops were halted by railroad workers and Kornilov was arrested on September 1. He escaped but died in battle while commanding White Army forces in the Don region in early 1918 (Pipes, *A Concise History of the Russian Revolution*, 124, 128–37).

XXII. Hospital, somewhere in Petrograd, April 4

Dear Dot:

The papers are full of what the members of the Duma and the different committees are saying, what they want, and what Russia should have, until you never know what to believe. It seems that every political party has a paper now. Since Russia is a republic everyone lets off steam. Wherever Boris goes he says he finds meetings, meetings, meetings, but from accounts there is more hot air shot off in the Duma than there is on the street.

The Russian is not known as a rule in America, outside of official circles at Washington. Few people have met the real Russian. I used to think all Russia was full of spies and that it was impossible to travel on account of passport regulations. As a matter of fact, it was easy to travel in Russia even before the revolution. The only exception was that you could not travel freely in the army zones, but that is true of any place in the world. The passport has been an institution in Russia so long that Russians never kicked about it. It was a habit to hand your card to the police to be viséd when you arrived and left a station. They are still keeping up the regulations on the passports and Boris tells me that you must have a passport visa just as you did before if you want to enter or leave Russia.

Boris also reports that German spies are spending money here in Petrograd as they never spent it before. They are certainly trying to stir up trouble.

The government has abolished capital punishment, which pleased a great many of the Soldiers' and Workmen's Deputies. Some of these men I would hate to meet in a dark alley. They tell me that when the order was read to them they cheered for five minutes.

I have received a great deal of mail from you the last few days and wonder what you think is happening, as no doubt the papers are full of the doings here. As soon as I am able to leave the hospital, I am going back to my hotel and will probably go to Finland for a week if I can arrange with some sanatorium there to take me in.

The papers print a statement that the Russians have been attacked on the eastern front near Covel and suffered quite severely. When these notices were posted in front of the newspaper offices, Boris tells me, the people became much excited and soldiers made speeches demanding to be sent to the front to help their brothers.

Boris says that thousands of Germans are coming into Russia now from Sweden on forged passports and by bribing officials at the border.

Don

XXIII. Hospital, somewhere in Petrograd, April 8

Dear Dot:

I did not intend to write at all today, as this is the first day that I am allowed to be up in a chair by the window. This hospital faces a little square and I have been watching squads of soldiers learning to drill. I have been on my back so long that it is a relief to see someone moving around. I tried to walk today but was unable to stand.

I heard early this morning that America had declared war on Germany on Saturday.

Grant, the Englishman, was in today with a lot of cigarettes—that is English cigarettes. I kept asking for these cigarettes and he got permission to take a vacation for two days and went to Finland to get them especially for me.

My doctor says things are getting very bad and that he fears serious trouble is coming. Tomorrow I am told that I will be given a light diet. They had promised it before this, but keep stringing me along.

Don

XXIV. Hotel Astoria, April 15

Dear Dot:

As you see, I am back at the hotel once more. I did not go to Finland. I am still shaky, but have been walking a little each day. In a few days I will be as strong as ever. The nurse at the hospital has promised to bring me white bread every day, as the doctor ordered me not to eat any more Russian black bread.

Wherever I go people smile when they find that I am an American; they expect America to give Russia a great deal of help.

While I was riding the other day, I saw the reception tendered Mme. Catherine Breshkovskaya,[61] who is called "The Grandmother of the Revolution." She has just returned from Siberia and you could not get near the railroad station on account of the thousands of people who cheered her all along the line of march. She was met at the station by Kerensky, the Minister of Justice.

---

[61] The "Babushka" (Little Grandmother) of the Russian Revolution, Yekaterina Breshkovskaya (1844–1934), was born into a wealthy aristocratic family. Her revolutionary work began with the education of peasants on her father's estates. She left home at age twenty-six to join the followers of anarchist Mikhail Bakunin in Kiev; in 1878, she was arrested and sentenced to twenty years in a Siberian labor camp. Released in 1896, she resumed her political activities and, in 1901, co-founded the Party of Socialist Revolutionaries, whose chief goal was the redistribution of all land to the peasants. In 1907, she was again arrested and exiled to Siberia for life. After the February Revolution, political prisoners were released, and Breshkovskaya was given a seat in Kerensky's government. She opposed the Bolsheviks and, after the October Revolution, left Russia for Czechoslovakia.

The report that one of the Socialist exiles by the name of Lenin, who has been living in Switzerland, is coming back to Russia, and that arrangements are being made by the Soldiers' and Workmen's Deputies to give him a great reception. There is a great deal of peace talk here. Many people say that it is the work of German agents who are trying to cause dissatisfaction and trouble for the new government. The commander of the military district here has ordered all workmen to obey the new government and has forbidden peace talk.

Miliukov has issued a statement that if Russia should desert the Allies now it would mean the loss of her liberty.

The Committee of Labor Deputies have issued a statement in their official paper in which they state that they are going to form a committee on foreign relations and will have this committee open negotiations with the enemy at once. They are demanding a voice in the management of things at the front. This also spells trouble.

The government has made a statement through Kerensky that Russia does not want Constantinople. Premier Lvov has also announced that the new government does not want to dominate over small nations, and all that they want is independence, and that Russia in common with all other nations should have the right to determine her own destiny.

Don

XXV. Petrograd, April 23

Dear Dot:

Today I made a photograph of Catherine Breshkovskaya, "The Grandmother of the Revolution." I found her very interesting and only wish that she had been able to speak English. As it was, Boris did the interpreting. She has spent over forty years of her life in Siberia. She escaped once, but was sent back for participating in the 1905 revolution.

I also met Marie Spiridonova,[62] who has also just returned from Siberia. Her face is disfigured. She says this was done by police agents when she was sentenced to Siberia. I understand that the men she accused of doing this have been killed.

Every few days we get more exiles from Siberia. I am told that there have been over 100,000 released already. Every place these people pass through gives them a

---

[62] Maria Alexandrovna Spiridonova (1884–1941) was a socialist revolutionary. Her assassination of a police official in 1905 was the most famous terrorist act by a woman in Russia, and her subsequent abuse by police made her a martyr. Having spent eleven years in a Siberian prison, she was freed after the February Revolution of 1917. She led the Left Socialist Revolutionaries (SRs) faction into alliance with the Bolsheviks, but was imprisoned after the Left SRs broke with the Bolsheviks in 1918 (Pipes, *A Concise History of the Russian Revolution*, 157, 184–86). Spiridonova was arrested by the secret police during the Great Purge of 1937–39 and sent to forced labor camps, where she was summarily executed in the summer of 1941.

great reception. Money is being gathered by popular subscription to help them and the government is also appropriating money for their benefit. Exiles throughout the world are invited to return to Russia at the expense of the government. All they have to do is to apply to the Russian consul or ambassador and he will give them money to return. Millions have been appropriated for this use.

Miliukov, the Minister of Foreign Affairs, has made an announcement that a separate peace is impossible unless Russia should be crushed. This has done a great deal of good, as all of the socialistic papers were stating that peace would be made in a short time by their party.

The Russians are having a loan campaign here now. One notice states that the revolution will be lost if everyone does not come forward and give money at once so that the government can go ahead with the war.

Nicholas Lenin, whom I mentioned last week in one of my letters, has reached Petrograd and is quite a hero. This man was given a special car through Germany when he left Switzerland for Russia. Everyone here says that he is a German agent. Anyway, he is spending money very freely, I hear.

We are now going to have a congress of soldiers, workingmen, and peasants, and all you hear the soldiers talking about is this congress. Also, delegates are beginning to arrive from the front. I was talking to an officer yesterday and he told me that conditions at the front are getting serious in some districts. Each company of Russian soldiers has a committee now that makes laws of their own. He says it is very hard to get the soldiers to do anything; also that a great many of them are leaving and going home, as they say, "for a visit." From reports that he could gather from other officers along the different fronts on a trip that he has just completed, he says that over a million and a half soldiers have gone home, and that none of them, so far as he could learn, had returned.

It is impossible to get near the railroad station ticket office now. I do not know where all these people are traveling to, but they fight to get tickets. Every train that arrives in Petrograd is loaded to the doors. Even the city ticket offices have long lines before them.

Food is getting scarce again and with the disputes daily between the government and the Council of Soldiers' and Workmen's Deputies, I do not know what is going to happen. Petrograd is getting full of pro-Germans.

The workingmen are making wild demands. One that they made a few days ago was that the factories should only work four hours a day and that they should have a 100 percent, increase in wages and a month's holiday at Easter, also one at Christmas with wages paid, and an extra two months' holiday with wages paid, which they could use as they wished.

This Lenin that I mentioned is making speeches daily urging Russia to make peace at once.

An article appeared in one of the papers today that America was contemplating sending soldiers to Russia. This is a mistake and should not be done. Russia has plenty of men. What she needs now is a railroad force, that is, a couple of thousand railroad men who could reorganize the broken down transportation system. Russia has plenty of ammunition at Vladivostok, but it cannot be moved because there is no one who can straighten out the congestion at the railroad centers between Vladivostok and Petrograd.

Lenin's work here is the most dangerous of all. The paper that is backing him says, "We do not want any help from America." Lenin is getting popular, as he addresses the soldiers in the different barracks almost daily and tells them that the war must end so that they can go back to their homes and be there when the land is divided.

The weather is getting warmer now and I have stopped wearing an overcoat, with the exception of days that are a little chilly, of which we have had one or two the past week.

They are arranging for a big demonstration May 1st. It is to be a labor parade and I am told that there will be a great many people in line. I am making arrangements to take a picture of this and I went out to the Duma today and received a red card enabling me to work along the line of march.

Don

XXVI. Hotel Metropole, Moscow, April 26

Dear Dot:

I ran down here for a visit and to see how things are. I find Moscow entirely different from Petrograd. Here the working people are busy night and day and manufacturers and other business men tell me that while the people want the war to be finished as soon as possible, still they are willing to sacrifice a great deal.

Moscow is really Russia. Petrograd is not Russia, never was Russia and never will be Russia.

The servants here in the hotel, I am told by the manager, are being organized by people from Petrograd. He says that the socialists are working night and day and he expects trouble to come from it later. He says that the demands he hears the servants are going to make will render it impossible for him to keep his hotel open unless he raises his rates about 1,000 percent.

I had a great deal of trouble in getting a railroad ticket down here. The tickets are in the hands of scalpers who buy up all of the tickets for the train. You must buy your ticket through a commissioner who buys it from them. This makes it very expensive to travel, that is for the Russian not so for me, as the ruble is worth about half what it was before the war, and I figure that as my dollar buys more rubles I can afford to pay the increase.

I find that there was very little rioting here during the revolution, although they expect trouble in a short time. I was talking to a family today who said that this time next year things would be very bad in Russia. They fear the socialists will begin fighting amongst themselves before the summer is over. They believe that Lenin is a German agent and that already emissaries of his are working in Moscow.

I was told by an officer here that someone is trying to cause trouble amongst the different regiments located in the city. I find a better class of soldiers in Moscow than I did in Petrograd. I lay this to the fact that before the revolution the soldiers who were stationed in Petrograd were, as a rule, men who had bought their way out of the army so far as fighting was concerned. They belong to regiments that always remain in Petrograd and never went to the front.

The shops here do not charge as much for things as Petrograd shops do. The stores seem to have more food also. In fact, I find everything cheaper here, even the hotels. The shortage of shoes, however, is as bad as in Petrograd. If you want a pair of shoes you must stand in line all day before your turn comes to enter the shop, and you must have an order from the government before you can buy shoes.

I am going to return to Petrograd in time for the May 1 celebration, as I am told that we may have trouble that day.

In Moscow they very much like the Foreign Minister, Miliukov, but they tell me that his greatest enemy is Lenin, who is saying that Miliukov is a representative of the Emperor. In Moscow they are satisfied with the new government, but are afraid that it will be broken up in a short time. Moscow papers have articles daily demanding that Lenin be arrested as a German spy.

I was talking to a soldier who went through a big gas attack a short time after the revolution. He said the Germans came over under a white flag (down at the Dvinsk front [see figure 3]) and asked the Russians to move their gas back ninety versts,[63] which is about 60 miles, and that they would do the same with their gas. He promised there would be no more gas attacks. The Russians did this, and after a German committee had gone back and found the gas at the distance agreed upon, they picked out from the Russian troops a few men and had them go to the German lines where they were to see that the Germans had done the same. These men who were taken from the Russian lines sent back word that they were going to stay a few days longer and enjoy themselves with the Germans. Before they returned a strong wind blew toward the Russian trenches and with that wind came gas. Twenty-five thousand Russians were gassed and the Germans captured their positions. A week later German officers came over with a white flag and said that it had been a mistake and that the officer who had been responsible for the gas attack had been shot by the Germans. The Russians were invited to send a committee to see his grave. The committee came back and reported that they had seen the grave all right, or at least a cross sticking

---

[63] A Russian measure of length, about 0.66 of a mile or 1.1 kilometers.

in the ground. The Germans did not give back the position that they had captured during this gas attack, but the Russians are fraternizing with them again as if nothing unpleasant had happened. Of course things like this could not occur if it were not for the Soldiers' Committees.

This soldier, who is an intelligent fellow, also said that a great deal of vodka is being sent over from the German lines to the Russian lines and that the officers cannot do a thing, that the committees of soldiers are absolutely in control at the front now. The soldiers have the right to vote an officer out of a company or a regiment, and even a general cannot issue an order unless the committee approves it. In other words, it would be impossible for an order to be given to attack unless the committee first approved this order.

German agents are exciting the peasants and telling them all kinds of lies, and they are also starting propaganda against the United States. Their stories are that America and England are now going to make the other nations do all the fighting and will be in a position when the war is finished to do as they please, and that Russia will be divided up to suit them. I was in hopes that when the revolution was finished all of these people would have been imprisoned or killed, but it seems that where we had thousands before the revolution we now have tens of thousands, and they are all supplied with plenty of money.

Coming down to Moscow at every station I found hundreds of peasants lounging around as though they had nothing to do. One of the men in my compartment said that it was this way all over Russia. He also said that at a great many places the peasants, when they heard that Russia was a republic, had immediately sent out of the villages the priests and school teachers and had closed the schools. That is their idea of freedom.

In Moscow, you can buy liquor, that is, if you want to pay the price that is asked for it. The theaters are all open and doing a land-office business.

I went out to a Russian film company here and saw them working on a play on the life of Rasputin, and also plays about the revolution. They have a good studio and showed me one of their finished pictures which was fine. With better directors they could make some wonderful films now that would make a hit in America. American films are very popular in Russia; that is love dramas. Charlie Chaplin films are not liked here. Russia cannot see humor and jokes as we do.

Moscow is flying the red flag, as Petrograd is, although you do not see as many soldiers wearing the badge of red cloth on their uniform as in Petrograd. The Moscow soldiers want the Petrograd soldiers to be sent to the front to fight, while they are sent to Petrograd to protect the government.

I am leaving tomorrow for Petrograd and will write you on my arrival there.

Don

XXVI. Petrograd, Tuesday, May 1

Dear Dot:

I have had one big day today. The socialists, anarchists and Kronstadters held their May Day parade. There were half a million people in line, men and women and soldiers. They all had banners and most of the banners were against the war and for peace at any price.

At five o'clock this morning, they began to meet in the main section of the city. At this hour I was awakened by the playing of a band across the square. Boris and I rushed to the window and found thousands marching along. The main parade came along the Nevsky at about nine. They marched into the Nevsky from the Morskaia as far as the Liteiny, and from the Liteiny on to the Field of Mars where they passed along the sides of the graves of the martyrs of the first revolution. I made pictures downtown of this procession and later went to the Field of Mars. There a truckful of anarchists from one of the districts gave me permission to put my camera on top of the truck where I made scenes of the mob passing. It seemed as if they never would stop passing. In one division were 15,000 anarchists. Most of the anarchists were armed with rifles and they carried black flags which said, "Down with the capitalists. Stop the war. Divide the land."

I understand that Lenin made addresses in different sections of the city. I am at a loss to know why permission was given for this demonstration, and I don't understand why the government allows these people, especially the anarchists who call themselves the "Black 400," to come out armed. If the government is weak it is going to have a short life. This demonstration was staged by the Soldiers' and Workmen's Deputies, who I think are backed by German agents.

The strain between the Provisional Government and the Soldiers' and Workmen's Deputies has almost reached the breaking point. Last week the government issued a manifesto to the people of Russia explaining the government's aims as regards the war. As I understand, they have sent a note to the Allies in which they pledge their support to the end of the war and promise to abide by all former treaties made by the old government with the Allies. The government was forced to give this out to the public on account of Lenin, who is now the leader of the radical socialists. His speeches against the Provisional Government and the Allies have already led to one riot in Petrograd and it was only by vigorous action that this riot was suppressed and peace restored. There have been several incidents like this since Lenin arrived in Petrograd. Lenin might say that he is not in the pay of the Germans, but take it from me, Germany is not giving a special car to anyone to travel through Germany and back to Russia who is at war with them. The best thing for Russia to do is to kill Lenin. The least they could do is to arrest him and put him in prison, and if they don't I expect to write you a letter, someday, that this cur is in control of things here. Every day he is gaining strength and getting the support of the lowest element in Petrograd. If Lenin succeeds in overthrowing the government, there will be rioting in Petrograd.

He is preaching to the soldiers daily not to fight any more and tells them that they are being sacrificed by the capitalists. Lenin is a brilliant man and is smart enough to know what the poor Russian wants to hear. These poor fellows believe that if Lenin is put in power the war will stop, the land and all the money will be divided amongst them, and they will never have to work again.

I went out to the home of Francis Judd, an American who represents the Baldwin Locomotive Works here and made arrangements to meet Guchkov, Minister of War, after dinner tonight. Judd is a friend of Guchkov and can get me passports for all the fronts.

Don

XXVII. Petrograd, May 2

Dear Dot:

This afternoon, after returning from the embassy where I found some of your letters, I was sitting in the hotel when I heard a band playing in the street. At first I paid no attention to it. Then Boris came rushing in and said, "There is trouble. Troops are marching to the Mariinsky Palace." I couldn't believe him at first but put on my overcoat, grabbed my cameras and went out. Sure enough, regiment after regiment was coming up in front of the palace. They were under arms and I noticed all of them had their cartridge boxes on their belts while some had bandoliers over their shoulders, all filled with cartridges. They were addressed by several men from the balcony of the palace. Boris said the people who were doing the talking from the balcony were appealing to them not to endanger the revolution but to go back to their barracks and avoid disorder. Most of them stood in silence. There was no cheering. Later a man standing in the center of these soldiers was raised to the back seat of an automobile and made some remarks. I was not surprised when Boris told me that he said, "Soldiers, the time has come for you to act. The government is composed of capitalists. It is worse than the old government. Soldiers, you must take the opportunity now that you have it and throw these people out, so that Russia can go forward. Soldiers, they will send you to the front. You will be sacrificed, and we will lose our freedom." Then these men certainly did some cheering. Later they marched away, the regiments going in different directions. I rushed back to the hotel and left my camera, and I couldn't do any more photography that day.

I took Boris and went up to the Parisian Restaurant on the Morskaia, where we had dinner. While we were at dinner the manager asked us to help him move a table away from the windows. I asked him why. He said there was trouble brewing. A few minutes later we heard several shots. Outside we saw nothing unusual. All was quiet on the Nevsky until we had crossed the Catherine Canal. While we were crossing this little bridge an automobile dashed by us carrying a big black flag with the skull and cross bones on it. I noticed a machine gun with the barrel pointing over the back of the car. We walked up as far as the Sadovaia and then we began to meet lots of people on the sidewalks. Many were carrying revolvers and guns. In a few minutes armored cars came along the street. Automatically Boris and I flattened ourselves on the sidewalk, as I was afraid they would open fire on the crowd. Later we went up the street, where we met a mob of about 10,000. From the banners they carried and the speeches made by people standing up in the automobiles, Boris concluded they were for the government and against the anarchists and socialists. Up by the Nikolai Station we met another mob, 60 percent of them armed. They had black flags and were carrying banners calling on the people to act at once: "Down with the capitalists and ministers" and "Kill Miliukov." This kept up until the early morning, I guess, for when we returned to the hotel at one o'clock, many crowds were still parading around.

As it is very late I will close. Tomorrow is likely to bring further excitement and I may get some more pictures. It is just as I told you in another letter, if you remember. That trouble would come if these mobs were allowed to continue their demonstrations.

Don

XXVIII. Thursday, May 3

Dear Dot:

This morning I was up at seven o'clock. Boris had my coffee ready for me when I awoke, but no bread or anything else. We started out about 8:30. On the Nevsky we found the shops all open. At the consulate I was told that everything was quiet and that they didn't expect trouble, but Lee added that you can never tell what will happen here anymore.

I then asked Boris to take me to the Jewish market. This is one of the sights of Petrograd. It covers about four blocks and is full of little shops owned by Jews. You can buy everything under the sun there. Everything stolen is brought there, and if you want to buy a machine-gun, a rifle, or anything else, you can find it. This is one reason why the Jews in Russia have such a hard time. They will buy anything they think they can make money on. The people say they are buying up army guns and that they are in the pay of the Germans.

I saw thousands of soldiers in the old clothes section selling their uniforms, underwear, shoes, and whatever they had. You can trade a pair of new shoes for a pair not so good and get a little money on the side. We spent the whole morning in this place. I looked at a great many pieces of jewelry. Most of this is loot, stolen during the revolution. I saw a watch that had blood-stains on it. A diamond necklace I could have bought for one-tenth of its value.

At the Nikolai Station when I went to see about railroad tickets for a trip to the country next week, we met a mob. I don't know which side this mob was on but I saw that they had started a little excitement. We hailed a droshky and went to the hotel, where I got my cameras and then returned to the Nevsky. I went up to the corner of the Sadovaia and the Nevsky and climbed up on the balcony of the third house from the corner. I sat down on the balcony, as I had a hunch that something would be doing around this neighborhood before the afternoon was over. Sure enough, I was right. At about 3:30 a mob came down the Nevsky from the Morskaia, and another mob came from the Sadovaia by the library side, where they met. Well, they started by arguing and trying to push each other aside, and then began to tear down each other's banners. Someone let fly with a gun and for a few minutes it was simply hell on that corner, with everyone lying down flat on the pavement. Amid clatter of feet, the screams of women and the popping of rifles you could not hear yourself speak. In fifteen minutes it was all over. Most of the people had got up and run away. The crowd that was for the government was in control of the street but six of them were lying dead on the pavement and about twelve or fifteen were wounded. The anarchists or socialists or whatever they are had run away. We left the balcony after a half hour's wait and had coffee in the Café Empire, which lost a couple of its plate glass windows during the excitement when everybody tried to rush into the restaurant and some didn't wait to go in by the door.

At six o'clock, while we were in front of the Kazan Cathedral on the Nevsky, shooting started again and a few more people were killed—how many, I don't know. At 6:30 another skirmish started between the mobs in front of the American Consulate. Four people were lying dead on the sidewalk as I passed, and I noticed they were soldiers. During the rest of the evening until 10 or 10:30 a constant uproar prevailed on the Nevsky. Thousands were marching for and against the government until finally it reached the point where you did not know what was what. Boris and I decided to take off our hats and cheer every mob that passed. About 10:30 one of the largest mobs came up the Nevsky from the Morskaia. When they were entering the Nevsky, I was at the door of the Singer Building watching them come up the street, Boris said, "Look what's coming." There was a mob approaching from the other direction. These men carried big black flags and banners. I made the mistake of waiting until the mob that was for the government was in front of me. I had intended to let them pass me but was pushed along until, before I knew it, I was facing the other mob. This bunch of anarchists were armed. When within a few feet of us, they all began to talk and shout at the same time. I backed up against the front of a little delicatessen shop. Well, we didn't have to wait long, for talking led to action. In a minute shots rang out and everyone started to make a break for safety. Windows were smashed and I was almost pushed through one. We fell down on the sidewalk, and after lying there about fifteen or twenty minutes we got up and ran around the corner. I don't know how many were killed, but it gave me a taste of what these mobs really do. When I left the street a few minutes ago parades were still going on.

Several thousand people went to the home of Miliukov, where they were addressed, I am told, by an officer. Miliukov thought the crowd was for the government, but when he came out on the balcony of his home, to his surprise, he found they wanted to lynch him. But he was brave all right. Instead of running away he addressed that mob and said he had heard they wanted the life of Paul Miliukov. He said he wasn't afraid for his life but he was afraid that Russia would lose its freedom. When he had finished, most of the people were cheering, but agitators in the crowd began making speeches and soon the mob was clamoring for his life. That is the way here in Russia—the one who has the last say, wins. You can talk for five hours to a crowd of Russians and they will believe every word you say. You could lead them around any way you wanted to, but if someone else got up he could change their minds in the next five minutes. I don't know why this is, but it is true.

I am now going to bed. No one knows what will happen tomorrow, and I want to be on the ground early.

Don

XXIX. Petrograd, May 5

Dear Dot:

All this trouble, I understand, has been brought about by the politicians and the refusal of Miliukov to publish the secret treaties of Russia and the Allies. The government held meetings all last night and did not adjourn until early yesterday morning. The papers say that the soldiers and workmen are the power in Russia now, and the Soldiers' and Workmen's Deputies are announcing that they will construct a new government at once.

Notices are up asking the people not to meet on the street any more. Meetings are allowed only in halls, theaters or public buildings. On top of this, however, there are notices, in most cases pasted over the government notices, calling on the people to kill all the aristocrats, divide the land, and stop the war. Monday is the day decided upon by this bunch of cut-throats to overthrow the government. The notices are printed on big sheets which attract much attention, and there is another notice, signed by the Committee of Soldiers and Workmen, saying that at last the mask has been removed and that this government is worse than the old government. "They think we are ignorant and don't know anything," says one proclamation. "Miliukov is a sly person and is deceiving Russia. Down with Miliukov and down with this temporary government."

Premier Lvov has stated in the papers that he will not modify the note sent to the Allies and that the ministry will resign first. Miliukov also has a statement in which he tells the people that if things go on as they are the world will begin to distrust Russia and that by behaving in this way they only play into the hands of their enemy, Germany.

Don

XXX. Petrograd, May 7

Dear Dot:

Just a few lines to let you know that things are going along a little better today. With the exception of a great many armed soldiers on guard on the streets, conditions are normal. These troops are out in great force. They are openly saying that if the workmen start any more trouble, they will shoot to kill. For the last day or so, the workmen have been very quiet. Boris says they won't attempt any new demonstration until they get better organized. Lenin has stepped out of the limelight for a few days.

Don

XXXI. Hotel Astoria, Wednesday, May 9

Dear Dot:

From reports now at hand it looks as if the Germans are going to make a drive against the Baltic coast, with Petrograd as their goal. Guchkov is issuing daily appeals telling the people that Russia is facing a crisis; that the Germans are using every means possible to have the men desert at the front.

The Germans are scattering by aeroplane daily newspapers, supposed to be printed in Petrograd, asserting that the land is being divided and that soldiers not there will not get any. If this keeps up there will be very few soldiers left at the front unless something is done to stop it. German intrigue is working now as never before. Some of the papers are publishing long letters supposed to have been written by Rasputin to the ex-Tsarina.

The socialists here who are led by Lenin are trying to cause trouble for the American Embassy; they protest against the hanging of someone in San Francisco who is supposed to be a labor leader.[64] Francis, the Ambassador, was having a late supper with some of his friends when he was notified by telephone that the mob was marching to the embassy. The government also heard of it in time to rush a hundred soldiers to the embassy.

I am told that Johnson, the Ambassador's secretary, says that Francis took his revolver and stood by the door and was ready for any trouble this bunch of cut-throats

---

[64] On the night of April 8, Ambassador Francis received word that a mob "waving black anarchist flags" was on its way to attack the embassy. Francis pulled out his revolver and "vowed to shoot anyone who tried to get inside the embassy," but the crowd was dispersed soon after setting out (Rappaport, *Caught in the Revolution*, 170). The protest was over the recent conviction of labor organizer and political activist Thomas M. Mooney for his alleged involvement in a bombing at the July 1916 Preparedness Day parade in San Francisco that resulted in ten deaths and forty injuries. Mooney was sentenced to death, but the sentence was commuted to life imprisonment in 1918. Believed by many to have been wrongly convicted of a crime he did not commit, Mooney served twenty-two years in prison before being pardoned in 1939.

might start. The government had given orders to the troops they sent, that if the mob started to attack the embassy they were to shoot to kill. Francis issued a statement afterward saying that, although he was told of the mob coming, he didn't take it seriously until he saw the soldiers coming to protect the embassy from insult. All these things are the work of German intrigue here in Petrograd. The Germans are exciting these people with stories of how the socialists are being treated in America. These socialists are daily agitating the people to trouble; as a rule the people won't listen to the calm citizens who tell them the truth and contradict all these terrible stories. Francis, the American Ambassador, Miliukov, and several other Russians gave an address at the hall in the Duma the other night to an immense crowd. I went over to the meeting with Mr. Lee, Vice Consul, and while we were waiting for the crowd to gather, someone made the remark, "Why don't we see any Americans?" We didn't have to wait long. The first American to come was a gentleman from Georgia with a very beautiful lady on his arm; she was a Russian and had a skin as white as ivory; she was certainly beautiful. The gentleman from Georgia was as black as the Ace of Spades. He is a cook in one of the clubs here. A few minutes later I noticed in the crowd three ladies who were also from America. Two of them were very black and one of them was a mulatto. I knew they were Americans from the flag they wore on their dresses.

When the crowd had gathered, we had, I should say, about thirty Americans. Half of them were negroes.

They have issued an order here in Petrograd that alcoholic drinks with a small percentage of alcohol can now be made and sold.

We hear through the papers that Elihu Root[65] is going to head a commission to Russia and a railroad commission is also being sent to re-organize Russia's broken-down transportation system. Several of the socialist papers have already begun to attack Root, saying that he represents the capitalists only. By the time he reaches here I doubt if he will be able to accomplish anything. By that time the Germans will have bought up all the papers in Petrograd and probably Moscow in order to do their dirty work.

---

[65] Elihu Root (1845–1937), a corporate lawyer, served as U.S. secretary of war in the cabinets of William McKinley and Theodore Roosevelt (1899–1903), as secretary of state during Roosevelt's second term until 1909, and as a Republican senator from New York (1909–15). At the outbreak of World War I, he openly supported the Allies and was critical of President Woodrow Wilson's neutrality policy. In June 1917, three months after the United States entered the war, Root, at age seventy-two, headed a mission sent by Wilson to arrange American cooperation with the new revolutionary government. Financial aid was possible only if the Russians fought on the Allied side, but Root was not impressed by the Provisional Government's will or popular support. "No fight, no loans," he wrote. The commission left after less than a month in Petrograd. Rappaport says that Root was unknown in Russia and went through the diplomatic motions with little grasp of the players or background (*Caught in the Revolution*, 190–01).

There is still a great deal of talk here about Russia making a separate peace. This will not happen as things stand now, but if the government does not take a strong hand, it might be accomplished later.

On the Dvinsk front, according to the newspaper bulletins, fighting has stopped entirely, although the Germans are continually sending over aeroplanes to drop proclamations that there is a movement being started in Germany to make immediate peace with Russia. From other reports I have been given, the attack on the American Embassy the other night was the work of Lenin. The better class of people are already accusing him of trying to start a counter-revolution and of being a German agent. Lenin and his gang of cut-throats have taken the home of a former dancer, who was quite popular a few years ago in Russia.[66] From this house he addresses great crowds; but the loyal people here, and those in favor of the new government, always manage to be there to hiss him. A great many fights take place in front of this building; troops have had to be called out to stop some of them. The crowds break up the meetings of the anarchists on the Nevsky whenever they try to hold them. Some of the anarchist groups have issued a statement that they want nothing to do with Lenin and won't recognize him.

We are also getting daily reports now that republics are being set up in different sections of Russia and that most of the landlords' properties are being taken by the people. You see this means trouble and Russia seems to be going back day by day, instead of forward. Hundreds of landlords' homes have been attacked and the inmates killed in the most cruel manner.

So many soldiers have deserted from the front that in a great many cases they have seized the trains, thrown out the passengers, and demanded the train to go where they wanted it to. When the railroad officials have refused to do as the deserters wanted them to, they have been attacked and killed.

Guchkov says that although there have been a great many desertions, the army is stronger now than it was a week or so ago. I doubt very much if the army will ever be as of old and have the fighting ability it once had. In some places, however, when the soldiers arrive at their former homes, they are asked for their papers showing that they have permission to leave; when they fail to produce the papers, they are given very harsh treatment by the people of their villages or towns. From what I have seen it is a wonder to me that there haven't been more desertions. By law now, the soldiers

---

[66] The mansion, on the north side of the Neva near Alexandrinsky Park and the Peter and Paul Fortress, was built in 1904–06 for Mathilde Kschessinskaya, prima ballerina of the Imperial Ballet, and a close friend of Nicholas II (in her youth, she was the mistress of the future Tsar). Shortly before the February Revolution, she fled to France, abandoning her home. Lenin's supporters took over the mansion and used it as their headquarters, bringing in typewriters and printing presses. Government forces took over the mansion after the failed Bolshevik coup in July, and found a stockpile of machine-guns, provisions, and documents which, it was claimed, showed that Lenin was in the pay of the Germans.

at the front have the right to express their views on anything; this they are doing daily. The soldiers don't have to attend mass, if they don't want to, and there has been a law abolishing the censorship of all letters, newspapers, and pamphlets at the front. There is an order issued that the soldiers must obey orders and observe the strictest discipline, but just as this order is being nicely carried out, other orders come along and upset everything. Take the matter of salutation between a soldier and an officer. That was abolished during the revolution. The only order a soldier most obey now is the order "Attention," when given by an officer. A soldier can salute his officer if he wants to, but it is not compulsory. No officers are allowed servants from the army, that is, they are not allowed to detail soldiers as private servants. Soldiers cannot be punished without first being tried by a court martial. If an officer strikes or inflicts physical injury upon any soldier, he is tried by the soldiers. All of these little laws please the soldiers very much; but eventually they will wreck the Russian army, for an army cannot live without discipline.

The Minister of War has made a trip to the front and says that a new plan is being tried there: committees of the different regiments will establish discipline and order. An order has also been given that Petrograd troops can now be sent to the front.

A notice that is attracting a great deal of attention on the Nevsky is one that asks the people to let Lenin share the fate of Rasputin.

On May 1, the day of the big parade I wrote you about, there were about 400 platforms here in Petrograd, built by the socialists so that their agents could address the people. I stood around and listened to a great many of these people airing their views. Most of them talked themselves hoarse before the morning was well on. We expected to have serious trouble during the day and the socialists were looking for it; and the reason there wasn't any was that they met with no resistance. The socialists cry, "down with the capitalists!" Well, if the capitalists were to leave Russia I don't know what would happen.

The sailors have had their request granted, that officers of the navy should wear no epaulets or insignia of any kind or rank, but should dress as they do.

General Alekseiev, commander-in-chief of the army,[67] granted me permission to take his photograph and was very much interested in what little news I had to tell him of America.

---

[67] As chief of staff of the Southwestern Front, General Mikhail Vasiliyevich Alekseiev (1857–1918) planned the 1914 offensive in Galicia. When Grand Duke Nicholas stepped down as commander in chief in August 1915, and Tsar Nicholas II assumed command, Alekseiev was appointed chief of staff of the General Headquarters (Stavka), serving as *de facto* commander in chief, in charge of all military operations. During the February Revolution, he sent a telegram to the Tsar advising him to abdicate. In August 1917 Alekseiev became chief of staff of the Stavka under Commander in Chief Kerensky. He thwarted the alleged coup by General Kornilov, arresting him at army headquarters on August 30. After the October Revolution, he joined forces with Kornilov and established the White Army in the Don region. He died of heart failure in September 1918.

At the embassy, daily, hundreds of Russian officers are applying for permission to go to America and become officers in the American army, saying they can help train our new army.

Since the order was issued forbidding all public meetings, things are more quiet, although they are now holding their meetings in halls and private homes. In a way this is worse than if they appeared on the streets, for we don't know what they are really planning. The socialists here are like the IWW in America. While the last riots were at their height on May 4, I ran across one mob of 10,000 workmen, 80 percent of them armed; when Boris asked a few of them what they were out for, they didn't know; they only showed him a printed slip, telling them to be at a certain place at a certain time. Take it from me, this Lenin has certainly got these people well trained considering the short time he has been back in Russia.

General Kornilov is issuing another warning that the Germans are going to attack.

We now have a law that anyone trying to excite the people on the streets, will be arrested and tried, and that anyone attempting an armed demonstration or shooting from rifles in the street, will be brought before the government, and that little mercy will be shown.

A newspaper called *Pravda*, the mouthpiece of the Bolsheviks, has tried to tell the people that they are not responsible for the shooting the other day, although on that day they came out and said that if the government didn't resign the working people should take their guns and make them do it.

The Soldiers' and Workmen's Deputies say they have patched up the differences between the government and their body. I believe this is only to gain time and that they are planning day and night for their next move. The cry from their side is that there must be a coalition ministry. They say in their papers that they can overthrow the government any time they wish to, that they haven't done it because they haven't been sure that they have had the right to do it and that they want to know if they represent the will of the people of Russia. All this trouble has been caused by the first note Miliukov sent to the Allies.[68] That note said the war would be carried on by Russia to a successful finish and that they would live up to all former treaties made with the Allies.

General Gurko,[69] who commands the armies on the Western front here in Russia, has given out a report through the War Office that the Germans have removed

---

[68] See n. 19.

[69] Vasily Iosifovich Gurko (1864–1937) was a commander on the Northern and Southwestern fronts from 1914 to 1916. In October 1916, he replaced General Alekseiev as chief of staff and from March 1917 became commander of the Western Front in Latvia and Poland. However, he was relieved of his command after only two months for expressing support for the monarchy. He was imprisoned at the Peter and Paul Fortress for two months, and then exiled to Britain.

three divisions to France. He has also issued a warning to all Russia that if something isn't done to stop the soldiers from fraternizing with the enemy and telling the enemy what is going on behind Russia's lines, Germany will crush Russia and Russia will lose her republic.

Some of the papers say that there has been no firing on the Russian front for a week. This is not so, for an officer of the 8th Artillery Brigade, who just returned from his division, reports that they are having quite a little battle along his position. I asked him about the fraternizing and he said that there had been some along his front, but that he did not censure the Russian soldiers. As you know, he said, they are weak. A great many people in the government say that this fraternizing between Russia and Germany must be stopped at once, but these people are overruled by the socialists, who say that in that way Germany will hear how easy it would be for her to become a republic as Russia has done. The socialists of one of the working districts here have organized themselves into an order known as the Red Guard; they are all heavily armed and gave a demonstration yesterday afternoon, down on the Nevsky, of how strong they were. The government as usual didn't interfere. That very fact, I think, has encouraged them—and they will give other demonstrations.

Don

XXXII. Sunday, May 13

Dear Dot:

Kerensky, the Minister of Justice, is getting stronger every day. He is gradually reaching out; and if I am not mistaken, in a short time he will be the whole cheese here.

The papers say we are going to have a coalition ministry and that they will allow socialists to be represented in this ministry.

About four o'clock this afternoon Guchkov, Minister of War, resigned. I do not know who is going to take his place. I saw Guchkov early this morning. At that time he had no intention of resigning, I know, for he gave me passes and letters of introduction to several generals at the front. He also gave me a letter to General Kartzov who is stationed at the Riga front; while we were talking one of his secretaries said that the general had been killed. Guchkov asked him if it was by members of his regiment. The secretary said, "No, by someone unknown."

Russia is slowly and surely being led by its anarchy into a civil war. When Guchkov resigned, he issued statements showing that he had the welfare of Russia in his heart and was working for Russia and Russia only. He also attacked the socialists and anarchists and said they are being led by German agents in this propaganda of peace. He prayed that they would see before it was too late that Russia would lose its revolution if they did not stop their campaign at once.

General Kornilov also resigned as commander of the Petrograd garrison here. His excuse was that he was being interfered with by the Council of Workmen and the Deputies Committees.

Lenin has, I think, left the city. We have not heard anything of him for a few days.

The soldiers held back the celebration Saturday in honor of the law that has just been passed granting them an increase in salary. This increase is going to cost the government about $25,000,000 a month.

I guess I shall have to get new passes now that Guchkov is no longer Minister of War. So I'll stay in the city a few days longer before going to the front.

Don

XXXIII. Tuesday, May 15

Dear Dot:

I have made a picture of Charles B. Crane of Chicago,[70] who, I understand, has been made a member of the Root Commission and will join them on their arrival here in Petrograd. Crane was out to see the ambassador today and when I called to get a picture of Francis, at work in his office, Crane agreed to pose for a picture with him. Crane is very well posted on Russia and has had a great deal of experience here. He is a good man for the Root Commission for he understands Russia's condition better than most Americans do. There is also a commission leaving Russia, which will be announced in a few days, I understand.

The soldiers are holding a congress here now and thousands of delegates from the front are in Petrograd attending this. They are the ones that kept pestering Guchkov, the Minister of War, and the other high officials of the army, accusing them of trying to rule the army as it was ruled under the old regime. There is also a convention being held here in which the people are asking that all citizens may have the right to keep arms in their homes. This, I think is in order that the workingmen in Petrograd may have arms.

The papers are telling us daily now about the Stockholm peace convention of the socialists.[71] A socialist paper states that no separate peace will be made unless it is a just peace for Russia. This is going to be impossible, because the moment the soldiers think that peace is going to be made, they will all start for home.

---

[70] Charles Richard Crane (1858–1939) was a wealthy American businessman with international contacts, particularly in Eastern Europe and the Middle East. Crane contributed heavily to Woodrow Wilson's 1912 election campaign and was rewarded with several appointments, including the Root Commission.

[71] In 1917, socialists of various national and political backgrounds planned to gather in a neutral country for a peace conference to show the way to permanent world peace. The attempt at informal diplomacy received much attention, but the conference never took place.

Hundreds of conventions are being held here in Petrograd. A convention of thieves was held the other day in a town a short distance away! They have demanded the right to have representatives sitting in the new council which they say is going to be formed. One of the Petrograd papers states that hundreds of pockets were picked at this meeting.

General Brusilov says that the Germans are now giving vodka to the Russian soldiers along the front, that this vodka is brought over under flags of truce and that in a great many instances it has had to be stopped by the Russians under artillery. He warns the people that if discipline is not established at once Russia will be ruined.

Kerensky is now making speeches and handing out long statements daily. Everywhere you go you hear about this wonderful man.

Miliukov has also handed out a statement that America is going to loan Russia a lot of money. He denies that Japan is preparing to bring an army into Russia.

The Labor Council has issued a manifesto addressed to the soldiers at the front saying that this war was brought on by the emperors and capitalists of all countries, and that now that the Tsar had been kicked out, it is the duty of the people to stop the war--that they must wait, however, until the Kaiser has been destroyed before they make peace and that they must defend the revolution with all their power. They also warn the people that the German army is not like the Russian army, that the Germans still believe the Kaiser. They tell the soldiers that the men they were fraternizing with at the front are not ignorant soldiers, but General Staff officers of the German army dressed as common soldiers, and they pray that the soldiers at the front will obey all orders and not endanger the liberty which Russia had gained.

From inside information, I understand that Miliukov is going to resign in a few days. Lee, the vice-consul, tells me that the railroad commission is now on its way.[72] I gave the story out to one of the Russian papers today and they had a long interview with regard to it. According to Lee, these men are our best railroad men. If that is so, they can do a great deal of good, more good than if we sent a million soldiers to Russia. What Russia needs most is locomotives, railroad cars and steel rails, and someone to untangle the railroad tie-up here.

Don

---

[72] The United States Railway Advisory Commission, headed by John F. Stevens, arrived at the end of June and spent about fifty days in the country. Its assignment was to conduct a survey of all Russian railways and make technical and management recommendations. A second mission, the Russian Railway Service Corps, consisting of more than 300 railway engineers, was hired by the Provisional Government for duty along the Trans-Siberian Railroad. By the time the unit arrived in Vladivostok on December 1917, the Bolsheviks had come to power and its services were no longer desired.

XXXIV. Thursday, May 17

Dear Dot:

I have missed writing you for a couple of days because I have been so busy making pictures of the new cabinet. Miliukov has resigned and M. Tereshchenko[73] is in his place. Kerensky is now Minister of War. He is a socialist, which gives the Socialist Party six members in this Coalition Cabinet. Kerensky is what I call a socialist-democrat. He has asked the people to prepare for the Constituent Assembly. Tereshchenko, the new Foreign Minister, is about thirty-two years old, and has a very good name here. The workmen, however, say he is a capitalist and are already printing things against him in their papers. He is very rich. His family made their money in the beet sugar business. He has been in the cabinet before, occupying the chair of Minister of Finance. Kerensky is now undoubtedly the most popular man in Petrograd. He is about forty years of age, and has done a great deal to keep the radical crowd from doing a lot of fool things.

The socialists now seem to think they have complete control. There are about five million of them in Russia and, as I understand it, they want to rule the country. Russia has a population of 180,000,000 people.[74] Kerensky has promised, I understand, to make the program of the sodalists moderate in its demands.

I met Kerensky after he had taken his position, and he willingly posed for a picture for me. I also requested that when he went to the front on his next visit he should allow me to go with him. He gave instructions to his secretary to issue a new pass to me and to notify me when he went to the front. He said I could go to the front with him any time I wished.

From what I hear, Kerensky is dying. When you meet him however, you cannot think there is anything the matter with him. I understand he has stomach trouble. Well, if he has been eating black bread all his life, I don't wonder. I have been here only a short time and if black bread put me down on my back as quickly as it did, I do not see how Kerensky lives at all.

---

[73] Mikhail Ivanovich Tereshchenko (1886–1956) was a Ukrainian landowner, owner of several sugar factories, and financier. From 1915 to 1917, he chaired the Military Industry Committee of the Kiev district and was deputy chairman of the All-Russian Military Industry Committee. After the February Revolution, he was appointed minister of finance, and in May succeeded Miliukov as minister of foreign affairs. He was arrested during the October Revolution and imprisoned in the Peter and Paul Fortress. He escaped in the spring of 1918, and fled to Norway and then France.

[74] There are no reliable numbers for Russia's population in this period. The only census conducted during the Tsarist era (in 1897) estimated the population at more than 125 million. Thompson's estimate looks high, although it should be noted that in this period Russia included not only what later became the Soviet Union, but also Poland and Finland.

Well, dying or not, Kerensky is going to make a name for himself here. I only hope he does not weaken. He is up against a strong gang here—the socialists and anarchists, who are undoubtedly being influenced by German money.

Kerensky's first statement as Minister of War was that fraternizing between Russians and Germans must stop at once. He says it is a shame, that the whole world is shaking its finger and saying, "Look at Russia fraternizing with her enemy!" He says the Russian soldier should remember that this does not happen on the French front. I am not afraid for the present of Russia making a separate peace with the Germans. If the government as it is organized now is strong, Russia will yet be able to hold its head up when the war is over and say, "We did our part."

The Council of Workmen's and Soldiers' Deputies have sent word to the socialists of Germany and Austria asking them not to allow any arms to be used against France or Russia while peace terms are being made.

The Germans have purchased about all the papers in Russia, I think. They are continually hammering out German propaganda, asking the soldiers why they are fighting. They say, "Why do you kill us? We are your friends. Russians, this war is unpleasant. Stop it. The time has come now when you should go back to your land. Do you know that the land is now being divided by the capitalists and that you will have none if you do not immediately, as an armed force, go home and take what is yours?" These proclamations are sent out; then there are German agents on the spot to tell the soldiers who can't read what the papers say.

This kind of propaganda has gained a foothold in the Russian army. As a general rule the Russian does not really know what he is fighting for. Nobody had ever told him what the war was about. They have no idea of the issues involved. Now the Russians are leaving the trenches and the camps and wandering over the country trying to find their way back to their homes (most of them don't know how to get back home). They hear about peace, and they know that means they will not have to lie in the trenches this coming winter. Undoubtedly the Russians are tired of this war. I do not blame them. They have been lying in the trenches, they have been fighting, they have covered themselves with glory. No army can say, "We have done better." On top of this, with the political factions fighting for power, the poor Russian soldier's mind is becoming so befuddled that he does not know what to say or what to do.

But I know this: the Russian is a fighter and right now, demoralized as the Russian army is, if some army were to start a real advance and had a few powerful and popular leaders at the head of it, there would be millions of Russian soldiers to follow. What Russia needs at the present time at the front is a leader, a Napoleon, someone who has the nerve to do things, no matter what the public says or how many mobs appear on the streets in Petrograd.

Everything Russian is judged by what happens in Petrograd, and as I told you long ago, Petrograd is not Russia.

As soon as I can, now, I am going down to the front I will write you how things are going there.

Don

XXXV. Sunday, May 20

Dear Dot:

As usual, I have failed to keep my word to write to you. I have been intending to go to the front, but each day I put it off.

From the reports I get and what I have seen the last few days, the soldiers at the front are still deserting by the thousands and are very much peeved with the program of the socialists, "peace without annexation." The soldiers who have just come from the front say that they have done a lot of fighting and that the soldiers who are with the Allies on the western front have also done a lot of fighting, and that what they have they should keep. They say the war should not stop until they have taken enough to repay them for what they have suffered in this war.

The generals stationed here who have resigned have agreed, I understand, to hold up their resignations; they announce that the commanders will all remain at their posts. This, in a way, is a very good thing, for the commander at the western front, General Brusilov, is one of Russia's best generals. Also, his staff is one of the best in Russia, and if he had left, they would probably leave too.

The only thing I fear now is that anarchy is going to get the upper hand. Thousands are crying out that they want the army to do a little fighting. A short time ago they wanted the war to stop. Russia is a funny country; you never know what to expect.

The Russian government has finally awakened to the fact that if Germany wins this war Russia will be worse off than she was before. For the last few days the cry has been that the war must be carried to a successful finish, that the Allies should be helped, and that all possible aid should be given to the soldiers at the front. Just as soon as the radical socialists get wind of this I expect to hear of another big demonstration urging that the war must be stopped at once.

Kerensky says it is impossible for a counter revolution to take place, that the government is too strong.

Poor little Romania is in a devil of a position. I feel sorry for Romania. Romanian officers I meet are very skeptical about what is going to happen. Some of them frankly say that they are sorry Romania entered the war. I realize myself that if Russia were to make peace poor Romania would be the one to suffer most; she would be in a position where she could do nothing and would be crushed. Still the Romanian troops are holding out to a man, and there has been no fraternizing on the Romanian front. Even the soldiers from the Russian army who are with the Romanians in certain places have been forbidden to fraternize along their front.

Kerensky has begun to use the iron hand with Russian soldiers who have deserted. He has had a notice published that Russian soldiers have so many days to return to the front. After that date those who have not returned will be considered deserters and tried before the courts. The other day he had a house on Ligovsky Street surrounded. A lot of deserters had taken up quarters there. He used a Finnish regiment, and those men, who had threatened to die fighting, when the soldiers lined up and surrounded the building, came out like little lambs and surrendered.

A general congress of soldiers representing the different fronts and workmen from all the districts of Russia has been called for a meeting on June 14. They are to discuss war, peace, land, labor and army questions, and demand that the Constituent Assembly date be announced at once.

I went to Finland the other day with Kerensky. At one little station Kerensky was received by thousands of people. He gave them a short address and was asked to visit the troops stationed at a barracks in that town, which he did. I do not know what he said, but after he had finished they cheered him and followed him to the station. Several attempts have already been made on his life.

As a general rule, at this time every year they begin to bring in wood for the next winter. You see no wood at all being brought into Petrograd. There are several reasons for this: one, that the peasants are refusing to work; another, that the railroads are so congested and broken down. Then, too, the landowners refuse to sell their wood, realizing that Russian money is not worth much now.

I also understand that the government is going to seize all the platinum mines. 95 percent of all the platinum in the world is mined here in Russia. The owners of the platinum mines have made fortunes since the war started.

The railroads are getting more congested every day. In Russia there are only about 50,000 miles of railroad. This is only one mile of railroad to over 100 square miles of territory.

I understand that the fairs are going to open again this summer. Before the revolution, or before the war, there were over 1,500 fairs a year. They were a great event in some cities and were attended by thousands and thousands of people, who did quite a business exchanging their produce for goods offered by the merchants. Most of the business at them was done by the Germans. Since the war the business has fallen down. Now, the fairs are to be held as they were of old, but not with German goods.

I am told that the Russian peasants are not putting in their crops as they did of old. The government has issued special appeals to the peasants to sow their land and grow as much grain as possible.

Don

XXXVI. Hotel Astoria, Thursday, May 24

Dear Dot:

Just arrived back from a trip I made with Kerensky to the front. Kerensky had a special train, and as usual he made speeches wherever the train stopped. There is talk now of organizing a new army. A good many officers have been asked permission to be allowed to organize Death Battalions.

A lot of Germans northeast of Krevo tried to come over from France and fraternize. They were driven back by Russian artillery fire and a great many were killed or wounded. This is what should be done to all who come.

The Peasants' Congress now in session here has given its OK to the new coalition government, and an order has been issued that agitators shall not be allowed to enter military zones except by special permission.

Kerensky is receiving a great many petitions from regiments stationed in the interior to be allowed to go to the front and help hold the line.

General Ruzsky, who is now here in the capital, says that Kerensky will do a lot of good, that his personality and popularity are already being felt at the front.

In Southern Russia, the workmen are causing a great deal of trouble by asking for an increase in wages. The manufacturers in that district now pay over 120,000,000 more a year than in the past. The workmen have threatened that all factories working on army orders will strike at once if their demand is not met. In a great many places in this territory, the only law is the Soldiers' Committee. This has taken the law into its own hands and smiles on acts of lawlessness; and the peasants are burning and sacking the mansions of the wealthy.

Disorders have also started in the Minsk district. Kerensky has announced that he will rule the army by force and that discipline must be maintained even if he has to use force. But he also says that it is still optional with the soldiers whether they shall salute their superior officers, and he tells the soldiers that they still have the right to speak and hold meetings and express their own political views. He has issued a statement with about twenty paragraphs. The fourteenth paragraph states that no soldier can be punished without trial, while at the same time an armed force can be used if necessary against those refusing to obey. The Provisional Government, which is now Kerensky, has its hands full. The way I size it up is that they are nearly all adventurers; each one wants to become famous, and all of them have their eyes on the presidential chair.

Take the Prime Minister, Prince Lvov. He got his job because he was always criticizing the old government and was always against it. Russians I talk with who know him, say that he has a poor reputation and is just a weak old man.

Guchkov, the first Minister of War, who resigned a few weeks ago, wanted to be dictator of Russia. He is also an adventurer. He came from a family of Moscow merchants. I understand from people in Moscow that he and his family were very unpopular, although one of his brothers was once mayor. During the South African war, Guchkov fought with the Boers against England.

But Kerensky has come up more quickly than any of the others. He is a young looking man and was elected to the Duma by the socialists on account of his extreme opinions. Not so long ago he was just a little lawyer at Saratov. Even friends of his now say that his honesty in certain affairs has been questioned and that for the position he holds he has had very little experience. He first broke into the limelight a few weeks before the revolution, when he made a speech against the old government and insulted the former Empress. When the revolution was at its height, and the Bolsheviks wanted to kill all the members of the Duma for some reason or other, and were actually at the Duma crying for the lives of the members, Kerensky jumped up and shouted "tavarish," which means "comrade" in English, and waving his arms launched into a famous address. He is a great orator and knows how to talk to the Russian in a way that he understands and likes. When Kerensky talks, these Russians stand around with their mouths open; they just eat his words as fast as he talks. In this address Kerensky said, "Don't kill these men but go at once and arrest all the old ministers and the officers of the old government." By his presence of mind and his nerve, and his bravery too, I think, in the face of these men, he so kept their minds away from what they had intended to do, that instead of killing the men they had intended to kill and even Kerensky himself, they decked him a hero in a few seconds, from that one word "arrest" and the way he said it. When the mob left they were cheering Kerensky, and before the day was over, Kerensky's name was being talked of throughout Petrograd. This was Kerensky's first step into fame. For the work he did that day, naturally they had to repay him and his reward was Minister of Justice. At the same time, on account of his socialistic views, he was elected to the first Council of Soldiers' and Workmen's Delegates, and he made himself a link between this body and the government. Both sides have always accused him of betraying them.

The first thing Kerensky did when in power was to abolish the death penalty. He abolished it even for spies. He also issued an order that all the criminals in all the prisons of Russia should be freed, and not satisfied with this, he introduced the first Russian law court. The court, as he had it, consisted of one judge, one soldier and one workman. The soldier didn't have to be educated; neither did the workman. It didn't matter whether they could read or write; they both had equal power with the judge and equal pay. These three were to deal out justice. Well, among the first few cases that came up before one of these courts there was the case of a workman who was suing his employer. This workman said he had been given a raise in salary from his employer since the revolution, but he was suing for wages fifteen years back. Did he get them? He did, and interest also. This is only one instance out of hundreds. Kerensky was always reaching out for popularity. When he became Minister of Justice he was supposed to take an oath. He put this off for several days, till the rest had taken their oath, when he finally got ready to take his, he named a day and sent word to the senators and the old judges and all the high officials and a great many other men who had grown old and were responsible now in Russia, telling them to assemble in the Senate at six a.m. in full uniform. While they stood around and waited, Kerensky, dressed as a workman, entered the door, shook hands with the porter, and then after a wait of half an hour or so, said he was ready to take the oath. When he had finished, he left without shaking hands with anyone. According to Russian custom it was a great insult to require all these people to be on hand so early in the morning and then fail to shake hands with anybody, especially as some of Russia's best judges and most eminent men were standing about and had willingly come at that hour as a favor to Kerensky. After having himself appointed Minister of Justice, he abolished all ranks, decorations and honors. He also had a proclamation issued that all honors which had been made in the past should be taken away from the judges who had rendered long and loyal services for them. Kerensky did all this to please the socialists. When he passed one of these orders, he would rush madly to some socialist meeting and announce what he had done and be cheered wildly. Finally, not satisfied with what he had done, he tried to issue an order and have it made law, that all decorations should be taken away from the officers. In this plan he met a stone wall. In Russia there have been hundreds of decorations given for bravery. Thousands of Russia's best men have sacrificed their blood; you see them with legs or arms off, blind and disfigured, but wearing on their breasts the large black and yellow ribbon called the Order of St. George. Kerensky wanted to take it away from them, this little medal which many a man had fought for and for which he was perfectly willing to go through life maimed or crippled, and which is the only thing he has in lieu of a pension. Kerensky wanted not only to take this decoration away but to abolish all decorations for the future. In this he was supported by the Soldiers' and Workmen's Council, though the men who upheld him had not as a rule been to the front. The plan was about to succeed when a poor soldier with half of his face blown away, with one arm gone and a wooden left leg, got up and, indicating the little St. George Cross hanging on his breast, said, as he pointed his finger across the hall, "You see that woman and those five little children sitting over there? That is my family. I couldn't even leave them outside because they are cold, sick, and feverish. I brought them here where it is warm. I am a member of this convention. I fought at the front. Look at me. I asked nothing from the old government because I was satisfied with this decoration. My family are satisfied. But try and take this away from me, this which my family have suffered for, and my children as well, and I will fight all of you." Well, the meeting was in an uproar. The outcome was a decree that no more decorations were to be given.

Kerensky, I understand, brags about his great number of friends. It is the same in Russia as in America. The moment a man gets into politics and holds an office, he has a pack of leeches around who will sell their soul for money or a position in public life. Now that Kerensky has power, thousands of people are patting him on the back and saying, "You are a great man." They want a position, that is all. I have seen people stand at a public reception and cheer and smile at everything Kerensky said or did. Ten minutes later out in the street they were making fun of Kerensky. It is just the same the world over, I guess.

Kerensky has appointed all of his friends to vacancies in the Ministry, and if there is no place for them, he makes one. He is also dismissing a great many judges in order to find places for his friends. Before the revolution in Russia, a judge was never dismissed except for the most serious reason.

Kerensky is now trying to make himself popular with the higher classes. He has become so popular with the socialists, that I firmly believe he thinks everyone likes him. After he had become Minister of War he had a lot of regiments march to the Mariinsky Palace. He told them they were not citizens but just privates who had revolted. This he did, I am told, to gain favor in the eyes of the upper classes. It did him no harm in the eyes of the Soldiers' and Workmen's Delegates because he explained it to them in another light and had it so printed in the papers. The newspapers who are against the Soldiers' and Workmen's Council then began to say things like this: "Kerensky, the savior of the country—Kerensky, the next dictator, the Napoleon of Russia, has been found." After that he began to play with both sides. This is going to be his downfall someday. He cannot play with two sides in Russia; he might in some countries, but not in Russia.

Kerensky is now moving different regiments along the front. From army officers I gather that he is getting ready to have an advance made. In most places the soldiers have already voted not to attack. Some regiments, however, have agreed to do so, and Kerensky is having these regiments moved to the front so they will be together. This is all very well, but it will not succeed. If he advances in one section, or persuades the soldiers to advance, what will happen to the front if the soldiers in the other sections don't advance? An advance must take place along the whole line, not just in one place.

I don't think Kerensky likes Prince Lvov very well. Lvov in a way is against the socialists when it comes to the land question and says that the only people to decide the land question are the Constitutional Assembly. Lvov says that if this question is decided before the Constitutional Assembly meets, it will bring civil war in Russia.

The Provisional Government and Russia's financial and economic situation are laughable. The first Minister of Finance after the downfall of Nicholas was Tereshchenko. He is a lucky man; has been lucky all his life. I cannot understand why the anarchists have not killed him. They say that all the rich should be killed and he is one of the richest men in Russia. He professes to be a socialist. I doubt if he is in his heart. He owns a lot of sugar refineries, but for the position he now occupies he has had very little experience, in fact none at all. He has done nothing worth mentioning except to make a few speeches. He became popular through some of his first speeches, in which he said he was going to change the tax laws and that the burden would fall upon the rich. Then he introduced a lot of new tax laws and state monopolies. His one idea, as I understand he has told his friends, is to be Minister of Foreign Affairs.

The socialists are crying that Shingarev, who at the beginning of the revolution was made Minister of Agriculture, should be made Minister of Finances.

There is very little business being done here in the stock market. The stock exchange was closed as soon as the revolution began and had only been opened a short time before that, having been closed since the beginning of the war. I doubt if the stock exchange will open for a year or so yet. This is very hard on the people of Russia, who have not been able to sell their stocks or raise any money on them.

The demands of the workmen in regard to wages are unreasonable. The workmen of Russia are only about one-half percent of the whole population, and they want to dictate to the rest of Russia. The majority of the population are peasants. These people cultivate their own lands and are independent but as yet have had no vote in the government. In 1910 the total balance of Russia's trade and commerce amounted to only 15,000,000 rubles and the workmen demanded 9,000,000 rubles more wages. The factories have refused this fantastic demand and their only hope is that they can close out their stock of goods. They even offered to allow the workmen to take over the factories and work them on a percentage basis, but the working people have refused this. The manufacturers cannot meet these demands and on the other hand they do not dare close their factories, having been told by a committee that if they do they will be killed. They are trying to get around the situation by using up all their fuel and raw materials as fast as possible, hoping that they will not be able to buy any more fuel or materials with which to run their factories. So now that the workmen have made and been granted their demands and been upheld by the law in so doing, they are gaining nothing by it. In a short time I expect to see nearly all the workmen out of work.

As for peasants, their idea is that freedom means no more taxes. Since the revolution the government has been unable to collect any taxes from them. Private landowners have stopped paying taxes for the simple reason that in most cases their land has been taken by the peasants.

The government has issued a Liberty Loan at 5 percent and are forcing the people to subscribe. They are meeting with very little success. It was only at the start that the loan was successful at all. The socialists say they will not allow the government to pay any loans made either before or after the revolution. They say they don't mind people subscribing to the loan, but after this announcement people are not keen about subscribing. The result of this is that Russia's finances are being slowly wrecked by incompetent ministers. Russian money is getting lower every day. There is no silver; stamps are used for small change, and the banks are issuing treasury notes which you are obliged to accept by law. All this is helping to depreciate the value of the ruble throughout Russia.

Don

XXXVII. Saturday, May 26

Dear Dot:

Just returned from a two days' trip to Tsarskoe Selo (see figure 2), where the palace of Mr. Romanov and his wife is.

When I arrived at the station at Tsarskoe Selo, I was met by soldiers who asked me my business. On presenting my credentials I was allowed to leave the station and take a droshky to police headquarters in the center of the city. There I made my request to be allowed to go to the palace and photograph the former Emperor in the yard. One of the officers in charge, who spoke English, invited me to stay for lunch, which I did.

It is very interesting, the change here from what it used to be when I was here in 1915. The soldiers then were a better-looking class, they were chosen men. They are far from it now.

Tsarskoe Selo has a population of about 40,000, quite a number of churches, the old palace and the new, the soldiers' barracks, some hospitals, and a good many little shops. The palace of the Tsar isn't a very stately looking building. If it weren't the palace, it would command very little attention. The revolutionists have made a small cemetery directly under the Tsar's windows where they have buried their dead killed during the revolution. The officer from the police station who went around with me told me that the former Tsar stood at his window and watched the burial of these people.

I visited the court photographer's house. He is dead now and his wife is trying to run the shop in a small way. He has all the plates that have been made of the royal family during the last thirty years. In going over those plates I saw pictures that some day will be priceless. They also had a number of pictures of Rasputin made at different times. The photographer's wife said that Rasputin had been around the palace a great deal but she had not heard of his ever seeing the Tsar more than a couple of times; she said she had inquired of the servants at the palace if Rasputin had ever seen the Tsar, and that they had told her only a few times.

My police friend told me that when Kerensky entered the palace the first time after he had become the power behind the new government he was as nervous as he could be, and that when he was taken into the room where the Tsar was, he didn't know what to say. The Tsar himself stepped up and held out his hand saying, "I am glad to meet you. I am only sorry I hadn't met you before for I should have made you one of my ministers. I never knew you were such a great man or that the people loved you so much." Kerensky was evidently unable to reply as he had intended. What he said was, "I am also sorry not to have met you before."

The officers here are under the impression that the royal family will have to be moved. Almost every day they have to change the guard for making speeches against the royal prisoners.

I made a long distance picture of the Tsar and his son walking in the yard. The servants must have told him, for the Tsar sent word to me to come up, saying that he would allow me to make a picture as close as I wished. I told him that I had met him before, in 1915, and had made pictures of him then at the front and at Lemberg. He remembered, and immediately spoke of Memes, the English photographer.[75] While I was making pictures and the camera was being reloaded so that I could put in some new film, several of the soldiers came up close, while the Tsar was watching how the camera was loaded. Three were smoking. One of them elbowed the Tsar away and at the same time blew smoke directly in his face. But the Tsar didn't show that he was annoyed by this. After I had made some motion picture film of him and his son, and also some still photographs, I saluted and said, "Goodbye." He answered, "Goodbye." While walking away I glanced around. He was still looking after me and talking to his son.

That evening I had my friend send for some of the servants to come over. Several of them had been with the royal family for years. Of the eight servants whom I talked with that night, two were loyal and refused to answer questions, or evaded them. The others began to tell the most outlandish tales I have ever heard. I knew they were lies, because when I would ask them the same question over again in a few minutes they would give a different answer. Most of the stories, which they evidently thought everyone wanted to hear, were scandals connected with the royal family.

The next day, I went to the home of Anna Viroubova,[76] that is, the house she occupied while at court. A great many people thought, from her being so closely connected with the former Empress, that she had lived at the palace. This is not true at all. She had a house across the way, and it was the habit of the Empress to go over there and visit. It was at her house that the Empress first met Rasputin. Viroubova is now in the Peter and Paul Fortress and will probably remain there a long time unless the present government takes pity on her and puts her in a hospital. I have been told that her health is broken down and that she grows worse each day. For a woman crippled as she is, and dependent upon crutches entirely, it is a shame, no matter what her crime, to keep her in a prison like the Peter and Paul Fortress. I don't know whether I ever told you that she was hurt in a railroad accident several years ago. From time to time I have been gathering information about Rasputin and when I get the whole

---

[75] George Mewes of the *Daily Mirror*. See n. 39.

[76] Anna Alexandrovna Virubova, née Taneyeva (1884–1964), was the best friend and confidante of the Empress Alexandra. After a brief marriage to a court officer that ended in divorce, she became one of Rasputin's adherents. She was severely injured in a train accident between the capital and Tsarskoe Selo in January 1915; she found herself a paraplegic, but credited Rasputin with saving her life with his prayers. Arrested in March 1917, she spent five months in the Peter and Paul Fortress. Investigators who probed her political role and links with Rasputin concluded that she lacked the intelligence to have any influence over the empress. She died at the age of eighty in Helsinki.

story I will write you a long letter and give you the inside details. The more I investigate the more I find that Rasputin, although he probably did have a great many crimes to answer for, was the most over-estimated man in Russia. If he had not been killed and had appeared later in America, I should have said that some clever American newspaper agent had got hold of him and staged all those sensational stories so as to make him a good drawing-card in vaudeville. In 1915, when I met Rasputin, as I told you when I was at home, I found him very interesting. Now that I find he was an uneducated man, I can hardly believe it, although all the conversation I ever had with him was through an interpreter. Even then I found him well posted, and with a knowledge of the affairs of the world such as few men have. They say that every time he saw a woman he lost his head. Well, we have a million Rasputins in America whom I know personally myself, and if their record had been published as his has, they would have a bigger record than Rasputin ever dreamed of having. But that is the way of the world. I will try to see a certain friend and sponsor of his again in prison, and get a story from her. I understand she is very talkative. Boris says he knows a place in Petrograd where Rasputin used to go, and that several of the artists living there can give me stories of him. I understand that Rasputin did most of his talking when he got drunk, and from all accounts that is why he was killed. If he had kept his mouth shut, a great many people say he would still be living.

And now you hear that Rasputin was the cause of the revolution, that his death awoke all Russia! That is a lie. German intrigue started the revolution, and that was what woke up Russia. I believe that if Rasputin had been living during the revolution, all they would have done would have been to throw him into prison.

The food in Tsarskoe Selo seems to be more plentiful than in Petrograd. The soldiers on duty there also are living better. They are drinking the imperial family wines. My friend told me they were afraid the soldiers would be ruined while on duty there, as they had begun to form a taste for expensive wines which they couldn't get at the ordinary barracks in Russia.

Don

XXXVIII. Hotel Astoria, Thursday, May 31.

Dear Dot:

The convention of soldiers who have a Congress here composed of delegates from the front are voting that they want peace without annexations or indemnities. They also say that they are loyal to the Council of Soldiers' and Workmen's Deputies and the Provisional Government, and demand that munitions and provisions be sent to the army at once. They say that the army in the trenches is willing to fight, but that they want means taken to end the war as soon as possible. They say that the Russian army has been fighting under conditions worse than the Allies, that the superior Russian soldiers have had to march against the enemy's bullets and break through the enemy's barbed wire with their bare hands, that they have to make charges without artillery preparing the way for them, and that the Russian army must not be used any longer as gun fodder. They urge the people of free Russia to rally at once and insist that the Soldiers' and Workmen's Deputies must not permit adventurers to lead Russia astray.

While they were holding their convention, the Cossacks in the Ural sent a resolution from their convention stating that they would help the Provisional Government, that the army should do away with fraternizing, and that there must be no more disorders. The Minister of Food Control made an address before this Congress stating that the food situation was better than before, but still a long way from normal. The Congress stated that the peasants are refusing to take paper money for their grain and demand instead that they be given tools and raw materials for the grain. The Minister announced that it was impossible for the government to provide the necessary machinery for the grain monopoly. He said that the army at the front had to have 400,000 tons of wheat a week and that last week they had only 45,000 tons. The munition situation is serious. He said that the factories have only about 25,000 tons on hand and need ten times more and that if the peasants and workmen do not grasp this situation at once civil war will ensue and Russia will lose her freedom. In some districts, however, the peasants are sending grain to the army without money; they are taking it to the railroad officials and saying that it is their gift to Russia now that Russia is free. I only wish this might happen everywhere. It would do more than anything else to encourage the men at the front.

The anarchist papers in Petrograd are crying now that the guards who are watching the Empress are not strict enough, and are careless in their duties, and that she can escape whenever she wants to. I was out at the palace the other day and found the guards sitting around smoking and playing games. They changed guards just before I left. It was done as I never saw a guard changed before in Russia. They did it with more snap than ever before.

The capitalists are being jumped on by everyone for not subscribing to the Liberty Loan. The better class of people also accuse the government of printing too much money, saying that there is no gold back of it.[77] The government says that if the people don't subscribe more liberally to the Loan they will have to issue more paper money at once to relieve the situation and that they will confiscate all currency that is being held by the people, who are hoarding millions and millions of rubles.

One of Boris's relatives, who has just returned from the southern part of Russia, where he has a farm, says that in that district German agents are working among the

---

[77] Russia adopted the gold standard in 1897. It was suspended in July 1914 for the duration of the war. Pipes estimates that over the course of the war the quantity of ruble banknotes in circulation increased four to six times. By the middle of 1915, prices began to rise and increased steeply in 1916 and 1917. Inflation had most impact on the fast-growing urban population (*A Concise History of the Russian Revolution*, 18, 67).

peasants and advising them to destroy their crops, telling them that if they don't they will be taken away from them. The German agents find it easy enough to persuade these poor ignorant peasants to commit outrages. If they succeed in getting them to destroy their crops it will mean that we will not have any grain next year.

The situation as regards wages is getting more serious. In the factories in Petrograd, the workmen are demanding from 100 to 200 percent increase. In the factories where this has been granted, they have come back and demanded more; this has only given the workmen an appetite for more demands. The factories here in Petrograd which were asked to give a raise of fifteen kopecks more an hour in pay, found when they started to sign the agreement that it dated from August 1, 1914. They had to have a directors' meeting at once and decided they would have to meet the demand though it cost them 6,000,000 in cash. Several manufacturers have been forced to hide until the people could quiet the workmen in their factories. An eight-hour working day is already in effect in most of the factories, and an English manufacturer told me that their output has decreased 40 percent since the revolution. The manufacturers are facing a daily increase in the prices of raw materials and are also unable to collect money on goods sold; they cannot find any means to raise more capital to meet the demands of the workmen.

We are now hearing daily in all the papers that the army should advance and defeat the enemy at once. This should be done so the troops cannot be withdrawn and sent to France. If they make an advance now it would give Russia an opportunity to retake a lot of her land, for I know Germany has withdrawn a good many divisions from this front.

Although law and order prevail in Petrograd and conditions at the front are improved, on the railroads in the rear the soldiers are still out of hand and in most places back on the lines, authority is very lax and weak, and the soldiers are looting wine-shops. Kerensky has issued a special appeal to the soldiers who are committing these acts, telling them that Russia will be lost on account of their outrages. In Petrograd when they find deserters, they fasten a huge card on them with the word "deserter" on it; when they catch a thief, they put the word "thief" on the card and lead him around with a chain. I have made several pictures of people who have been accused of different things being led around the streets of Petrograd in this manner.

In the province of Nizhnii Novgorod, thousands of criminal prisoners have asked permission to go to the front and fight. Their request has been granted and they will now be dressed as soldiers. I hope I shan't meet any of them. I don't want to lose my cameras.

There is an increase of drunkenness owing to the illegitimate sale of vodka. I have seen more drunken people on the streets in the last few days than I ever saw before. Notices are being posted by the Provisional Government saying that this is the work of the old government, which hopes to lead Russia into civil war. If the government doesn't take charge of the vodka, it will lead to serious trouble. I hear that in

1915 there was a great deal of drunkenness during the riots and that the reason the government overcame the mob was that most of them were drunk.

On the Russian front in several places, the Germans are withdrawing their big guns. If Russia could only get together now and attack, all of this would he stopped; if it keeps up, France will be made to suffer in a short time. The General Staff have issued a statement that everything is ready for an advance and that all that is lacking is the will of the people and soldiers.

The people who were sent to the front after the revolution are now causing a great deal of trouble with a propaganda they are spreading. I believe they should not have been sent to the front, but interned. Naturally they want to be back to their old positions, where they can graft and live easily.

I hear that Great Britain is sending labor leaders to Russia who will try to deliver a message to the working people of Russia from the English working people.

Don

XXXIX. Friday, June 1

Dear Dot:

Well, we have had more excitement. The anarchists and socialists who call themselves the "reds" have seized Kronstadt (see figure 2), the last defense of Petrograd and Russia's strongest naval base, and they have declared themselves a separate republic.[78] This fortress is only twenty miles from Petrograd. All of the Provisional Government's representatives who were at Kronstadt have had their offices taken away from them and Anatole Samanov[79] has declared himself President of Kronstadt. The factories have begun closing now on account of strikes. I am told at the staff headquarters that over one hundred have closed already. The workmen have made another demand; they have chopped off two hours and now only work six hours a day; and the women, who have been organizing, have come out with a demand that their minimum salaries should be $75 a month.

The anarchists are also holding demonstrations in Petrograd, carrying banners advising the people to take what is theirs and get rid of the capitalists. The Kronstadt people are going to cause trouble, according to the papers; they threaten to bombard Petrograd if anyone interferes with them! I asked an officer if this was possible. He said they had some guns there that would reach to Petrograd.

---

[78] See n. 45.

[79] No reference to Samanov was found in histories of the revolution. The most authoritative account of the Kronstadt uprising is Evan Mawdsley's *The Russian Revolution and the Baltic Fleet: War and Politics, February 1917–April 1918* (London: Macmillan, 1978). Mawdsley (29) lists two leaders of the Kronstadt Bolsheviks—Fedor Fedorovich Raskolnikov and Semen Grigorovich Roshal. Both were former students from Petrograd who had served prison terms for their political activities.

The miners now have asked a minimum wage of $125 a month and threaten to strike if their demands are not met at once.

Kerensky has issued a statement saying that the Constitutional Assembly cannot meet until November. This has caused dissatisfaction. Kerensky says that the fraternizing in some places has grown worse and in other places better.

The Cossacks have met at their barracks and are mad about a statement that has got out saying that they are deserting. They say they have never deserted and have never fraternized with the enemy, and are always on the alert at the trenches at the front.

Kerensky says that he has troops in ships which he can use if necessary to stop any trouble at Kronstadt. The chief topic of conversation here in Petrograd is Kerensky. For some reason or other the demonstrations of the anarchists on the streets are not being stopped.

Kronstadt is talking about its strength, but I think it is exaggerated. Kerensky says he will starve them out. Kronstadt's answer is that they will come down and knock Petrograd off the map and take what food they want. The leader at Kronstadt, Anatole Samanov, was a student in a chemistry school in Petrograd before the revolution. Afterwards he went home and became a "dyed in the wool" anarchist. He has been carrying on his little propaganda in a quiet way and is now the dictator of Kronstadt. If something is not done to stop his little program, it might lead to Russia being split in two. He says Kronstadt is going be a model for all Russia to copy, and things work out that way. He wants to be the Napoleon of all Russia and says he will be before he is through.

The deserters from the Russian army are now going to have a convention and state their demands. Captain Riggs[80] has arrived at Vladivostok to meet the Root Commission, which is coming by special train to Petrograd. He left with the new Russian Ambassador to the United States in his special car.

The sailors at Kronstadt, now that they are a separate republic, demand that the custody of the former Tsar be turned over to them and that he be transferred to Kronstadt where they will guard him themselves.

Don

XL. Monday, June 4

Dear Dot:

Tomorrow I am going to the front for a week or so.

General Brusilov has been made commander-in-chief of all the Russian armies in place of General Alekseiev, and General Gurko has been given Brusilov's place on the Western front.

---

[80] Captain E. Francis Riggs, a military attaché at the U.S. Embassy.

General Brusilov is one of Russia's best commanders, a brilliant man and a good strategist, and the one man Germany fears.[81] This is a change that is very popular in Russia, and Kerensky couldn't have picked a better man. When the war began, he was one of the Corps Commanders under General Ruzsky, who was one of the right-hand men of Grand Duke Nicholas.

Early in the war Brusilov captured Halicz, which was the first real victory for Russia and resulted later in the fall of Lemberg. In 1916 he was made commander of the Southern group of armies, and in that year began his great campaign. He was able to break through the German lines and roll them back over one hundred miles in some places, and he captured almost 400,000 prisoners with guns and valuable supplies, all of which made him a hero. The Germans had a great deal of trouble stopping that drive of his and only succeeded after they had brought a great many divisions up to face him. I have met him several times. I expect he will be allowed to do many things that some other generals might not be allowed to do. On Sunday we had a scare in Petrograd. A bunch of sailors landed from the Kronstadt garrison. They said they were being followed by thousands of others and some war ships. In a few minutes the report got around Petrograd that they were going to seize the city. I don't know what happened, for later in the afternoon we failed to see any more. Then the small bunch who had come in were given the laugh.

While these men were landing, a fire started burning in the Gutuyev quarters.[82] Several explosions occurred which, I understand, did quite a little harm. I heard one of the American newspaper correspondents say, however, that those men we saw had come on a regular steamer, that no more ships had arrived from Kronstadt, and that no one knew anything about what had really taken place there. If these Kronstadt people are going to have a revolution of their own, we may expect the same thing in other districts.

Don

XLI. Hotel Astoria, Tuesday, June 5

Dear Dot:

I am leaving Wednesday, June 6, for the front. Today I met Dr. Eugene Hurd of Seattle, Washington,[83] who is a colonel here in the Russian army. Hurd is a big, tall Westerner and has been in Russia now nearly three years, fighting with the Russian

---

[81] See n. 54.

[82] A port district of Petrograd.

[83] Eugene Hurd, born in Wisconsin in 1881, was appointed captain in the Russian Army in October 1914, and later promoted to colonel. He served as a medical officer at the front and received several medals for his service. In 1917, he joined the U.S. Army Medical Corps. As far as is known, letters or diaries from his experiences in Russia have not survived.

army. He was in Seattle with a very good practice, when the war broke out, and why he ever picked Russia as a field of operations I do not know; but I understand he wrote a letter to the Tsar himself requesting permission to come to Russia and fight with the Russian army. Hurd comes from a family that dates back to all the wars, and they have all been doing their bit for the last hundred years. Hurd had his letter answered in this way. The Russian consul at Seattle bounced into his office one day and handed Hurd a bunch of money and a railroad ticket to Petrograd. Hurd left the next day for Vancouver where he took the steamer, and after a few weeks arrived in Petrograd. A short time afterward he was commissioned a colonel in the Russian army and has been decorated five times for bravery.

He organized a flying hospital column, and I hear Russians wherever I go speak about this man. He has a hospital down at the Dvinsk front (see figure 3) where I will make my headquarters when I cover the front in that district. I understand from some people who have been at his place that when he was asked to take charge of this hospital, which is the division hospital for that front, he found only one building, a shack made of canvas and logs. Although he has been there only a few months, he has now the most modern field hospital in all Russia.

Florence Harper met him while he was in Petrograd, and he arranged for her to go to the front. She writes me that she is in the hospital now, assisting in the surgical ward, and visits the front from time to time. I look forward with a great deal of pleasure to visiting Dr. Hurd, as I hear he has plenty of chickens, eggs, pigs, and fresh milk—and white bread. That is almost too good to be true. I had come to the conclusion that there was no more white bread to be had in Russia.

I will not take Boris to the front with me but will use the interpreter who is working for Dr. Hurd. The latter tells me he is going to build me a little log cabin all for myself and will have it ready for me when I arrive.

At Kronstadt the anarchists are holding over one hundred officers of the old army and navy and are subjecting them to the most shocking ill treatment. The prison these poor men are in is very crowded and filthy. Several of the prisoners have been shot by the guards. From stories that I gather, many of which I believe are true, conditions are simply horrible in the prison at Kronstadt. Kerensky says the stories are true.

The working people have been granted their six-hour labor day. Another order that has been issued is that all members of the Russian Red Cross who are under forty must go to the front and fight, and that older men will take their places in the Red Cross.

The socialists, or radical socialists, have made a demand upon the government that all secret treaties must be published at once. I think that is a German scheme to embarrass the Allies, as they are under the impression that there might be something that would cause dissatisfaction. From what I know, however, there is nothing of which the Allies need be ashamed.

In some districts now they have started the whipping-post and are using it quite freely, according to reports. I am under the impression that they could use it here in Petrograd.

Boris, who has just come in, says that Kronstadt has made peace with the Provisional Government, that they have patched up their differences and that officials will be appointed at Kronstadt who will be acceptable to the Provisional Government of Petrograd.

Last night the women met and have given out a statement that they are going to organize a regiment and go to the front themselves to fight This meeting was addressed by Col. Popov of the 12th army. They say they will fight under the same conditions as the men. I asked Boris about this and he says it is true, and that his girl has already signed a paper of enlistment.

I have been to the palace of Mme. Kschessinskaya, who was one of Russia's greatest dancers and quite a favorite with the royal family.[84] She was connected in a great many scandalous stories with the Emperor's name. This palace of hers has been wrecked. I made a great many scenes of it. I understand that she is entering suit against the government for damage done. She has tried several times to regain possession of her palace, but it is in the hands of the anarchists, who refuse to be moved. Nikolai Lenin is using it as his headquarters. In the grand saloon there is a big press where a socialist newspaper is printed and proclamations are run off by the thousands to be scattered among the people of Petrograd. The Roman bathroom, which has a tub made of some kind of marble, is being used by a lot of clerks as a room for keeping records.

Kschessinkaya is still in a way very popular, in spite of her name being linked with that of the Romanov family. She has appeared before so many audiences in Russia and all over the world for that matter that she has a following which has stood her in good stead. A great many of the papers are calling upon the government to give her back her home and throw out Lenin and his gang.

The clamor for putting the ex-Tsar in the Peter and Paul Fortress is growing daily. Where formerly only a few of the soldiers and anarchists wanted it, now it is being heard everywhere. Lenin demands that the ex-Tsar should be transferred to Kronstadt or sent to the Siberian mines. The sailors stationed at Helsingfors[85] have demanded that Nicholas be given to them; they say they will take him to Petrograd and keep him until he is placed on trial, and that if their demand is rejected, they will bring warships and force it. They say this must be Russia's last revolution and that the only way to make it the last is to imprison the ex-Tsar. Thousands of handbills are being thrown broadcast from automobiles in Petrograd saying, "Try him at once, Nicholas II." Kerensky has taken the trouble to increase the guard over the ex-Tsar

---

[84] See n. 66.

[85] Helsinki in Finland. Helsingfors was the original Swedish name.

and has issued a statement that it is impossible for him to escape. On top of this, however, the labor council in discussion today demanded that Nicholas should be sent to Kronstadt.

I was told at the General Staff today that Root is to arrive here next Monday. I am sorry I will not be here to make a picture of him, but I have left my camera with one of the regiments so they can take some pictures of him.

From reports the Romanian front which is held by the Russian soldiers has had a little trouble. Several of the regiments there have refused to obey orders but the difficulty has been finally ironed out. Several officers have had their epaulets stripped off and their swords taken away by the committees of the different regiments. I understand that at one time two or three regiments were opposing each other and only gave in after a great deal of arguing. This is the first serious trouble that has happened there.

The President's message, which has been published here, has caused a great deal of comment, and from what Boris says the press is about equally divided. The socialist paper controlled by Lenin, however, says it is unacceptable to the Russian democracy. But the papers that are supporting Kerensky state that America is holding out her hand to Russia.

Well, as I want to get started I will have to close. But before closing I want to give you an idea of what starting means. After I had got my military permit stamped and OK'd at the General Staff office, I had to take my order and go to the railroad station to get a seat on the train. When I arrived at the station I had to stand in line; and I should have had to wait there for three or four days if I hadn't got Boris to go to the line and pick out a soldier and offer him 100 rubles for his place. Boris did this, and after a half hour's wait I had my ticket. Now I must send Boris to the station two or three hours before I go so that he can rush and get me a seat. The trains are packed to suffocation. It is impossible to get a berth any more, as the people refuse to allow anyone to travel in comfort. Where they are all going I do not know. The trains go out jammed to the doors and come in the same way. It is the same everywhere you go.

I will have trouble, I think, watching my cameras on this trip. I am afraid someone will steal them or that they will get broken in the crush.

Don

XLII. Dvinsk front, Thursday, June 7

Dear Dot:

I arrived here this morning at nine o'clock. I do not know the name of the town, but I was met, after I had left the little narrow military gauge railway, by a soldier who seemed to know me and said he would take me to the Colonel's house. I did not know whether he had the right man or not but I let him take my things in the little Russian army wagon, and away we went. After a drive of an hour we pulled up in front of a building flying the Red Cross flag and also the Stars and Stripes, and then I knew I must be at Dr. Hurd's. I did not have long to wait. In the doorway, filling up the whole space, and with a good old Western smile on his face, was Dr. Hurd himself. He was out in a minute. He had just been notified and was in the operating room when I arrived. He then told a man to take my things, saying to me, "You are shaking." It was true; I was shaking from head to foot. I could not get my legs steady.

I was rushed into a real, honest-to-God dining-room. A sister came up and spoke to me in French and asked me if I would have breakfast. Then I was asked if I wanted to wash. When I came back to the dining-room, the sister asked me what I would have for breakfast. I said, "Anything." She said, "Name what you want, and you can have it." I told her I would like to have some ham and eggs. Ten minutes later the ham and eggs were set down before me, made just as we have them in America. There was also good coffee with real cream in it and sugar on the side, and white bread toasted, and good country butter. Well, I ate eight eggs, and a great big slice of ham that covered the plate and was a quarter of an inch thick, and about eight slices of toast and three cups of coffee. I was then given a drink of good American whiskey. It was real American whiskey. The bottle was corked and the seal unbroken before I drank it.

I was then rushed out of the dining-room over to my little log cabin which the doctor had made after he invited me to make my home with him while I was at this front. I have plenty of blankets on my little bed and pictures—I do not know where he got them—hanging on the wall. Late magazines are on a little log table and I also have a real lamp that burns oil, a reading lamp. He has made me a dark room and has had troughs fixed so that I can develop my film here if necessary. This doctor is a prince.

In the afternoon after lunch—a meal I could never describe; you would think me foolish if I did, but it was the best meal I have had since I left you at Topeka, Kansas—I was shown over this place. I cannot believe that this has all been done in such a short time. It shows what an American can really do when he is put to it. He had nothing, and where he got all these things I do not know.

The soldiers in this hospital do not have to sleep in tents, for he has had log houses built. Some of these hold seventy-five wounded, and he has a Russian bath house that twenty-five people can bathe in at one time. It is a real Russian bath, and a wonder. The floors everywhere are as white as marble.

The doctor has his own meat-house, and it is full to the door with hams and sides of bacon. He has a regular blacksmith's shop where all the repairing of ambulances is done. He has his own milk cows and a pig pen. He tells me he started with two pigs and now has a couple of thousand. He has chickens, ducks and geese and has also got hold of two fine turkeys which he says he is saving for Thanksgiving and Christmas. His barn for the horses is as good as any barn in America, and then he has another building where he stores grain with which to feed these horses. He has also had gas-masks made for the horses and the milk cows and says he would have made them for his pigs but that he could not catch one to take his measure.

The soldiers here have a committee also, but they do not interfere with Dr. Hurd's management of the hospital. He has one of the best equipped places in all Russia and is liked probably better than any man we have ever sent from America to Russia. His name is known from one end of this front to the other. Even the peasants flock about this wonderful American doctor. No one has ever come to this hospital, peasant or soldier, without having his wants attended to. If we could only have a few more men like Dr. Hurd of Seattle, it would be a great thing for America.

Now that America is in the war, Dr. Hurd is anxious to go back and do his bit at home. I told him that what he is doing here will more than amply repay him for not doing so, but I am afraid that when he hears that Root is in Petrograd and that his old friend, Stanley Washburn,[86] who is now a major, is with Root's Commission, he will leave and go back. But in America, although few doctors have had the experience and training he has, his services will not be given the reward they should be given. Dr. Hurd has never dabbled in politics and I am afraid he would never get the rank he has here in Russia. He was telling me this this afternoon, and it was overheard by a Russian. As if by magic the report spread over this little colony. A petition is already being sent around the hospital, another to the front and a third for the peasants living in the villages in this district, asking them to sign and ask their great American not to leave them. I myself will do all I can to persuade him to stay and keep up his great work. Dr. Hurd knows the Russians and how to handle them, and the Russians know that Dr. Hurd is not here playing politics but has come of his own free will to do something for Russia, a country that has no claims upon his services, and that he is doing this for 300 rubles a month. Now that the ruble has fallen so low in value, he is working practically for nothing. Dr. Hurd is a wonderful man, Dot. Just think, he left a practice of over $12,000 a year to take up this life! When you meet men like him who are doing great things, it makes you proud to be an American. Although I have been here only a few hours, I am already received with open arms because I am an American; I am being taken in on the record that Dr. Hurd has made.

Dr. Hurd is going to teach me a new Russian card game tonight. He tells me that I can only stay up until nine o'clock at the hospital, as at that time everyone must be in bed. The hour of rising here is six a.m. and breakfast is at seven. The doctor is in the operating room at 7:30.

Don

---

[86] Stanley Washburn (1878–1950) was a correspondent for the London *Times* on the Russian front from 1914. He published three volumes of *Field Notes from the Russian Front* (New York: Charles Scribner's Sons, 1915–17), one with photographs by George Mewes of the *Mirror*.

XLIII. Friday, June 8

Dear Dot:

Outside of the usual artillery compliments paid by the Russians and Germans to each other every day, you would hardly know you were at the front or that Russia was at war. German aeroplanes pay daily visits and throw proclamations by the thousands to the soldiers. These machines are fired at, and it is a treat to us. They are immediately attacked from eight different points within half a mile of the hospital where we have aircraft guns stationed, not such guns as you see on the Western front, but Russian artillery, fixed up on a platform on a high post so that they can be moved around easily. The German aeroplane has to be in a certain position for these guns to do any damage. They have to spot the aeroplane at a great distance and then begin to shoot.

New regulations have been published for the Russian army establishing the rights of the men in the fighting service. The decree says that all men who are able to fight shall enjoy while at the front all the rights of free citizens, but that their conduct must meet the requirements of the service with reference to discipline. They have the right to belong to any political party they desire, to speak, write or do anything they wish of any nature, and to have complete religious freedom. All mail addressed to the soldiers must be delivered, without exception, no matter what it is. When not on active duty they are allowed to take off their uniforms and dress in civilian clothes. The order also says that the relations between the fighting men must be based upon a strict regard for discipline, and that the soldiers and officers should both try to establish more friendly relations. It also states that the compulsory salute has been abolished, and establishes in its stead a voluntary mutual greeting. An exception, however, has been made when soldiers are on parade and for ceremonial occasions. When they are not on duty they can leave the barracks, ships, or quarters without asking permission. They are also exempt from capital punishment. In actual battle, however, the officer in command has a right to take all measures he may wish, even to the use of armed force, to have his orders fulfilled. No punishment is to be used that will offend the soldier's honor and dignity. If the soldier commits a criminal act he is to be tried.

The country around here is absolutely different from the neighborhood of Petrograd. In the villages you do not see as many men as you ought to see. I am told that they are not in the army but have gone to the cities, where they are now working, the wages being so attractive that they cannot resist the chance.

I notice that no land is being cultivated nor crops planted. Some peasants in this territory seem to think they do not have to work anymore and that they will be taken care of. They are right, in a way, in this neighborhood, for it is in an army zone and they are able to steal enough grain and food to live on.

The peasants here at the front seem to be satisfied with their freedom now, but they ask a great many foolish questions; when you ask them what they want they are like the rest in Petrograd. We ask them if the war should be carried on to a successful finish, and they cannot see why it should be. When they are asked if they are not afraid of the Germans coming, they say it would make no difference to them, that they have the land and would pay taxes to the Germans just as they are now paying them to the Russians. I was surprised to hear them speak of paying taxes, but they say that taxes are still being collected in their district.

I asked a peasant today if he knew that America was now with the Allies. He had never heard of America. I had this translated several times; I could not believe that such a thing was possible.

At the front here we have a great many socialists also. The Russian socialist is not a dreamer, as a great many people think; the belief now is that the Germans themselves will destroy Kaiserism and join hands with the Russian socialists. They are hungry for power and want to try out all their ideas. But I am afraid they do not want to pay the price and fight for them, as they will have to do to get absolute control in Russia.

The soldiers here at the front are very much disgusted with the soldiers of Petrograd. They say they are cowards and threaten that if they come to this front they will be very badly treated.

Prince Lvov has issued a long statement in which he says that Russian ideas are like American ideas and that some day the two countries will resemble each other in government and ideals.

Don

XLIV. Saturday, June 18

Dear Dot:

I got up at 4:30 this morning after sitting up pretty nearly all night playing poker with Dr. Hurd. One of the doctors came over and gave Dr. Hurd a vacation for a couple of days, so that he could indulge in a little extra sleep. We began playing poker, he and I, and the sky was the limit. We both played pretty tight, though, and neither one of us lost much; I was set back $115, but I have asked for revenge, and I hope to win it back. But I am willing to stop right now: Dr. Hurd is some poker player.

Senator Root has arrived in Petrograd, and I understand he has created a very good impression. A Russian officer who was visiting us yesterday said that the press would not have much to say about Root, as the papers were in the control of the Germans. He was very sorry, for he would like all Russia to hear what Root had to say and what message he had brought from America.

The general in charge of the 8th Army at this front says that an order has been issued to all commands that there must be an attack or offensive started by the Russian troops at once, that this inactivity at the front is playing into Germany's hands, and that we must show Germany at once that Russia is with the Allies and is still in the war.

I am going to go along the front now and take in different places. According to one of the nurses, the Petrograd papers report that a lot of socialists are coming back now from America. I hope this is not true, for several that have already arrived in Petrograd are stirring up a lot of trouble and accusing America of a good many things that are not true.

I am told that a few weeks ago the Russian army did not care to do any fighting. Now they are eager to discuss anything that will lead to an advance, and are ready. This is in the front line trenches. Back of these trenches, where the soldiers are counted by the millions, they are still hesitating. Here at the front the men want to fight and are going to fight.

At this front there is very little fraternizing. I saw one case, but it did not look as if it was of importance. Most of what I have seen has been just trading between soldiers; very little talking has been done. The Russian soldiers trade articles with the German soldiers. I notice, however, that this is all done on the Russian side; the Russians are not allowed to do any trading behind the German lines.

Everywhere I go the soldiers greet me with open arms when they find I am an American. They ask hundreds of questions through my interpreter about what America will do and when the American soldiers are coming to Russia. I tell them what America is in this war for, that we are fighting for world democracy and that Germany is not, and that America will spend, if necessary, every cent she has to crush Prussian militarism. The men always cheer these talks and I feel quite encouraged to give more as I go along. The officers tell me I do a lot of good in speaking to the soldiers this way.

The soldiers here all say they would like to get hold of Lenin and that they would make short work of him. They tell me that the villages back of the lines are full of German agents who are trying to make the soldiers go home, but that when they find them in their trenches at the front they make short work of them.

Since I have been down to the front I have greater faith in Russia than I ever had before, but I still find a feeling even here against the Jews. This is a feeling that will not die down.

Don

XLV. Galician front, July 3

Dear Dot:

Well, Russia has at last started her offensive. It was started by Kerensky himself, who after traveling along the position here for about thirty miles addressing different regiments, led the attack himself. So far the Russians have bagged over 10,000 Austrians. This attack is in charge of Gen. Brusilov. The advance was not carried through without trouble. The twelfth and thirteenth divisions refused to obey Kerensky's order and were surrounded by Cossack troops, especially after they had retreated in the village of Joukov, which was shelled all afternoon with shrapnel. About five o'clock in the evening the Cossacks charged and captured 500 of these mutinous troops and the others immediately surrendered.

The Russians are not losing as many men in this drive as one would expect, but the Russian aeroplanes report that the Germans and Austrians are bringing up heavy reinforcements. The army has already captured the enemy's strongest position here at Konichy, which is near Brezrzany, in Galicia. They have made their biggest gain here in prisoners, taking more than 10,000, and a great many guns. From here to Zlochow, a distance of about thirty miles, the attack is progressing with success. As I understand it, this is the key to Lemberg, the Galician capital, and if the Russian success keeps up they will again have Lemberg in their hands.

Officers say that this advance has been due mostly to Kerensky, whose speeches to the soldiers have finally made them see that they must not believe the German propaganda which is being thrown daily into their lines. Officers have sat down and cried when they realized that once more the Russian army is fighting as of old and that the Russian soldier has entered into the war with all his former spirit and dash. This goes to show that when the Russian soldier is fed with Russian propaganda he can be influenced as easily as he can be with the German propaganda which was slowly turning him from the welfare of Russia. Even men who have deserted who have heard of this great advance are returning and asking pardon for what they have done and for permission to join in the advance.

The Russians have also used one of their big Zeppelins here which is dropping over half a ton of bombs at a time at the enemy's rear. I understand that this Russian Zeppelin, or airship, was hit and several of the men seriously wounded, also the officer in charge.

The Russians have also blown up one of the enemy's ammunition trains. The soldiers along here are like a lot of children, they are so happy with their success.

Don

XLVI. Somewhere on the Russian front—Galicia, July 8

Dear Dot:

I am told that we are now less than sixty miles from the capital of Galicia—Lemberg—and that the Austrians and Germans are already evacuating the city. In Monday's fighting in the neighborhood of Zlochow, the Russians captured over forty machine guns and 6 or 7,000 prisoners. This advance now covers, according to officers, a stretch of 600 or so miles; they have already captured over 20,000 prisoners and the complete reports are not yet in.

The Death Battalions which I wrote to you about a month or so ago are doing great work in this advance. They wear an insignia on their sleeve of black and red stripes with a cross to resemble a death-head and cross-bones. They are called the "squadrons of death." Even the artillery regiments have their death squadrons. The Germans have issued proclamations by aeroplane that they will hang every one of these death battalion men they capture.

Major General Hugh L. Scott[87] is here at the front with Colonel Robt. E. L. Mitchee, Judson, Bentley, and Mott and they are witnessing this great attack.

It was almost as if it had been staged especially for Gen. Scott and his staff; they could never have arrived at a better time. Previous to their arrival there was nothing doing on the Russian front; this great advance ought to be of great value to them now that we are beginning to raise an army in America such as we never had before.

June 18 will go down in history as one of Russia's greatest days. The 11th Army will get the most credit for this. To date they have the record of covering themselves with the most glory.

The Austrians and Germans are bringing up great forces and on Tuesday started an offensive which was stopped after two attacks had been launched and utterly failed.

I am now going back to Petrograd to develop the film I have made on this trip. I do not dare to hold it too long.

Don

XLVII. Hotel Astoria, Tuesday, July 11

Dear Dot:

Back in Petrograd again as you see, I have just finished developing all my film and find that I have some of the best pictures I ever made in my life.

I also find that things are getting a little serious here. The Germans now are working as hard as possible trying to create disorders here in Petrograd, so that the drive at the front will be stopped.

The anarchists' headquarters in the home of one of the former ministers here has been attacked by government troops and they have been thrown out. These people called themselves anarchists, but from reports I gather that they were nothing but a bunch of murderers and thieves who went around posing as anarchists in order to have a chance to carry guns.

While Francis was making his speech in response to a crowd of about 15,000 people who had marched to the embassy, one of Lenin's agents started a disturbance.

---

[87] Hugh Lenox Scott (1853–1934) served as chief of staff of the United States Army from 1914 to 1917, including the first few months of American involvement in World War I. He was a member of the Root Commission.

He was immediately beaten up pretty badly by the crowd and was only saved by the prompt work of the military men who rescued him.

The government has abolished all decorations, except those awarded for services of distinction in the war.

I made a photograph of Root and the Commission today and also met Stanley Washburn, who has been with the Russian army for almost three years. He is one of the best posted men I know of as regards Russian military affairs and in fact everything Russian.[88]

I hear that the Russians are retiring again and are losing the territory that was captured by them in their great advance on June 18. I hope this is not true.

I got a letter today from an officer I met in Tarnopol[89] before the big drive in June. He tells me that he expects trouble with his regiment and that he is going to get leave of absence and come to Petrograd to see me.

Speaking of Tarnopol, I should hate to be in that town during the retreat. Most of the people I saw walking around the place seemed to be German sympathizers. Although they did not say anything to me, from the looks they gave me I am of the opinion that they would have liked to knock me down.

Gen. Kornilov, one of the generals in this great advance, has a good chance of being commander-in-chief of the Russian armies; I think Brusilov has a great many enemies who are accusing him of things he should not be accused of. They claim that he sacrifices too many men to accomplish what he wants, that he could do it with less sacrifice.

This drive of the Russians has done more to create a better feeling towards the government than anything else could have done. Everyone likes what has happened with the exception of the anarchists and radical socialists, that is, Lenin's crowd. Boris tells me that already they are working night and day to do something to stop the drive.

The papers today are full of accounts of what Gen. Kornilov's Cossack cavalry are doing. They also say that the Germans are bringing up great reserves to try to stop the Russians. In a way, I am sorry I did not stay to see the finish of this. On top of this great drive, in Russia, we are having a shortage of food here in Petrograd which is really getting serious. There is another report on the streets that the government has no more money.

Don

---

[88] See n. 86.

[89] Tarnopol (today Ternopil) is a city in western Ukraine on the banks of the Seret River. During World War I the city passed from German and Austrian forces to Russia several times. In 1917 the city and its castle were burned down by retreating Russian forces.

XLVIII. Thursday, July 12

Dear Dot:

I spent today at Kronstadt, where I made a lot of photographs, and visited the prison where the anarchists are holding a good many Russian naval officers. By striking a match, I was able to see two of the men. They were the worst wrecks I ever saw in all my life; both of them had gone mad.

I met the President of Kronstadt and his committee, and was allowed to photograph them. My first request to visit Kronstadt was refused; I was told I would be arrested if I landed there. So I hunted up the ugliest Russian I could find and photographed him, and called him the President of Kronstadt. Then I had two of the theaters on the Nevsky Prospekt run the film. Twenty-four hours later, the real Kronstadt President was down here, very mad. I told him this man had come to me and said he was the President of Kronstadt. I said I was very sorry it had happened and that I would come to Kronstadt and make a scene of him among the people of his Empire, and take it back to America and show the Americans that the President of Kronstadt, which is now a separate republic, is a handsome looking man. That is how I got to Kronstadt today.

I took in a picture show tonight and saw several scenes of President Wilson which were cheered by the people. They are beginning to get acquainted with Wilson now. The papers print a great deal about him and about the speeches he is making.

Don

XLIX. July 13

Dear Dot:

The first women's regiment has gone to the front. This was organized by Maria Bochkareva, a woman born in a peasant home who is herself a peasant. She cannot read or write. The women when they left for the front vowed never to retreat. This regiment has a number at the War Office but is called the Battalion of Death by everyone you meet. A great many regiments of women have now been organized, two of them here in Petrograd and one in Moscow; there are now 20,000 of these women, armed, uniformed, and trained. They came from all walks of life, and have members from the best families of Petrograd.

Bochkareva has been to the front before and has been decorated three or four times for bravery. People say she is the first woman to be commissioned in the Russian army, but that is a mistake. In 1915 I met a woman who had served in the Russian army and had been promoted to a captaincy before they found out that she was a woman.

Bochkareva comes from a little village on the Volga and looks about thirty-five years of age. I had a talk with her and she told me she was one of a large family and that her father had been through the Russo-Japanese war and had lost a foot. She said that she was married when she was young to a butcher in her village and that they had lived very happily together, but that when the war broke out in July 1914, her husband had been marched away with the rest of the men of military age and had been killed in one of the first battles he went into.

She said it was not so much her being all alone in the world that had decided her to take up the life of a soldier, as that she had no money and that she saw suffering in the village the like of which she had never seen before. This made her want to join the army to avenge her husband's death.

When she applied for permission to go with a certain regiment she was refused; but finally, after a week's persuasion, she induced them to consent. She said that she had been wounded three times and had been decorated for bravery under fire. After her last wound, which she said took place in 1916 and which kept her in the hospital for months, just before the revolution, she had gone back and joined her regiment. Bochkareva was a revolutionist herself and her regiment was composed mainly of revolutionists, and was one of the first to go over. She said that she had never been so happy in all her life as when she realized that Russia was free. She had always thought that some day it would come to pass, but that it would never be her fortune to see it. When the revolution was over and she thought that things would be better, to her surprise she found hundreds of her regiment deserting; none of them would obey their old officers; riots were a common thing in their regiment and finally grew to be a daily occurrence. Murders were committed before her eyes. It was then, hearing that other regiments were acting in the same way, that she decided to raise a regiment of women and then get other women organized to equip and train other regiments and shame the men into going back to the firing line. If they refused she was going to make the women themselves lead the attack. After that she did not think the Russians would hesitate any more.[90]

---

[90] Maria Leontievna Bochkareva, née Frolkova, (1889–1920) left her abusive partner to join the Russian army in Tomsk in November 1914 after Nicholas II granted her personal appeal. Male soldiers treated her with ridicule or sexually harassed her until she proved her courage in battle. She was twice wounded and decorated three times for bravery. After the February Revolution, Minister of War Kerensky charged her with creating an all-female combat unit. Her 1st Russian Women's Battalion of Death initially attracted around 2,000 volunteers. At the time, writes Rappaport, Bochkareva was "probably the most talked about woman in all Russia." Her regime proved too strict and harsh for many recruits; by the end of intensive training, the battalion had 250–300 members. The unit was sent to the Russian Western Front to participate in the Kerensky Offensive of July 1917 and involved in one major battle, near the town of Smorgon. The unit performed well in combat, losing fifty dead and wounded. Bochkareva was wounded and sent back to Petrograd to recuperate (Rappaport, *Caught in the Revolution*, 193–202). The unit disbanded after facing increasing hostility from the male troops remaining at the front. Bochkareva was arrested in 1918 after leaving General Kornilov's White Army headquarters in the Caucasus, and scheduled to be executed. The sentence was stayed and she was granted an external passport. In April 1918, she left Vladivostok for the United States, where she met with President Wilson and implored him to intervene in Russia.

I met an American just after I had visited Bochkareva'a regiment. He said, "I understand that the high school girls here are organizing a women's regiment calling themselves the Death Battalion." Well, these girls are not school girls but women from all walks of life, as I told you. They have been trained by drill sergeants detailed from the War Office. All these sergeants were men who had been decorated for bravery and they entered into the training of these women with their whole heart and soul while they remained in Petrograd. When they had finished, the women were drilled as well as any soldiers in Russia have ever been drilled. Two hours a day they spent in rifle practice and eight hours a day in training. Although ten hours was a hard day's work for them, when they had finished their training for the day you would go around to the barracks and find them dancing and singing in the courtyard until the bugle was blown ordering them to their beds. They were reluctant to go! They were a happy lot. Never in Russia have I seen such a happy bunch of women. Little did they dream, as they drilled and marched day after day, what they were going to face in the future.

To give you an idea of the women who have joined this regiment, one of them was Marie Skrydlova, the daughter of Admiral Skrydlov,[91] one of Russia's greatest admirals, a man who distinguished himself during the Russo-Japanese war. Marie is about eighteen or twenty, very attractive, although not beautiful, very talented and belonging to the Russian aristocracy. She speaks several languages and had been educated abroad, I understand. She had given up her life to war work since Russia entered the war, and had devoted all her time to the Red Cross till this Death Battalion was organized and she joined it.

During the revolution this girl saw horrors that few people saw. She told Florence Harper that her father was attacked by soldiers who had been in his command and who tried to kill him; she begged them to spare her father and they did so. She said that the mob broke into the Marine Hospital where she was and murdered officers in their beds and that one patient whom she tried to defend was killed before her very eyes; she said that men she had sat up nights with had turned on her now that Russia is free and cursed her as she never heard a person cursed before in all her life, calling her an aristocrat. She said that after what she had seen in that hospital and what had happened the following week, when some people in the apartment building where she lived were murdered in cold blood and several young girls were outraged, she had taken off her Red Cross uniform and vowed that she would not lift a hand while

---

In April 1919, she returned to Tomsk and attempted to form a women's medical detachment under the White admiral Alexsander Kolchak, but was captured again by the Bolsheviks. She was shot by the Cheka on May 16, 1920.

[91] Maria Skrydlova, "tall and aristocratic ... a talented musician and linguist" (Rappaport, *Caught in the Revolution*, 196), was Bochkareva's aide-de-camp. Her father, Nikolai Illarionovich Skrydlov (1844–1918) served as commander of the Pacific and Baltic fleets and on the Admiralty board in Petrograd. He retired from active service in August 1909 with the rank of admiral. In October 1918, Skrydlov was arrested by the Bolsheviks and executed.

such people were in power. Later, when she heard that the Women's Death Battalion was being organized to help save Russia, she had gone to Bochkareva without even putting her hat and coat on, running most of the way, she was so happy that at last she could serve Russia as she wanted to serve her.

The Death Battalion is like the Legion of France. Everyone in it seems to have a history. One girl I talked to told a story that made me sit and look and wonder if all women in Russia were like that. A few of the women I talked to had seen the war as no one has seen it in America, and all of them were anxious to go to the front and do their bit.

When these women appear on the streets drilling they are hissed and hooted at by the men; and when they appear alone on the streets and soldiers push them off the walk, these girls turn and fight and drive the Bolshevik cowards to cover. I remember when they appeared at St. Isaac's Cathedral while the Death Battalion of men were being blessed before being sent to the front; the anarchists and Bolsheviks said they were going to break up this meeting and not allow the battalion to leave. In this Death Battalion there were old men, some of them seventy years of age, who had come from all parts of Russia. Their wives and daughters had come with them and many of these joined the Women's Death Battalion. We have already heard that some of them have gone through fire in a charge and covered themselves with glory. Most of the soldiers I have met at the front ask me not to judge Russia by the Petrograd Bolsheviks, deserters and traitors who are there by the thousands, but to look around and see the real Russians for myself. As for these women, when they march down the street and are hissed and hooted at, they shoot back at the Bolshevik soldiers and scream at them, "Go back, you dirty cowards. Aren't you ashamed to let women leave their homes and go to the front for holy Russia?" When this is said to the Bolsheviks they don't know how to answer.

When these women were blessed in front of the Kazan Cathedral a few hours ago, you couldn't get near. Very few people knew that they were going to leave, as the government had to keep it quiet. The Bolsheviks have said that they shall never leave for the front, and that if they try to go they will kill them all. While they were at the cathedral, they were supposed to be under the protection of the church; the lamps and other paraphernalia the priests used in blessing their ikons and flags were carried out to the front, which made the square and street the church itself. Even this did not stop the hoodlums. Stones were thrown and in a few instances the Bolsheviks tried to mingle with the crowd and create disorders. The better class people heard what was happening, however, and immediately rushed these people out of the crowd. When the regiment started to march back to the barracks, where they were under government orders, the crowd had dispersed in the front; later they were taken out by the back way and rushed to the station. Thousands of people rushed down town that they might pay their respects to these brave women of Russia.

I was always against woman's suffrage before, but now that I have seen these women and talked with them and heard their stories and seen them drilling and willing to fight beside the men, I have become a suffragist. I have nothing against suffrage any more.

Emmeline Pankhurst has been in Russia now for a few weeks. I understand she was sent by Lloyd George to help line up the women of Russia, but that for some reason or other she has been interfered with constantly by Kerensky's orders.[92] She has been a daily visitor to Bochkareva's regiment and has talked with almost every one individually. They all love Mrs. Pankhurst, and I know that her smile and words of cheer, even though they have to be interpreted, will help these brave women when they reach the front and see what work is laid out for them.

Boris tells me however that there are a lot of girls in this regiment who ought not to be there. He says they have been put in the regiment by the anarchists, socialists, and Bolsheviks, and that they are sure to cause trouble in the ranks, being nothing better than spies.

When these women left for the front they were given second-class railroad carriages. That was the only distinction shown them. They are equipped exactly as the Russian soldiers are, and as they marched along the street to the railroad station their pans and pots made quite a racket. They have also been supplied with 200 rounds of ammunition; their equipment must weigh about sixty-two pounds. I noticed that most of them carried their powder puff in the leg of their boot.

Here in Petrograd they tell us that the government will never let them go into the trenches. But I know Bochkareva; she is out for a fight and will not be contented until she leads her battalion into action. If she does, I am sure she is going to make

---

[92] "As a lifelong radical and political activist," writes Rappaport, "Pankhurst had always been sympathetic to the revolutionary cause" and had entertained prominent Russian political exiles at her London home. When the war began, she put her women's suffrage campaign on hold and traveled around Britain rallying women to support the war effort. She welcomed the February Revolution but feared that Russia would lose its freedom if it withdrew from the war. She volunteered to go to Petrograd to boost Russian women's support for the war effort. British Prime Minister David Lloyd George enthusiastically supported Pankhurst's mission. Arriving in Petrograd in early June 1917, Pankhurst and her young associate Jessie Kenney had a hectic schedule of meetings, receptions, and interviews, including visits to Maria Bochkareva and the Women's Death Battalion. However, the Provisional Government refused to grant permission for her to hold outdoor meetings, fearing that her pro-war stand might provoke the Bolsheviks. By the end of August, as foreigners and Russians started to leave the city ahead of the advancing German army, Pankhurst must have realized there was little she could do. "[D]espite the best of intentions and her energetic commitment, Emmeline Pankhurst's mission to Russia had been a failure," writes Rappaport. "She had little or no comprehension of Russia's women ... Why should she—an Englishwoman from a position of relative comfort and privilege—preach to women such as they, who had spent their entire lives struggling to survive against political and social oppression of a kind that was way beyond her understanding or experience?" (*Caught in the Revolution*, 187–90, 191–93, 249–50).

a record. These girls that she has trained will be more than willing to sacrifice their lives for "Holy Russia."

Don

L. Saturday, July 14

Dear Dot:

The other day I met Williams[93] who represents the *New York Times*. I met him in Belgium early in the war. He was a pastor and had a small church near Boston, and as I got the story from von Hay, the U.S. consul then at Ghent, his beloved people had sent their dear, little parson (he is not little, being about six feet tall, also quite good looking and a very brilliant young man) to Belgium so that he could get first-hand information about the cruel war that was going on and come back and tell them in Sunday sermons what was really happening. Williams has turned up here in Petrograd and is seeing everything of importance that is happening. He has taken up with a very well-known Russian who has an income and I understand has held several good positions in public life here. The two of them are getting into places where other people find it hard to go. Williams ought to be able to hand out a very good story of Russia. He says he is going to stay here until the trouble is over.

Williams brought up a friend of his to my room the other night and introduced him. This chap left Russia fifteen years ago and went to New York; there he studied in night schools and worked in factories, and has come back here since the revolution. He began to ramble about what America had done to him. How could I argue with him? Finally, I ordered him out of the room; I told him if he did not get out I would break his head open. He is one of the worst enemies we could have at the present time. I heard him making a speech, before I had been introduced to him, and Boris says he is telling people that the draft in America is a joke and that we had to force our men into the army at the point of a bayonet. He is not the only one who is talking this way. There are hundreds of others, in fact thousands, who are back here spreading lies about America.

All these men have money. If you ask them how they came back, they say they came on tickets furnished by the Russian consul. There is a law now that all subjects shall have their fare paid back to Russia. I asked this fellow where he got his money; he said he was working for the Committee of Peace and was allowed 100 rubles a day

---

[93] Thompson confuses the lives of two men named Williams who were in Petrograd during this time. Albert Rhys Williams was a minister and journalist who worked for the *New York Evening Post*. Most of Thompson's description is of this Williams related to being a pastor in Boston, being in Belgium during World War I, being tall, smart, and good looking. However, the last portion of the description seems to be of Harold Williams, who was also a journalist, but from New Zealand and working for the *Times of London*. The woman he is referring to is likely Ariadna Tyrkova-Williams.

and expenses. He also said that this committee had its headquarters at the home of Lenin. Well, it is German money.

These people say we have a president by the name of Wilson who is worse than the Tsar was, and that our police are worse than the Cossacks, and that the workmen must wake up in Russia to the fact that America has gone into this war with England and that the two of them are out to wreck Russia. This is one kind of exile that has come back to Russia only to do harm. The exiles who have been in Siberia, some of them all their life, don't say a word. Their only hope is that Russia will now take advantage of her freedom and become a great country. These are the people who have suffered, and if anyone has the right to speak, they have, not a lot of these anarchists from America. Every one that America allows to come back will cost us a man on the Western front. When I see these men on the street attacking the country that welcomed them years ago, I feel as if I wanted to kill them. Although I'd hate to kill a man in cold blood, if I ever get the chance the next time there is an uprising here and there is any shooting going on and I see any of these men spreading lies about America, I am going to do a little shooting myself. I know I shall never regret any life I take in this way. I feel that I have as much right as if I were in the trenches firing upon the enemy opposite.

Don

LI. July 15

Dear Dot:

This morning I visited the Peter and Paul Fortress, and was allowed to make photographs. This fortress, which is also a prison, has about eighty cells, I am told. The windows are up at the ceiling, which makes it impossible for a prisoner to look out. The furniture consists of an iron bed and an iron table, fastened to the wall. The air is suffocating in these rooms. They only have a straw mattress with a pillow to match and one or two coarse blankets. The prisoners, most of them former ministers of the old government, are given the same food as the soldiers. It consists mostly of black bread and some kind of a soup. They are not allowed to purchase anything from the outside, though I am told that if friends of theirs are willing to bribe some of the soldiers, dainties can be slipped in to them. I went up to the cells of Stürmer and Protopopov but saw neither of them until later. Anna Viroubova,[94] who was a close friend of the ex-Tsarina and was also supposed to be close to Rasputin, was walking slowly up and down her cell, using her crutches. I do not know just how she was injured; but it happened in some accident before the revolution.

The officer who was showing me around told me that Protopopov spends most of his time pacing up and down his cell and hardly speaks to anyone at all. He said,

---

[94] See n. 76.

however, that most of the others had a friendly good-morning or good-night for the guards.

I hear that the former Tsar is asking to subscribe to the Russian Liberty Loan.

The guards tell me that the trial of these people held here will take place very soon. I asked him what would be the charge against them. He said there were so many that he could not name all of them. When you talk to Russian officials, however, they say that they doubt very much if any direct charges can be proved against any of the ministers.

We also are told that all court martials have now been abolished and that all anti-Jewish laws have been thrown out. Jewish chaplains are now at the front and we also see daily Jewish officers in the army. At the front I have seen thousands of Jews in uniform and 10 percent, of the Death Battalions are Jews.

We now hear nothing but Kornilov, in fact, he is getting almost more popular than Kerensky. But Kerensky doesn't want anyone to become popular, and I am looking for him to sit down on Kornilov[95] shortly. Kornilov is a Cossack and has a chance to do some great work if he is only given the opportunity. It was largely due to him that the revolution was accomplished with so little bloodshed. He is like the Grand Duke, a man who believes in discipline. He is the man I told you about when I was at the front the other week when the twelfth and thirteenth regiments refused to obey orders; he had artillery turned on them and blew about 1,000 deserters to pieces. He made a great record during the Russo-Japanese War and although he was offered a great many soft berths under the old regime, he preferred being in command of an army at the front. When the revolution broke, Kornilov was in Petrograd and he was the first man the Duma looked to to preserve order. He was military governor of the capital after the revolution. The people know Kornilov and trust him, and even now they give him the credit for establishing order after the revolution and saving the city from riot and bloodshed. Kornilov rose from the ranks; he had been a private. During the big retreat of the Russians in 1915, he was captured. He escaped from a prison camp, and since then has been more or less in the public eye. He is a great deal like men who have made themselves famous in American history.

I should like to see Grand Duke Nicholas made commander-in-chief of the Russian armies and Kornilov placed in charge of one front and Brusilov in charge of another. With these three and a good strong man at the head of the government here in Petrograd, things would go ahead with a push. But I am afraid now that Kerensky is doing so many foolish little things trying to play with both sides that we are going to have to pay for it.

Boris tells me that tomorrow we are going to have trouble with Lenin and his bunch of cut-throats. They are going to try to overthrow the government. I asked him where he got his information. He says that his brother belongs in a society which has

---

[95] See n. 60.

received word to keep off the streets tomorrow, until the trouble is over. I am getting my cameras ready. If there is any trouble I will get some good pictures.

I went out to Lenin's place and tried to see him and make a picture of him. I saw him after a wait of two hours and asked him to pose for a picture. When Boris told him I was from America, he told Boris to tell me he would have nothing to do with me and that we had better leave Petrograd. I told Boris to tell him that I was not going to leave Petrograd and that I would stay as long as I wished.

I have made photographs of Lenin and a man named Trotsky who has come from New York. Trotsky I find a very mysterious man. He does not commit himself. He knows New York better than I do and knows about everyone you mention and seems to have the American situation at his fingers' tips. I asked him how long he had been in America. He did not seem to know.

Don

LII. Monday, July 16

Dear Dot:

Today may go down in history as one of the greatest days in Russia. A second revolution is now being fought on the streets here in Petrograd.

I am going on with this letter at a quarter after three, Tuesday morning, July 17.

I am at my window here in the hotel. There is the constant roar of a big mob. Going out into the hall and looking up from one of the windows facing the Morskaia, I can hear the roar of rifles, the snarl of machine-guns and the roar of another mob in the direction of the Catherine Canal.

This trouble started even before I had word of it. I would have been likely to know it, as I was around most of the government offices during the day. I think it even took them by surprise.

Yesterday afternoon after lunch, Boris and I dropped into the coffee shop next to the Europe Hotel and had coffee and listened to the orchestra. Boris is engaged to be married and I wanted to look the prospective bride over. Although Boris is a soldier and has been wounded twice, I still feel as if he were just a boy and I should give him fatherly advice and watch out for him. I had heard from another fellow who is a comrade of Boris's and mine, that this woman was not the right sort for Boris. Well, we saw the woman. She was decked out in her best, and just as I was about ready to give her my OK, and tell Boris he had used good judgment, she pulled out her cigarette case and lit a cigarette and I noticed that on one side she had the tell-tale little white papers, cocaine. Well, coming out I told Boris there was nothing doing. All the way to the hotel we argued. Finally, he gave in and said that he would look around and pick out another girl. He is bound to get married, as he is under the impression that two can live as cheaply as one. I don't believe it, never having seen it proved.

When we were just about a block from the hotel, we met two regiments on their way to the Duma. They carried banners saying that the capitalist ministers must be thrown out at once and that if they didn't resign the people would make them. When Boris translated those banners to me, I, like the other people on the sidewalk, couldn't believe it.

I went on to the hotel and decided that I would lie down and sleep until dinner time, as the soldiers I had just seen hadn't looked as though they meant anything serious. About 4:30 my phone rang and one of the British officers here in the hotel told me there was trouble. I asked him where it was. He said it was near the Duma, that the English Embassy had just phoned him this news.

I immediately got up, put on my boots, incidentally took my revolver and some cartridges, and told Boris to take the cameras. When we got downstairs we found our chauffeur sitting in front asleep, and after giving him a punch to wake him up we told him to drive to the Nevsky. When we got to the Nevsky at the corner of the Morskaia, we didn't see anything out of the ordinary. By the time we reached the Sadovaia and the Nevsky, however, we saw some soldiers passing in a limousine, all of them sitting with rifles. I mentioned the fact to Boris, saying that looked bad. Later, we met quite a number of closed cars—in fact, up to this time, I had failed to see any open cars. We drove around the city and across the Neva a couple of times and found plenty of armed people, but most of them in cars, touring cars and limousines. No trucks had appeared up to this time.

At seven o'clock I ordered the chauffeur to drive to a little French restaurant on the Morskaia where we could have dinner and then start on a round again. We drove to the Admiral Arch and just as we got through it the car gave a sudden stop. The first thing I knew I was on my back in the street and a great big Russian had his foot in my face. Well, I cussed, but cussing in English does no good in Russia. You must learn to cuss in Russian. Five minutes later I told Boris he must teach me every cuss-word in the Russian language. These anarchists took the automobile away from me and immediately started around the corner with it.

Going back to the hotel, my chauffeur and I met some Bolsheviks who had a lot of hand grenades.

The chauffeur asked the anarchists for some of them. They refused, then offered them for a ruble apiece. When he started to pay for them he found he had no money and asked me to loan him some; but as I didn't know what his standing was, I asked him what he wanted the grenades for. He said, "I want to get our car back. One of these grenades will recover the car." He could have had 100 rubles after that. So then we started out on a still hunt for our car. When we got to the Nevsky Prospekt, it was a blaze of rifle fire and machine-guns. At 12:30, or almost one, while we were up on the Nevsky by the Fontanka bridge, across the street from the palace, the firing started from soldiers in automobile trucks. They were answered by other people from the corner of the Sadovaia. In this way we were caught between fires, which caused us immediately to throw ourselves flat on the street. There we lay till a little after three. We had company, however; between these two points, there must have been between 1,800 and 2,000 people lying flat on the street. When the firing died down a bit, everyone made a run for the cross streets; it was a case of elbowing your way through. I have seen the Russians run and some of them have speed when they want it, but this time no one had anything on me. I cut the air so that I would have made a Kansas jack-rabbit look sick if he tried to follow me. In the get-a-way, I lost Boris and the chauffeur.

Arriving at the room here, I found Boris. Later the chauffeur came in followed by several officers who are friends of mine. They were later joined by some of their friends I hadn't met before. Now we are all here together; and as soon as I have finished this letter, we are going out again. The officers have taken off their swords, decorations and shoulder straps.

They tell me this trouble began with some soldiers refusing to start for the front; they think it was a put-up affair, in order to excite other troops. On top of this, there is a story being handed around to all the soldiers by the Lenin press, that thousands of soldiers are being killed at the front and that the government is systematically killing all socialists, workmen, and Bolsheviks. After these forty men had refused to go to the front, the Maximalist leaders[96] started a mutiny in one of the Petrograd garrisons, telling them this story which the Lenin people had spread in the other barracks. On top of that, a fake notice was printed, supposedly signed by Kerensky, saying that the death penalty had been re-established. At first only one regiment fell in with the scheme, which is nothing more than German agents' work. Other regiments failed to join this first mutinous regiment, although gradually they did later in the evening. By this time I don't know how things stand. At first the soldiers were satisfied just to make a demonstration. I understand that was all they had been asked to do. But after they had made this demonstration, motor trucks carrying machine-guns began to appear, even to their surprise, which gave the impression that there was a general movement against this government. Poor fools, they probably think they must join the right side. I find Petrograd mobs easily influenced; they all go over to anyone who seems to have the upper hand.

During the first part of the evening, there were not many civilians out on the streets; but by the time I returned to the hotel, everyone seemed to be out to see what was really happening. Undoubtedly Lenin plans to overthrow the government; and once he gets power he will start a peace campaign and try to make terms between

---

[96] Maximalists were so called because they demanded full implementation of the "maximum programme" in the expected revolution: full socialization of the land, factories, and all other means of production. Orthodox Socialist Revolutionaries wanted to start with land reform but defer socialization of other means of production. The Maximalists also rejected notions of a two-stage revolution. The group soon splintered. Some allied with the Left Socialist Revolutionaries, some joined the Bolsheviks, and others opposed the Bolsheviks.

Russia and Germany. That is what he has been sent here for, and he will not be content until he has accomplished it.

I don't know what the Soldiers' and Workmen's Delegates will do. They have issued an order that no soldiers are to carry arms on the streets. Now that the regiments have disobeyed this order, the government must do something and do it quickly. Although the shooting started with only a few shots, the town is in an uproar now. The regiment that began the racket was a pack of cowards, for when the shooting started on the Nevsky most of them dropped their guns and ran for their lives.

One of the officers here in my room is an officer of the first machine-gun regiment which started this trouble. He says that all the officers were driven out of their barracks before the troops began to march to the Duma, that the seventh machine-gun regiment has also gone over, that agents from Lenin's headquarters are behind this and Lenin had spoken to the men the night before, and that all officers were forbidden to attend the meeting. He says that his orderly went with the men but later left them, and that at Lenin's headquarters, when he left, they were handing out revolvers and rifles by the thousand to the working people who were arriving there every minute. He says that wagon after wagon full of machine-guns were driving up.

Our waiter, who is loyal, has just brought in a notice to the soldiers and workmen of Petrograd which Boris translated as follows:

> Certain persons who are unknown summon you, contrary to the unanimous general will, not excepting that of the socialist parties, to appear on the streets with weapons and invite you to protest in this fashion against the disbandment of regiments which have dishonored themselves at the front by criminal breach of their duty toward the revolution.
>
> We, the delegates of the Revolutionary Democracy of all Russia, declare that the disbandment of the regiments was the result of representations by the Military Committee and by the order of Minister of War Kerensky, whom you elected. Consequently, every act in defense of the disbanded regiments is an act against your brothers shedding their blood at the front. We remind you that no military unit should appear with arms without special authority of the commander-in-chief, who is in agreement with us.
>
> All who infringe this order we brand as traitors and enemies of the revolution. We are taking all measures in our power to see that this order is carried out.

The office of the *Novoe Vremya*[97] has been stopped and the anarchists are in control there. They call it a capitalist paper.

---

[97] *Novoye Vremya* (New Time) was a popular daily newspaper published in Petrograd from 1868 to 1917. The newspaper began as a liberal publication but later supported the Tsarist regime.

One of the other officers here states that the Russians are now falling back, and have met with some reverses. At headquarters they have a report that the Germans have retaken Calusz after a great battle and that thousands of Russians have been killed and captured.

General Popov just came into the room and has asked me to go with him as soon as they get his car out of the court of the hotel where they have hidden it. He has asked me to put two American flags on this car and use it as though it were mine. Two officers will go with us, both dressed as civilians, and find out how far this movement has gone. He tells me that so far this is what has happened.

At 6:45, the factory hands at Lessner, Nobel, and Paravaianen laid down their tools and with a shout started toward the center of the city. This had been all arranged in the big factories in different sections of the city, and the men had been instructed just what to do. As these men, fully armed, passed regiment barracks, the soldiers went out in the streets, at first just to look at them and see what was happening. Later, many of them, after a talk with this mob, came back to the barracks and began to talk in whispers to others. In a short time they were out on the street firing their rifles and creating disorder. These soldiers have set up machine-guns in the Lauskaya at the railroad station to prevent trains with reinforcements coming in on the finished railway.

Later, about nine, two automobiles appeared on the Liteiny bridge, and then the fifth company of the 180th reserve infantry regiment was seen on the Liteiny Prospekt shouting, "Down with Kerensky!" This mob had about 5,000 soldiers in it. It was led by the fifth company of the 180th reserve infantry regiment and there were 3 or 4,000 workmen, all armed, with them. They were on their way to the Kschessinskaya Palace. At the same time that this happened, the mob, led by the soldiers of the regiment called the Moscow regiment, attacked the Mihailovsky artillery school and stole all the cannon there. They now have a great many field-pieces and two or three howitzers.

When the soldiers in automobiles appeared on the Shpalernaya street,[98] there was quite a little fighting because they met government soldiers stretched across the street. These latter captured both the automobiles with only one machine-gun, although the mob had many more supporters than the soldiers facing them, they all retreated.

A little after ten, the mob led by this Moscow regiment, which had been reinforced by a machine-gun regiment, surrounded the Duma and demanded that certain ministers, a list of whom they presented, should be made to resign. But these ministers they wanted had resigned early in the afternoon.

About 10:45, the regiment I told you about, supported by the 4th Don Cossack regiment, appeared on the street the embassy is located on and immediately started

---

The paper was looked down on by the liberal intelligentsia of the early twentieth century and despised by the Bolsheviks, who shut it down the day after the October Revolution.

[98] Near the Tauride Palace, where the Duma met.

firing on the mob. Although the engagement only lasted a few minutes, about eighty Cossacks were killed and 200 of the mob attacking them.

Popov says that all the bridges are now occupied by soldiers of the mobs against the government.

At 11:30, the Nevsky was in control of the government for a few minutes, but the government soldiers were given orders to go back to their stations and not fire any more. The third rifle regiment is also out in the street, but as they are fussing amongst themselves as to what they should really do, not much support can be expected from them.

Since 11 o'clock, however, there has been firing. It is growing heavier all the time on the Nevsky. This is being done by large crowds of unorganized soldiers, Bolsheviks, and the Red Guard, armed with every conceivable weapon.

Lenin's headquarters has been turned into a fortress. They also have many machine-guns on the tops of houses throughout the neighborhood.

The Minister of Justice has issued appeals to a great many of the commanders of the different troops here, but the military authorities have said that they are powerless to do anything.

The soldiers who are members of the Bolshevik or Maximalist parties have taken all the automobiles.

General Popov's orderly has just come in to report to the general that the Cossacks have met the mob up by the Kazan Cathedral along the Canal and that they are fighting like cats and dogs there. This orderly had a notice which had been thrown out of an automobile that passed saying that troops were on their way to Petrograd to establish order.

When the *Pravda*, the anarchists' paper, was searched yesterday, a letter from a German baron who is now at Haparanda[99] was found, in which he said that there would be great rejoicing throughout Germany when the anarchists with the help of their brave comrades, the Bolsheviks and Maximalists, gained control of the city.

I am now going out to see what I can find out. I will write you a letter tomorrow with a full account of things as they now stand.

Don

LIII. Tuesday, July 17

Dear Dot:

Although it has been hell all day here in Petrograd, and thousands of workmen, anarchists, and Bolsheviks have come into the city from outside, and the streets are in an uproar, I am told that we will not have much more trouble. This I doubt.

---

[99] A town in northern Sweden, on the border with Finland.

The Cossacks have come out several times, but after having had a great many of their horses killed, and quite a number of themselves shot out of their saddles, they have returned to their quarters. Officers tell me that the government has not as yet taken any action. From the look of things, it seems that the government is deliberately holding back, hoping that the people themselves will become ashamed of their actions and stop. Once the government turns the Cossacks loose, there will be the greatest massacre in the history of the world right here.

I visited several of the Cossacks' and other loyal barracks and found the troops were paying little attention to what was going on. Most of them were attending to their regular routine duties or playing games. I talked to several and they said their officers had told them that they might be called in to do a little shooting. They said that the Bolsheviks were only a lot of cowards and that they were anxious to get at them and were sorry orders had not been issued before for them to clean up the city.

The Bolsheviks are demanding the removal of all the capitalist ministers. I understand that the government has offered to give the Bolsheviks a chair or two in the cabinet. They have refused the offer and demand that the Soldiers' and Workmen's Deputies have absolute control of the government.

Today, in different parts of the city, I have seen machine-guns in the middle of the street firing in every direction—why and what for, no one seems to know. At one time this afternoon I was in the street talking to some anarchists in a truck; all at once they opened up with two of their machine-guns. When I asked them what they were firing at they didn't answer. Boris asked them if they were for Lenin, and they said, "No," but that they had heard of trouble and were out to see the excitement. These men had five machine-guns in their truck and thousands of rounds of ammunition. What I am afraid of is that the army will get the wrong story of what is really happening here, and that there will be trouble at the front.

General Polovtsev,[100] military governor here, says that these armed disturbances must be stopped. He has requested all civilians to stay in their houses and keep their doors closed and locked until further orders. This to be done so that unidentified people cannot enter houses and commit acts against the safety of the city.

The Cossacks are out in great force this evening and are having fights in a great many sections of the city. The government is holding sessions night and day. So are the Soldiers' and Workmen's Delegates. The two are trying to reach some kind of an agreement.

Don

---

[100] Major-General Petr Aleksandrovich Polovtsev replaced Kornilov as commander of the Petrograd military district. He conducted the search for Lenin after the abortive July coup, and later worked in the Ministry of Foreign Affairs of the Provisional Government. He emigrated after the Bolshevik takeover.

LIV. Wednesday, July 18

Dear Dot:

We have had rain practically all day.

This afternoon a few of the leaders of the Maximalists went to Peter and Paul Fortress to talk with the people there. The day before, this palace had been taken possession of by the sailors from Kronstadt, who made an agreement with the garrison of the fortress that they should fight together. They have many guns and a large amount of ammunition and say that any attempt to interfere with them will mean the shelling of Petrograd.

About five o'clock I heard that the Kronstadt sailors had agreed to return to Kronstadt. We have a report that Doctor Roschal, leader of the Kronstadt anarchists, has been arrested. I doubt this. Innocent blood is being shed by hundreds of people in the streets here in Petrograd, and a few thousand have been wounded. Most of them are women, children and old men, peaceful citizens and passers-by. The mutinous soldiers, Bolsheviks, and anarchists are the lucky ones; they started this trouble and they are getting the least knocks. I wonder what the poor boys at the front who are putting up such a heroic offensive think, when they hear what the people at home are doing.

There is only one reason for all this, the German agents. They are responsible for this reign of terror. Thousands of soldiers and anarchists and Germans, dressed like Russian soldiers and supported by armed automobiles with machine-guns, are helping to bring Russia into civil war.

Several times today I have got Boris to ask these people what they were in the streets for, why they had come to the city, and why they had left their barracks; 70 percent of them couldn't give any answer. They couldn't even explain why they had been ordered out. The banners they carried completely contradicted those which say that all the power should be in the hands of the Soldiers' and Workmen's Deputies, as these bands of Maximalists, Leninists, and Kronstadters have refused to obey orders issued by this Council.

On top of this we hear that the front has had a great disaster due to this trouble here, that regiments, of their own accord, are leaving the trenches, and that troops in sections receiving orders to support attacking troops, instead of going to their assistance, immediately start committee meetings to decide whether they should obey their superiors or retreat. In other places, we hear, regiments of their own free will are abandoning their trenches, throwing up their arms and refusing to fight. Officers are wiring frantically here in Petrograd that they and their command are powerless, that the control has been taken away from them and that all authority is now in the hands of these thousands of committees at the front.

I am not going out on the street tonight, as it is too bad.

Don

LV. Thursday, July 19

Dear Dot:

The government has ordered the Kronstadt executive committee to turn over at once Doctor Roschal and his assistant, a man named Raskolnikov,[101] to be tried for these four days of rioting and bloodshed. Otherwise they will be blockaded until they meet the government's demands.

The Russian Congress, composed of workmen, soldiers, and peasants, has issued the most stirring appeal saying that Russia is now menaced by a breakdown at the front and by anarchy at home, that the country and the revolution are in danger, that the Provisional Government is now the government of national safety and must have unlimited powers in order to re-establish discipline in the army so that there can be a fight to the finish against the enemies of Russia. The Congress prays that all people who have the welfare of Russia at heart will join hands with them in this appeal they are making for Russia

Orders have already been given to fire on deserters at the front, and arrests have been made or issued for all who have been leaders in this trouble.

After the troops had settled down around the hotel here, they started to have their breakfast about five o'clock. A little later they began to move, under orders that the military authorities here had issued. The authorities first decided to get all their forces together before making an attack on Lenin's headquarters. The latter also had some troops stationed at the Peter and Paul Fortress. Then troops were marched to the square of the dancer's palace where Lenin is. These forces consisted of armed motor cars, cavalry, artillery and infantry, and thousands of volunteers. There were detachments from Boliensky, Petrogradsky, Semionovsky, Preobraginski, and a detachment from the Black Sea Brigade. The control of these troops was in the hands of Lieutenant Kousmine, who is second in command of the Petrograd District. The troops were divided into two sections. The first section, which I call No. 1, started to march across the two bridges, the bridge of the palace and the Berjivay, and others went along the Kronversky Canal. This was done in order to cut off the arsenal from the Peter and Paul Fortress and also from Kschessinsky, Lenin's headquarters. The other army, which I call No. 2, was sent to the Troitsky bridge to attack the headquarters of Lenin. I went with the first army.

Before they started, the artillery was taken to the summer garden and had their guns trained on the position I told you about. After this was all ready at about 7:30, the commander of these two armies went into a house, I following him, and called up Lenin's headquarters. After saying "Good-morning" over the phone he told them that he had instructions from the Council of Soldiers and Workmen and from the military commander-in-chief of Petrograd, that they must get out of the palace at

---
[101] See n. 79.

once and surrender themselves and their machine-guns and rifles to the government troops. He then called up the Peter and Paul Fortress, according to Boris, who was with me, they talked about the weather and various other things first, then the commander requested, not demanded, that they do exactly what the people at Lenin's headquarters had been ordered to do. Both places asked for an hour to think this over, and the commander very kindly granted them an hour's time. At the end of the hour, they found that Lenin and the Peter and Paul people had been talking with each other over the phone and with friends throughout Petrograd. So they immediately had the telephone service disconnected in that part of the city.

A little later, while I was standing down by the Winter Palace, out of sight, but where I could command a view of the Peter and Paul Fortress with my camera, a scouting party came back with word that there were about 100 armed anarchists in front of the palace and that when the scouting party was discovered they had been fired upon, but that no damage bad been done to them.

At about nine, word was sent to the fortress that they had only half an hour to surrender. Why this was allowed them, I couldn't figure out. At the end of the half hour, orders were given and two columns of troops started to advance over the Troitsky bridge toward Lenin's headquarters. An officer with a flag, which was supposed to be a flag of truce, though I could not see why they used a red flag, sent over from the Peter and Paul Fortress saying that the troops who were holding the fortress had no intention of resisting the government, and that the Kronstadt sailors, anarchists, and machine-gun soldiers from the different regiments who were in the fortress were there only by chance and had merely come to see their friends. While this man was telling his story, two sailors came out of the fortress and crossed over to the troops and began to talk to the government soldiers, asking them not to obey any orders to use force in taking the fortress. They said that this was a question for the soldiers and workmen to decide among themselves and that the commander-in-chief of the Petrograd district and the executive committee of the Soldiers' and Workmen's Council had no right to decide what they should do. Their talk stopped in a hurry, however, when they were told that they could either surrender at once or return to the fortress to their comrades. A little later, about 10:15, I was taken in an armed car to Lenin's headquarters, where I found government troops in charge. While I was there, about seven persons were arrested, three of them women. They, I am told, were the leaders. In the house we found about seventy brand new machine-guns and a great quantity of provisions and arms, and in the yard were a great many more cars. A list was also found of all the people who belonged to the Maximalist organization.

After this I returned to the Petrograd side and arrived in time to see government troops discover on the Bolozersky street a large nest of the Red Guards, where they found rifles, revolvers, flour, boots, machine-guns, and other supplies, enough to have kept them for a month or so.

As soon as Lenin's headquarters had been captured, the commander of the troops made his headquarters there. Presently, some sailors came over from the fortress and said they were willing to surrender themselves and their arms but wouldn't do it to the soldiers, only to the executive committee. They were told to go to the devil.

A little later several officers of the executive committee of Soldiers' and Workmen's Delegates went over to the fortress themselves. After about an hour spent in arguing with the people there, they gave in to the military authorities. This was at about 11:30. Immediately troops were sent for, who came into the fortress and began to disarm everyone. The soldiers in the fortress said they would have surrendered long before but that they had been powerless, as the anarchists had taken away their arms and threatened them.

Later, in the afternoon, at Lenin's headquarters, I was shown a lot of what they said were important documents. I didn't read them, but I am told they showed that Lenin was unquestionably connected with the Germans.

The troops who are guarding this palace now are a bunch of cyclists who came all the way from the Dvinsk front on their wheels.

The rooms of this beautiful palace are in the worst state of disorder you could imagine. I never saw such dirt. The floor was completely covered with scraps of anarchist literature, and all the beautiful furniture I had seen before was gone.

As I was leaving this place, I was surprised to hear Boris say to me, "I bet you are thinking the Russians are no good." I asked him why. He said, "Look at what you saw today, look at how they act. How can you like the Russian people?" He went on to ask me how could I like such a bunch of scoundrels who had come in and lived in a private house as they had for several months and then went unpunished and made a joke of the Russian laws. He is very much against the government. He says that if the government had acted a couple of months ago, all this trouble would have been avoided. Even now he is afraid the government will not be stern enough.

The workmen are now being disarmed throughout the city.

Lenin, who I heard was in the Peter and Paul Fortress, escaped during the excitement of the surrender in a small boat, in the disguise of a sailor.[102] One of the officers in charge at headquarters here says that the ministers who were in the fortress while it was in the hands of these anarchists had a trying time. They had been told to pack up their little effects, as they were going to be taken to Kronstadt and tried there.

When the fortress surrendered, Stürmer, the former premier under the old government, was so happy that be fainted from the long strain he had been under, and the wife of the former Minister of War under the old regime lost her mind completely and begged the soldiers guarding her to give her something to commit suicide with. She seemed to be afraid that she would be lynched. The prisoners would have been

---

[102] Lenin went into hiding in Petrograd and sent messages denying he intended to launch a coup. A few days later, he fled in disguise to a rural region near Petrograd, from where he made his way to Finland (Pipes, *A Concise History of the Russian Revolution*, 127).

taken away from the fortress, but the soldiers who had been on guard all the time there refused to permit it. The only thing that finally saved them from being taken to Kronstadt was the early surrender of the fortress.

Soldiers at the palace of the imperial family say that the latter were alarmed by the report that reached Tsarskoe Selo, while the trouble was at its height here in Petrograd. The Emperor was assured by the troops that no danger would come to him.

In the Viborg district,[103] the government is disarming, with the help of the Cossacks, all the Red Guards. They have recovered thousands of revolvers, rifles, and machine-guns already, most of which had just arrived from America.

Late this afternoon, three people dressed as sailors shot from a motor car at a group of officers on the steps of the Duma. They killed two soldiers. They immediately started away at full speed, but were stopped by a large truck, accidentally going their way. By this time hundreds of soldiers at the Duma had rushed out after them, and immediately started firing in their direction. About forty civilians were killed and a great many wounded by this firing. The three occupants of the motor car surrendered and were immediately lynched by the large crowd that had gathered. This is something new to Russia. They stretched them up to the cross arm of a telegraph pole, and didn't tie their hands. Then they drew them off the ground about three feet. All three of them as they were hanging tried to hold on to each other, but the mob knocked their hands away and they slowly strangled to death.

Don

LVI. Friday, July 20

Dear Dot:

I have had more narrow escapes today than I have had for the last few months. Now that I am sitting here in the hotel I can't for the life of me figure out why I am not lying dead on the streets.

I am a nervous wreck from what I have gone through today. On top of this I have the blues, for I see Russia going to hell as a country never went before.

Things are bad not only here, but at the front, from accounts that I got personally today from the general staff. The Bolsheviks, anarchists, and others who have been causing all this trouble, captured the wireless and sent lies to the front: that the city was in control of the Bolsheviks, that Kerensky was dead, that the Allies had made peace, and that America had just said that she also wanted to make terms of peace with the Germans. From this, supplemented by thousands of German agents at the front and German propaganda, I don't wonder that a lot of the weak soldiers were

---

[103] Industrial district on the north side of the Neva.

easily led to revolt at the front. I don't quite know to what extent it has gone; the officers themselves at the general staff seemed not to want to speak of it, so it must be bad.

My mind goes back to the boys I left at the front who, I know, are not retreating but sacrificing their lives for Russia. It may take Russia ten or fifteen years to appreciate what those men are doing, but I know that you at home will appreciate it. Many an American boy's life has been saved by the horrible sacrifices my friends at the Russian front are now making.

The newspapers can tell you that all of Russia's armies are retreating, but I know that those boys I met are still fighting as a Russian knows how to fight. Some of those I know haven't chests big enough for the St. George Cross. Today, the Premier, Prince Lvov, resigned. They say it was a resignation, but I think it was forced.

Kerensky, who I prophesied would be the whole cheese someday, has at last reached the top of the ladder and is now Premier of Russia. He is a hog, in a way, because he is also keeping the office he had before, Minister of War and Munitions. Kerensky, as things stand now, is absolute dictator of Russia. He has had his government endorsed by the Congress of the Workmen and Soldiers and also the Peasants' Council, and they have voted to give him all the power he wants, which practically means unlimited authority. One of the first things he did was to issue orders that all deserters should be killed, and that all the revolutionary agitators should be arrested and thrown into prison. The Admiral in command of the Baltic Fleet was arrested by Kerensky's order; as he had proved himself a traitor to Russia. While this trouble was at its height here, he was letting the Sailors' Committees see the government's secret telegrams.

This Lieutenant Dashkevitch, who was a member of the executive committee of the Workmen's and Soldiers' Delegates, was supposedly insulted today by Kerensky's Government, when a squad of eight soldiers knocked him in the back of his head with the butt of his rifle and took him off to prison.

The government is now sitting in its quarters and issuing notices every minute about what they are going to do. Well, they had better do it quick, or they will never do it.

The Germans had absolute knowledge of all this, and when the trouble started here on Monday the 16th, the Germans also started theirs at the front. This had been arranged probably weeks ahead and was timed to a T. Now all the work the Russians had done in all those weeks has been undone in a day. After the Russians had covered themselves with glory and captured 36,000 men! This Lenin, who escaped, dressed as a sailor, when the Peter and Paul Fortress was taken, and his confederate, Trotsky, who was a hash slinger in New York a few months ago, have done more to ruin Russia than any two men I know of in history. I think that Kerensky's only solution is to catch these two and give them the limit. I know that if I had the chance I would take a good deal of pride in shooting both of them.

I always have had it in for the waiters in New York, as you know, and you and I would have a home, Dot, if it hadn't been for the tips we have been forced to give to the waiters in New York while dining.

The other day a Russian socialist got into quite an argument here at the hotel when he said that Trotsky didn't get his money from the Germans, but was a former waiter in New York, and that all waiters were rich. I told Williams of the *New York Times* about it, as it is a good story; but Trotsky never worked in a first class restaurant. Trotsky has just enough education to do a lot of harm in this world. Lenin, his side partner, is a brilliant man and sincere, as I told you, in what he is doing, and believes that the only solution for Russia lies in a separate peace with Germany. Trotsky is out for fame, money, and power, and would sell his soul and his best friend's soul if it was necessary for him to climb up the ladder. But enough of this. Now I will tell you what happened today.

At two this afternoon, after a morning on the street, where I found everything quiet, I was told that there was trouble at the Nikolai Station. I arrived there a few minutes after two and at first I thought a mistake had been made, that whoever said there was trouble had dreamed it. But at three, or just before, troops who were coming out of the Nikolai Station were suddenly fired upon from the balcony of a large hotel, facing to the left, as you go in. They had a machine-gun in the window of the room and were firing out over a large balcony into the street at these soldiers who had just arrived.

Florence Harper, who had accepted an invitation to join me on this trip, immediately said she was going to leave. I tried to persuade her to stay, but she refused. Then I took my camera to the station in the center of the square. By this time the firing had been returned by the troops, who had recovered from their surprise. As I was just getting my camera evenly balanced and ready for action, firing started from another hotel window across the square to the back of me. By this time the troops pouring out of the station were firing in all directions. In a few minutes it died down, and one company of soldiers were given orders to search the buildings around the square. Then an officer I found out about later came up to the officer in command of these troops and told him to march up the old Nikolai street, as he had been sent to assign them to barracks. The officer in command told him that he had orders to go down to the barracks close to St. Isaac's Cathedral, and the man said the order had been changed. As the troops started into the old Nikolai street, they were met with a hellish fire. At the same time, a regiment of Cossacks came dashing up the street and into the square. An officer then came up to me and told me to scurry, which means run. I was more than willing to get away from this position, but by the time I unscrewed my camera from the tripod the Cossacks had been forced to fall back and firing now became general. In a few minutes the square was deserted, with the exception of troops firing from the side streets from all directions. I was absolutely alone, and I felt alone. After about half an hour of this, the firing ceased except on the old Nikolai street, and when the

Cossacks made their dash across the square and into the old Nikolai, I immediately started in the other direction. Going down the Nevsky, I ran for protection into a court. An hour later I started back to the old Nikolai street to see what damage had been done. I found it in the possession of the Cossacks, who refused to let me by until I had presented my pass. They were just finishing the round-up of the anarchists who had started this trouble, and were showing them little mercy, killing them as they found them in the houses. Most of the people who were killed during the fusillade were women and children. Three or four hundred were killed around that station this afternoon, if I can judge by the number of bodies I saw in some places.

I now hear shooting close up by the hotel. I'll stop and get ready and see what this means. I don't know what to expect. But no matter what happens, it will not surprise me.

Don

LVII. Saturday, July 21

Dear Dot:

Well, last night, as I was finishing your letter, trouble began. The chauffeur, Boris and I got the car and started up the street to the right of the Nevsky Prospekt where it cuts in here by the hotel. We kept on until we reached the Nikolai Station and then started down by the station into the Nevsky. About two blocks down we got into a rain of hell. I think everyone in that part of the town was firing on me. My heart got up in my mouth and I chewed it all the way to the Morskaia. How we ever took the turn as fast as we were going when we got there, I have never figured out, but we did. Reaching the hotel we heard of trouble down along the Neva, so we crossed to the other side and ran into several shooting affairs, near them, I mean, but did not get into any danger to speak of. We returned to the hotel about 12:30. An awful fusillade of machine-gun fire around the Cathedral of St. Isaac told me that I was in for another sleepless night.

The Bolsheviks had got into the People's Park with several of their pets—machine-guns—and placing these on the steps of the Stock Exchange on the other side of the river and on several bridges began to sweep the city. We had just started across the bridge when this trouble began, but we immediately turned back for the hotel and kept to one side of St. Isaac's Cathedral. My chauffeur then, as the firing was dying down, asked permission to go over to his house on the other side of the Neva. I told Boris we would sit on the steps of the cathedral for a while and wait until he came back, as he had promised to bring me some cigars that he said he could get at a shop in his neighborhood.

A few minutes after he had left us, the shooting started up. Boris and I went down near the People's Park and got caught between fires. We flattened ourselves, and then we saw a sight on the bridge that we did not think at the time was of any special importance to us. There were a street car and three or four automobiles reflected in the dark by one of the automobiles burning. After we had watched this for a while we saw one of the other cars catch fire. Meanwhile, by four o'clock, the government troops had the situation in control. A half hour or so later, we found ourselves looking at the body of our chauffeur. Our car was riddled from one end to the other. The chauffeur must have been killed instantly, as he had four or five bullet shots in his head, and from appearances his body had also been hit a great many times, not only in the arms and legs, but in the upper part. We got to the street after we had crossed the bridge where the Stock Exchange is located, and there we found the extent of damage the machine-guns had done. The front of the building looked like a Swiss cheese and the arcade was riddled with bullets. By six o'clock the city was quiet and I noticed that people who passed on the trams seemed surprised to see bodies and buildings scarred with bullets.

While this shooting was at its height, a steamer came down from Kronstadt with reinforcements. Undoubtedly they had made a miscalculation in time or the Bolsheviks had opened up the People's Park sooner than they should have, for the steamer arrived after the Bolsheviks had been practically beaten. When this boat, ablaze with electric lights and with a band playing the Marseillaise, steamed down the Neva, it met all the heavy machine-gun fire of the government forces. The artillery stationed in the Summer Garden had the aim to a T and sunk it with five shots out of the seven they fired. The troops, to make certain that no one would escape, kept a constant play on the Neva as the boat sank, and all those people who had come down from Kronstadt were killed.

Tomorrow being Sunday, I am going into the country. I have been promised a meal such as I would get at home. This Russian family have a real American Southern negro cook, and they say she will cook to order any dish I want. Well, it is going to be French toast and eggs fried with bacon and onions. Tomorrow I will go to sleep with my stomach full. I noticed the other day when I got weighed that I am getting so light I can hardly balance the scale with the smallest weight on. My stomach has the right to have a personal grudge against me, for it is so seldom that I give it even a taste of proper food. Well, I came to Russia against your wish and I am paying the price. If I ever get back home safely, this is the last trip I shall make. But there is no use in saying this. I shall be the way I always have been. A few weeks at home and then I'll pick up the paper at breakfast and read about something happening somewhere and I'll want to go there. Today I feel as you always want me to feel—sick and tired of being a war photographer.

Don

LVIII. Wednesday, July 25

Dear Dot:

The Russian army is now retreating. It is one of the greatest retreats in the history of the world. Tarnopol has been retaken by the Germans, 17,000 Russian soldiers have been shot for deserting; over one million men are retreating and today the Germans captured 90,000. The Belgian and English in command of armored cars are trying to help the Russian loyal soldiers at the front to stop this stampede.

On Monday, the Executive Council of Workmen, Soldiers, and Peasants issued a proclamation which will give you an idea of how quickly they change their minds overnight. Now they are backing Kerensky's Government. A few days ago, their leaders were against Kerensky. Here is a translation of the manifesto, made by one of the boys at the Embassy:

> Fellow-Soldiers: One of our armies has wavered, its regiments have fled before the enemy. Part of our front has been broken. Emperor William's hordes, which have moved forward, are bringing with them death and destruction.
>
> Who is responsible for this humiliation? The responsibility rests with those who have spread discord in the army and have shaken its discipline, with those who at a time of danger disobeyed the military command and wasted time in fruitless discussions and disputes.
>
> Many of those who left the line and sought safety in running away paid with their lives for having disobeyed orders. The enemy's fire mowed them down. If this costly lesson has taught you nothing, then there will be no salvation for Russia.
>
> Enough of words. The time has come to act without hesitation. We have acknowledged the Provisional Government. With the government lies the salvation of the revolution. We have acknowledged its unlimited power. Its commands must be law. All those who disobey the commands of the Provisional Government in battle will be regarded as traitors. Toward traitors and cowards no mercy will be shown.
>
> Fellow-soldiers: You want a durable peace. You want your land, your freedom. Then you must know that only by a stubborn struggle will you win peace for Russia and all nations. Yielding before the troops of the German Emperor, you lost both your land and your freedom. The conquering, imperialistic Germans will force you again and again to fight for your interests.
>
> Fellow-soldiers at the front: Let there be no traitors or cowards among you. Let not one of you retreat a single step before the foe. Only one way is open for you--the way forward.
>
> Fellow-soldiers in the rear: Be ready to advance to the front for the support of your brothers, abandoned and betrayed, fleeing from their positions

in the regiments. Gather all your strength for the struggle for a durable peace, for your land and your freedom. Without wavering, without fear, without disastrous discussions, carry out all military commands. At the time of battle disobedience and wavering are worse than treachery. Your ruin lies in them, the ruin of Russia.

Fellow-soldiers: You are being watched by those who work for Russia and by the whole world. The ruin of the Russian revolution spells ruin for all. Summon up all your manhood, your perseverance and sense of discipline and save the fatherland.

The General Staff says that at Dvinsk the enemy is conducting an enormous offensive, firing hundreds of thousands of shells every twenty-four hours. On top of this, however, we get news that the fighting has been renewed on the Romanian front and that the Romanians and Russians are making advances.

Kerensky is now at the front, doing a great deal to stop this retreat. As things stand now, the Council of Workmen's and Soldiers' Deputies is the power in Russia, and when you look at these men at Tauride Palace, where the government's work is carried on, the men who are now sitting in that committee, you feel that somehow things are going to be better. A great many of them, from what I gather are Russia's best men—that is, they are known to be honest; but if they were not socialists I would feel better.

Now that Kerensky has a blood and iron policy he should take advantage of the power and confidence that the soldiers and workmen and the government have placed in him and start a wholesale lynching of trouble-makers, especially German agents. What I am afraid of most is that the old regime will take advantage of the retreat and start a revolution of their own.

In the town of Stanislau, southeast of Tarnopol, there was hand to hand fighting by the Probrajensky and Semoszky regiments who remained loyal. Then the Russian guard corps retreated although the latter were not even pressed by the enemy. The Russian troops, when they were forced to retire, were attacked by the civilian population, who threw thousands of grenades at them.

The Russian woman's battalion is also in batlle along the front at Krevo. The commander, Maria Bochkareva, has been wounded twice. When they heard the soldiers were retreating and that a regiment had just abandoned a very good position, these women asked permission of the general in command, who was more than willing, for them to go in and hold this position. The official statement in regard to these women is as follows: "In the neighborhood of Vilna, in the district of Krevo, the women of the Death Battalion, after they had occupied their trenches, were immediately shelled by the Germans. Instead of retreating, they made an attack on a portion of the enemy's trenches east of Mihaloze, where they captured over 100 Germans and two German officers. They were forced by the enemy's terrible artillery fire to retire after they had taken two lines of German trenches in front of them. They were also fired at by Russian soldiers on their left."

General Kornilov, who is in command of the troops at the southwestern front, has issued orders that all troops refusing to obey orders shall be shot at once. Kerensky, I am told, has given his OK to this.

They say that old Kaiser Bill himself was at the front at Tarnopol and saw the advance. I suppose he'll be issuing a statement that God is with him again and has helped his glorious army in their work. Well, God is not with him in this dastardly work he is doing in Russia; the devil himself would not he his partner in this.

Don

LIX. Friday, July 27

Dear Dot:

The bodies of a few Cossacks were taken into St. Isaac's Cathedral this evening about five. There they will remain until tomorrow, when they will be buried with great honors. The government is giving about eight of these Cossacks a public funeral to convey the impression that only a few were killed. If the Cossacks really knew how many had been killed, nothing would keep them from attacking the Bolsheviks and making an end of them once and for all.

Maria Bochkareva, according to reports, has been taken with other wounded girls of the Women's Death Battalion to Minsk. They were then sent to Potollova. They will arrive here in the city in about twenty-four hours, I am told. They will be given a great welcome by over 200,000 soldiers, and the people will escort them along the way with banners and bands. The report we get here is that these women covered themselves with glory and that one of the German officers committed suicide when he found it was women who had taken his position and captured him and another officer and a great many men.

The retreat that is still going on is now endangering the Russian-Romanian or so-called Moldavian line. The Germans are now apparently trying to re-enter Bukovina.

General Kornilov the other day ordered the 11th Army to attack one of the divisions of this army and kill every one of them, which they did. The Russian army down near Tarnopol has retreated to the east of this place, to the Gizna River.

Hindenburg is claiming great victories from the wonderful showing of this army. That is not true; the victory is due to the lack of the Russian army and to the treachery caused by German agents working among these poor ignorant soldiers.

On the road to Vilna, Russian officers, when their regiments refused to advance, formed themselves into regiments and made an attack. Of one regiment organized in this way, out of 1,500 only one escaped alive.

On the Galician front, the retreat is at its height; the men are shooting down their comrades when they find them advancing. Troops of the 11th Army attacked the artillery on their way to the front, and killed all the men and officers, so that they could have their horses to retreat with. Hundreds of guns are falling every hour into the German hands.

On Tuesday, July 31, we are to have a meeting of the so-called Extraordinary National Council. It will convene at Moscow, and members of the Duma, men of prominence from the chief centers of the Empire, and labor delegates have all been asked to attend and decide how to save Russia. The only way to save Russia, so far as I can see, is to have a wholesale killing of the traitors here in Petrograd such as they are having at the front, according to reports we get. The reinforcements that have been sent from here to the front are behaving worse than the troops which have been there over three years.

The retreat at the front in some cases cannot be explained. Regiments which had always before been loyal have voluntarily quit fighting for no reason at all, and started to retreat. When this happens other regiments immediately follow suit.

We are told here that Kerensky is to blame for all this trouble, that the soldiers and workmen are to blame, that the socialists are to blame, and that Lenin is to blame.

I had an interview with the former Minister of War, General Sukhomlinov, while I was out at the Peter and Paul Fortress taking some pictures this morning. He is going to be tried some time for treason, and they also have his wife in another cell. From the stories I hear about what she did, I will bet he is glad she isn't in the same cell with him. The general told me through Boris that he was never in the pay of the Germans, that the harm was done at the War Office by other generals, and that his record, which he would lay before the court, would acquit him, if the court was composed of honest judges. The greatest enemy he has is Rodzianko, who used to be President of the Duma, and Miliukov, former Prime Minister. According to these people, this old general's criminal neglect of duty was the cause of Russia's retreat. He was an enemy of the Grand Duke and I think had a lot to do with the Grand Duke's transfer. His wife has been in the pay of Austria during the war and obtained a great many secrets by asking the old general to bring his work home. There she could have an opportunity to copy letters and plans.

Don

LX. Saturday, July 28

Dear Dot:

Today I received quite a shock when I found that the Russians had closed the frontiers and that no one can leave for three weeks.

I am now getting ready to start back home. I have developed all my film up to today's pictures, and I will develop them Sunday. I have also received a permit to take my film out of the country without being examined.

I worked it in this way. The secretaries and chief clerks of the Foreign Office are the same people who have been there for the last ten to thirty years. When the old government was overthrown, the ministers left their desks, but the machinery went on as usual. So I went up to the Foreign Office and had a talk with the old secretary. I cussed the devil out of Kerensky and said how sorry I was for the old government, and that I hoped Mr. Nicholas was well and enjoying life under these trying times and would come back some day and give these people their just dues. At the same time I casually mentioned that I had a lot of film which would show to the world the conditions in Russia caused by this new government. Then I asked him if, when handing a bunch of papers to Kerensky to be signed, he would slip in an order giving me permission to leave the country without having my baggage examined. He fell for it and was more than willing. I had been in Kerensky's office one day and saw Kerensky sign a bunch of letters without reading them, so I knew it could be worked.

Well, I have the letter signed by Kerensky. He doesn't know that I have it, but this letter will make it possible for me to leave Russia without having my baggage examined or my film censored. According to law, it has been censored already. These people have stamped it, sealed it, and given it their OK.

I am coming home by way of Japan and hope to leave Petrograd August 14, on the Trans-Siberian Express. I have a ticket for that day. It cost me about 400 percent more than it should have cost. The tickets for this train are in the hands of scalpers who charge the most exorbitant prices, but we have to pay them or not travel.

Today, the funeral of the Cossacks was held. These are the men who were killed during the week of July 16. About a million people turned out to see it. The Bolsheviks threatened to stop the proceedings; they must have been impressed by the great number of loyal troops who marched in the parade.

An amusing incident happened at the cemetery. The people were packed in there like sardines. As the bodies were lowered into the graves, a company of soldiers started to fire three volleys. By the time the first volley had been fired, I think everyone on the outside of the cemetery fence began to move on. The people inside thought that a fight had started between the Cossacks and the Bolsheviks, for in a few minutes about every tombstone in the cemetery was knocked over by the people running away. It was over fifteen minutes before quiet was restored and the people realised that it had only been a salute. This showed at what high tension the people's nerves are.

A strict censorship has now been imposed. Any one giving out any information about the army or navy, without first having it censored, is liable to two years' imprisonment and $5,000 fine.

Kerensky has issued an order making it impossible for generals to resign. General Ruzsky and General Gurko, who were at the front and in charge of the troops when the big retreat began, have been told to come to Petrograd. What Kerensky will do with them I don't know.

Kerensky was here today and walked in the procession behind one of the bodies.

On top of this, I hear that the national congress, which was to be held at Moscow, has been postponed and will not meet until the government's new cabinet has been reconstructed. I understand that the changes in the cabinet will not be made for a few days.

The Soldiers' and Workmen's Deputies have adopted by an overwhelming majority a resolution against Lenin, who is now hiding at Kronstadt.

I talked to one of the girls of the Women's Death Battalion, who has been brought back here to Petrograd. She is the daughter of Admiral Skrydlov.[104] She said that a great many of the women were killed and quite a number taken prisoners. They say their hardest fight was in the woods near Smorgon, the Novospassky Woods. She said that when the attack started the women advanced singing and kept on singing until they saw the first dead bodies of their comrades. She said that only a few of them lost heart when they found they had been deserted by Russia's soldiers and that only a handful of women were facing the enemy alone.

I am going out to talk to one of the other girls, who, I understand, knows a little English. I will get the story from her of just what really happened. This admiral's daughter is still suffering from shell-shock and cannot give a clear account of it.

Kerensky says he is going to put an end to soldiers' debates at once, and that when the Ministers' Conference meets he will ask their support in establishing strict discipline and reorganizing the army as it was under the old regime, till Russia is out of danger.

Kerensky is leaving for the front again tonight.

Don

LXI. Saturday, August 4

Dear Dot:

General Kornilov has been made commander-in-chief of all the Russian armies in place of General Brusilov, who has resigned, probably because he was forced to do so by Kerensky. There have been several other changes, but this is the most important.

Kornilov is one of Russia's best generals and I think if he is given full power, he will be able to straighten things out better than anyone else. The Engineers' Palace here in Petrograd is now the big recruiting barracks for the new Women's Regiments. At present, there are about 6,000 women drilling in Petrograd, Moscow, Kiev and other cities. These women are being equipped and instructors are being supplied as

---

[104] See n. 91.

quickly as battalions are formed, and they are drilling ten hours a day. About 40 percent of the women are peasants. I went out and made a series of pictures of them today.

I hear that Kerensky had a fight with one of the ministers of the cabinet, and that for a while we had no government at all, and that Kerensky had even rushed away to Finland in an automobile. How true this is I don't know, but I do know that all the ministers resigned but later reconsidered and withdrew their resignations.

Several of the generals at the front have issued an order that all soldiers who abandoned their trenches when the retreat was at its height shall from now on wear a mark of some kind on their coats until they have proved that they are brave soldiers and willing to fight for Russia. When they have proved this, the mark will be removed.

Kornilov's terms upon accepting the command of the army were that no one should interfere with his orders, that he should have the right to appoint anyone he wanted, and that he would establish order at the front and must also have the power to establish order in the rear, and that there must be discipline not only at the front, but also in Petrograd and other places.[105]

General Gurko,[106] who has been arrested, has been accused of a great many things, but I doubt if he is guilty of any of the charges. To my mind he is a very able general and is having these charges made against him by German agents working through the Socialists.

We are having many murders now here in Petrograd. Some soldiers drove up in an automobile in front of the Senate Building, killed the guards and stole a lot of valuable antiques worth a million rubles. Where we hear of one case like this, there are others we don't hear of.

Don

LXII. Sunday, August 5

Dear Dot:

I had a very interesting talk today with one of the officials of the Ministry of Trade and Industry. He says that during the first year of the war, Russia spent about two and a half billion dollars, that the second year she doubled it, and that the third year has cost her nine billion dollars, the revenue being less than half this. He also says that the government is issuing billions of rubles monthly and is being slowly ruined. At a meeting today, the executives of the Workmen's, Soldiers' and Peasants' Delegates voted by a large majority to uphold Kerensky. According to the newspapers, Kerensky has said that he will not resign and has withdrawn his resignation; but I am told by Russians that he never intended to resign and that this was only a bluff.

---

[105] See n. 60.

[106] See n. 69.

Miliukov has again come forward and declared that his party, the Constitutional Democrats, are ready to form a coalition government with Kerensky at the head. Other parties have done the same. If these people don't get together at once and form a strong government, we shall have a revolution that will make the other revolution look sick. The Russian General Staff says that the panic at the front has ended and that the troops are beginning to fight again.

The greatest help at present at the front is the example being set by the death battalions. By their acts of bravery, they have brought about a new spirit in the army.

I talked to-day with Memes,[107] an English photographer, who has done some of the most remarkable work I think any photographer has done during the war. He was a companion of Stanley Washburn[108] for over three years here in Petrograd. He has just returned from the front and says it was something awful during the retreat. He was with some troops of the British armored car division here. The Germans broke through. Some soldiers rushed by in trucks crying, "The Germans are coming." In a few minutes the camp was a scene of rioting. All the automobiles, which had been used as supply wagons were taken by force by the deserting troops. Soldiers he talked to said that the death penalty had been abolished and that they had nothing to fear. Most of the time they had to circle to go ahead, because the road was so jammed. The English officers did more to stop this retreat than anyone else; they put courage into the Russian officers and between them they were able to save a great many supplies that otherwise would have fallen into the Germans' hands.

Machine-guns were turned on Russians by Russians during this retreat, and in some places thousands were killed. I have had this same story from several Russians. They also say that all meetings are forbidden now at the front.

This afternoon I had quite an adventure. I had made a contract with a droshky driver to take me to the American Embassy and back to the cafe next to the Empire Hotel for four rubles. When I arrived and handed him the exact change, he demanded ten rubles for the job. I immediately said, "Nit," and started to walk away. He jumped down from the seat, followed me onto the sidewalk, grabbed my arm, and began to talk in an excited manner. I threw his hand off my arm and said, "Nit," and told him in Russian not to act that way. He still kept on. Each time I started away, he would follow me. Finally, I lost my head and got so mad that I smashed him in the face. Over he went. That was the worst thing I could have done; in Russia you can kick a man with your foot, but you must never lay a hand on him. I realized I had made a mistake, as a large crowd immediately gathered. Getting my wits together, I climbed up on the driver's former seat, took off my hat, bowed to the crowd, and said, "Tavarish," which in English means, comrades. Then I said "Americansky," which meant that I was an American, and pointing my finger down at the driver lying on

---

[107] George Mewes of the *Daily Mirror*.

[108] See n. 86.

the sidewalk, added, "Bolshevik, no good." As the Bolsheviks are in bad now, the crowd immediately turned from me to him. In a few minutes several people were striking him. While this was going on, I jumped down, went into the café, and stood in the window and watched the fight. Others began to arrive every minute and the crowd increased until I believe there were 2,000 people there. They took sides, and finally after half an hour the military police came and dispersed the crowd.

Don

LXIII. Manchuria border, August 15

Dear Dot:

As you see, I am now over two-thirds of my way home. I have just found that I shall not be able to make connections at Yokohama for America, as I thought I should. I shall be about three weeks in Japan until the *Empress of Russia* arrives.

On the train I met five or six Americans who were on their way home. One of them was a prison investigator for the YMCA who has visited and helped feed and look after the Austrian and German prisoners in Siberia. He told me that a great many of the Austrian prisoners are married to Russian-Siberian girls and intend to remain the rest of their lives in Siberia. He said that thousands of them had stated that they would never go back to their own country, as the possibilities in Siberia were greater for them than they would be at home.

I shall not change trains, as a great many of the passengers will, at Harbin,[109] but will go on to Vladivostok. I am told that enormous supplies are stacked up all around the town, waiting to be sent into Russia. Vladivostok has grown to be quite a city, and has over 75,000 inhabitants; it is now one of the most important ports in the world. Most of the buildings here on the Manchurian border are log houses, although in the bigger cities in Siberia they have modern buildings now and the older type have been abandoned. Concrete is used a great deal out here, or has been for the last few years. The buildings in which the troops are quartered are very modern and well equipped. The soldiers are now being reached by socialistic literature. I am told by officers that they will have trouble out here in a short time, just as they are having in Petrograd.

The food which the soldiers get in this part of the country is mostly black bread, soup and tea. This soup is a meal in itself; it is made up of cabbage, vegetables and meat. The bread is of better quality than in Petrograd. You can have all the white bread you want after you reach Siberia. There is no shortage of any food here; at every station you find peasants loaded down with white bread, fried meats, cakes, and other foods, and willing to sell them at a very small price.

The first prisoners the Russians took were sent to Siberia. The prison districts are scattered throughout the territory, each district having from 10,000 to 50,000

---

[109] Railroad junction with Chinese Eastern Railway. See n. 6.

prisoners. There are about four Austrians to every German prisoner. They do not attempt to escape, for one reason because they are over 6,000 miles away from home. The officers have privileges, club houses, etc., and the men also have very good barracks, and although it is true they were not fed or given the clothing that they should have had for this severe climate in the winter time, since America started to go through these camps and make their reports, they have little to complain of. A change had been made even before the revolution.

There have been many escapes, however, from the camps near the Chinese frontier.

Germans living in China started a campaign to help the German prisoners to escape, and other acts they committed were responsible, in a way, for the Chinese entering the war. After a few escapes, the old government built huge wooden stockades about the camps, on top of which they stretched rows of barbed wire and placed searchlights to command a better view of the prisoners. The prisoners were given the same food as the Russian soldiers. In a great many places they were quartered in brick barracks.

The officers were kept separate from the privates. One funny thing about this war that a great many people do not know is that when an officer is captured and made a prisoner, the government that captures him must pay him the same salary that he drew while an officer in his own country. Some officers with the rank of general cost the Russian Government a great deal of money; they made it a rule that these officers must pay for their own food. These officers often pool together and hire people to come and manage their food department; in some camps they have had noted chefs, also prisoners, whom they pay enormous salaries, as much as they ever made while they were chefs at famous hotels in Budapest, Vienna, or Berlin.

There is a big business done in the prison camps by people who sell American shoes. The Russians did not put their prisoners at work until they heard that Germany was using its Russians. When they did, the prisoners were more than satisfied; it kept their minds occupied, and the health reports went up. The Russians, however, have never worked prisoners who were wounded or crippled in any way, or officers, and they have made special arrangements for soldiers who were educated. Most of the camps have established orchestras, the Austrian camps, especially, and their concerts are attended by people from miles around. The work the prisoners have turned out in the way of curios is wonderful. You see it on exhibition at the Siberian stations, where you can buy it for a song. Many Siberian churches have been decorated by the prisoners in these camps. You see the touch of prison labor almost everywhere you stop in Siberia.

When they first heard that they were being sent to Siberia these prisoners trembled and many committed suicide; they expected they would be put to work in mines with chains around their feet and suffer hardships untold. Imagine their surprise when they arrived and found that they were better off here than they had been in prison camps in European Russia!

A lot of prisoners who came out here unable to read or write have been attending schools which have been started in these prison camps and are now able to read; some of them have become quite proficient in the studies they have taken up and will be able to command better salaries when the war is over, thanks to the education they have had in these Siberian prison camps. Schools for languages hare been started and prisoners have been known to master five different languages in two years' time in some of these schools. They have courses in scientific and research work that colleges would be proud of. Many of the camps are supplied with plenty of reading matter. Although the Germans send a great many papers they do not reach the men as quickly as the English and French papers. Neutral newspapers are the only ones that are not allowed.

In many of these camps in the last year the Americans have established tennis courts, theaters and football grounds; and the prisoners have made some of them very beautiful with rustic gardens and other decorations.

I will mail this letter at Harbin when we arrive there in the morning. They have Japanese beer on sale at this station where we are now. It is in Chinese territory, but the Russian officials, by arrangement with the Chinese, have their custom house here.

Don

LXIV. Tuesday, August 21

Dear Dot:

I am on a steamer bound for Japan. I left Vladivostok yesterday and managed to get fair accommodations. The boat is packed with Russians, leaving Russia for a safer place to live in, and I am told I shall find the hotels in Japan full of Russians who have left until conditions improve in their country.

We arrived at Harbin on August 18, at about nine o'clock in the evening. The train was at the station for about three hours, and I met several Americans, among them the American Consul and several of the Standard Oil boys. They told me that conditions were bad, that everyone had to carry a gun in Harbin on account of the holdups.

We left Harbin Thursday and arrived on Sunday, August 19 at eleven o'clock in Vladivostok.

There were about 1,500 people sleeping on the floor in the station. I finally got a droshky. The driver told me I could not get any accommodations, as the hotels were full, but I thought I'd try anyway. Well, I tried, but it did me no good. So, along with an Englishman I had run into, I started out for a ride. I think the droshky driver thought we were crazy. We kept driving around and whenever we saw a hill in the distance we would tell him to go that way. We did this the rest of the night till about seven-thirty the next morning. Then we drove back to the city and stopped in front of a restaurant and had breakfast. I then left my friend and went to the Consulate, where I was given a lot of magazines. From there I went to the police station, where I had my passport stamped, and finally to the steamship office, where I attended to my baggage. I breathed a sigh of relief when the steamer left Vladivostok for Japan.

The amount of supplies tied up in Vladivostok—I forgot to tell you—is incredible. All the hills as far as you can see are covered with them; some have been here for two years and the government has been unable to move them to the front. The Americans, however, who have shipped automobiles here, get by, I don't know how; they have been doing so ever since the war started. They have an automobile landed off the steamer here one day, and a couple of days later it is on the way to Petrograd. But they are Americans, not Russians.

Don

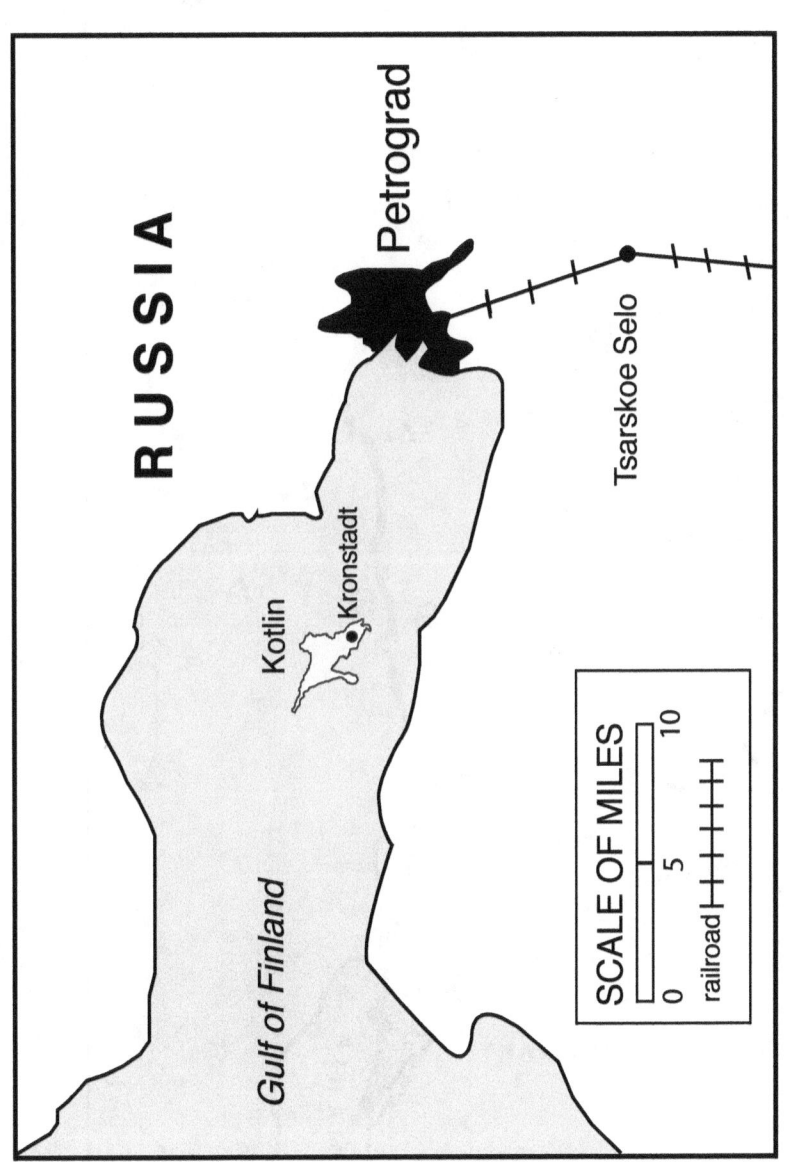

Figure 2. Kronstadt and Tsarskoe Selo. Map by Belén Marco Crespo.

Figure 3. Russian front, 1917.
Map by Belén Marco Crespo.

Figure 4. Just before the Russian Revolution.

Figure 5. Demonstration against peace.

Figure 6. Gun and ammunition cart.

Figure 7. Merry-go-round at the Russian front.

Figure 8. Rasputin surrounded by admirers.

Figure 9. A bread line in Petrograd.

Figure 10. Three generations of Cossacks.

Figure 11. Russian front at Riga.

Figure 12. Nicholas Romanov and his son, June 1917.

Figure 13. Men shooting from a motor.

Figure 14. The first red flags on the Nevsky Prospekt, Sunday, March 11, 1917.

Figure 15. Petrograd police station after the Revolution.

Figure 16. Half a million people demonstrating on the Nevsky.

Figure 17. Street scene in Petrograd.

Figure 18. A captured car, Monday night, March 12.

Figure 19. Picking up the dead and wounded after a street fight in Petrograd.

Figure 20. Types of Bolsheviks.

Figure 21. The Reds of Petrograd.

Figure 22. My room at the Hotel Astoria.

Figure 23. A deserted prison.

Figure 24. Soldiers' and workmen's deputies sitting.

Figure 25. A Russian nurse.

Figure 26. Women lined up for inspection.

Figure 27. Effects of street-fighting during the Revolution.

Figure 28. Armored cars in Petrograd.

Figure 29. Funeral procession in Petrograd.

Figure 30. Catherine Breshkovskaya.

Figure 31. Cossack general reviewing Bochkareva's Death Battalion.

Figure 32. Sole survivors of an entire regiment after gas attack.

Figure 33. Wounded Russian soldiers walking back from the front.

Figure 34. Demonstration by loyal Russians.

Figure 35. Mobs meeting at the Nevsky and Sadovaia.

Figure 36. Trotsky and Lenin. *See also* footnote 34, page xx.

Figure 37. Women making a demonstration against the war.

Figure 38. Russian soldiers leaving the front.

Figure 39. Russian Cossacks.

Figure 40. Kerensky just about to salute regiment passing on its way to the front.

Figure 41. Mobs listening to Kerensky near the Russian Admiralty.

Figure 42. Mobs on the Field of Mars in Petrograd.

Figure 43. Bochkareva and one of the companies of women soldiers.

Figure 44. Russian soldiers who had tried to cut this barbed wire of the Germans.

Figure 45. Russian soldiers advancing through the grass.

Figure 46. Left to right Bolshevik, German Agent, and Kronstadt [sailor].

Figure 47. Russian army on the retreat.

Figure 48. Dr. Eugene Hurd, of Seattle, Washington.

Figure 49. House used by me at the front.

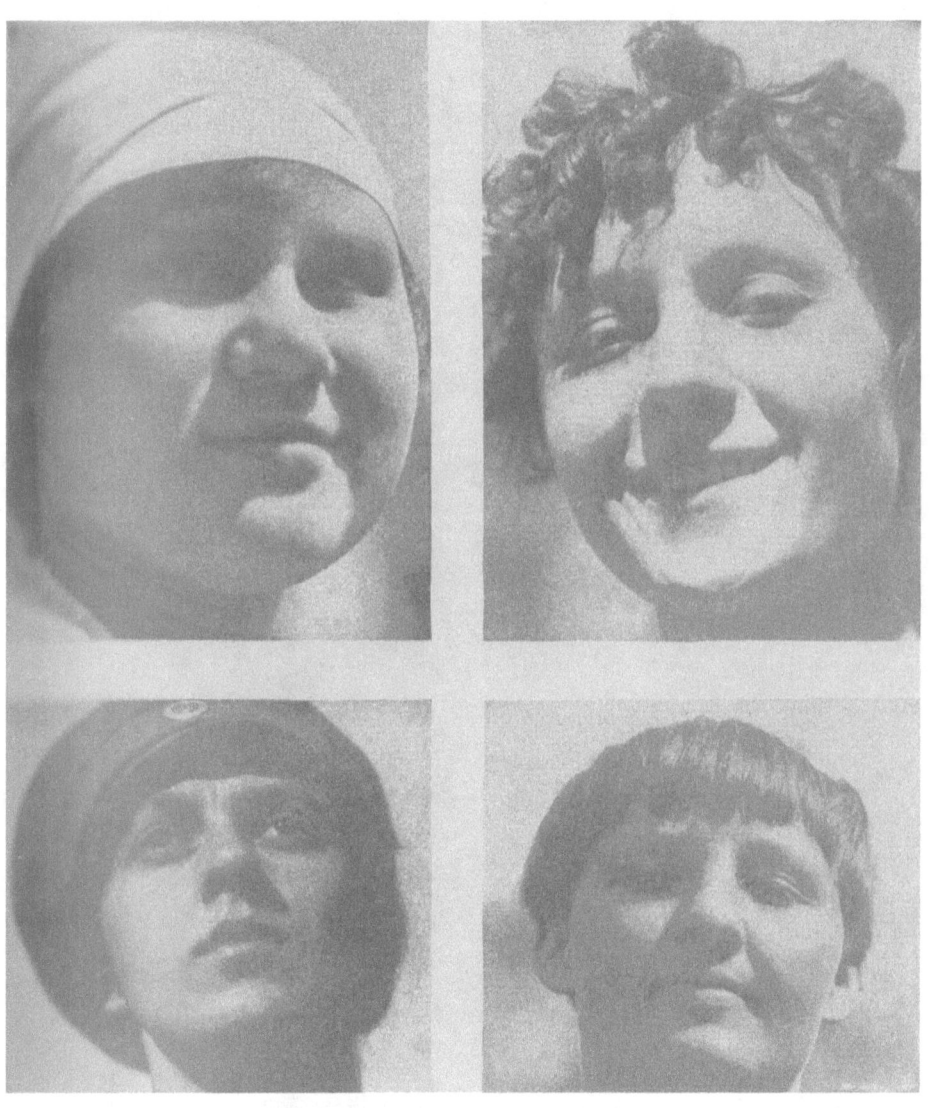

Figure 50. Women who joined the Women's Death Battalion.

Figure 51. Blessing of the Women's Death Battalions.

Figure 52. Florence Harper and Maria Bochkareva.

Figure 53. Bochkareva and Emmeline Pankhurst.

Figure 54. Lenin addressing a Petrograd mob, Monday, July 16, 1917.

Figure 55. Emmeline Pankhurst and Bochkareva reviewing Women's Death Battalion.

Figure 56. Mutinous soldiers.

Figure 57. Russian soldiers abandoning their positions during the great retreat in July 1917.

Figure 58. Lenin's arrival in Petrograd.

Figure 59. A Russian Death Battalion.

Figure 60. A crowded street tram in Petrograd.

Figure 61. Cattle cars were used to haul the wounded in.

Figure 62. With my camera in frontline trenches on the Dvinsk front.

Figure 63. Low bridge on Russian front line.

Figure 64. A soldier's funeral.

Figure 65. Petrograd mobs.

Index

Alekseiev, Mikhail Vasiliyevich, military commander 83, 83n67, 103
Alexandra, Tsarina 18n9, 22n16, 22n17, 50n43, 58, 61, 62, 63, 67, 80, 93, 98, 98n76, 100, 122
Astoria Hotel, Petrograd xix, 17, 18, 18n11, 20, 23, 33n30 44, 46, 53, 69; attack on 46, 53. *See also* figure 22

Bochkareva, Maria 116–17, 117n90, 119, 120–21, 120n92, 123, 141, 142. *See also* figures 2, 43, 52, 55
Breshkovskaya, Catherine 69, 69n61, 70. *See also* figure 30
Brusilov, Aleksei Alekseevich, military commander xv, 60, 60n54, 87, 90, 103–04, 112, 115, 123, 145
Bulgaria xiv, 7n8, 8, 11

Carpathian Mountains xiv, xv, xvi, 7, 7n8, 8, 60n54
Catherine Canal, Petrograd 27, 27n24, 29, 34, 39, 76, 124
Chicago Tribune xi, xii, xiii, xiv, xv, 6, 7n8
Cossacks xviii, 23, 25, 26, 28, 29, 31, 32, 33, 34, 38, 42, 47, 58, 100, 103, 113, 115, 122, 123, 128, 129, 130, 135, 137, 138, 142, 144. *See also* figures 10, 39

Daily Mail (London) xiii, xviii, 4, 5, 5n5, 6
Dosch-Fleurot, Arno, journalist 24, 24n18, 39
Duma xix, xxi, 21n15, 22, 22n16, 22n17, 24n19, 30, 38, 39, 44, 45, 47, 49, 50, 52, 53, 55, 56, 57, 58, 59, 61, 62, 63, 65, 68, 72, 81, 93, 123, 125, 127, 128, 135, 143
Dvinsk front 58, 58n51, 73, 82, 105, 107, 134, 141. *See also* figures 3, 62

Eastman Kodak 10, 10n14

Finland xxi, 19n13, 54n45, 58n50, 59n53, 68, 69, 88n74, 91, 106n85, 146
Fontanka Canal, Petrograd 31, 31n29, 35, 36, 39, 125
food shortages (in Petrograd) 17, 17n8, 20, 22n17, 21, 115
France (Western Front) xiv, xvii, 3n2, 9, 14, 24n18, 26n20, 85, 89, 101, 102
Francis, David, US ambassador 26n20, 38, 38n33, 42n38, 62–63, 80–81, 80n64, 86, 114
Frederiks, Count Vladimir Borisovich 57, 57n50, 60

Galicia (front) xiv, 7n8, 7n9, 60n54, 67n60, 83n67, 112, 113, 143
Greece xiv, 7n8, 9
Guchkov, Alexander, politician 51, 55, 55n47, 62, 66, 76, 80, 82, 85, 86, 92–93
Gurko, Vasily Iosifovich, military commander 84, 84n69, 103, 144, 146

Harbin (Manchuria) 14, 15, 16, 16n6, 148, 150
Harper, Florence, journalist x, xvii, xviii, xix, xxiii, 9, 9n13, 13, 13n4, 15, 18, 19, 23, 26, 28–29, 30–31, 33, 34, 35, 38, 40, 50, 63, 64, 105, 118, 137. *See also* figure 52
Hurd, Dr. Eugene 104, 104n83, 105, 108–09, 111. *See also* figure 48

intrigue and spying, German xxii, 5n3, 7, 8, 9, 10, 11, 14–15, 73, 80, 89, 131
Italy xvi, 8, 9

Japan xvii, xxv, 11, 12, 87, 144, 148, 150, 151

Kansas ix, x, xi, 4, 20, 27, 40, 108, 126
Kazan Cathedral, Petrograd 31, 33, 34, 35, 78, 119, 129
Kerensky, Alexander, politician xxi, 24n19, 49, 56, 62, 67, 67n60, 69, 70, 85, 87, 88, 89, 90, 91, 92–95, 97, 101, 103, 104, 105, 106, 112–13, 120, 123, 126, 127, 128, 135, 136, 140, 141, 142, 143, 144, 145, 145, 146. *See also* figures 40, 41
Kornilov, Lavr Georgiyevich, military commander xxi, 60n54, 67, 67n60, 84, 86, 115, 123, 142, 145, 146
Kronstadt (naval base) xx n34, 54, 54n45, 75, 102, 103, 104, 105, 106, 107, 116, 131, 132, 133, 134–35 139, 145. *See also* figure 2
Kschessinskaya, Mathilde (and mansion) xx, 82n66, 106, 128

Lee, Frank Charles, US vice-consul 26, 26n20, 29, 34, 35, 64, 77, 81, 87
Lenin xx, xx n34, xxi, xxii, xxiv, 70, 71, 72, 73, 75, 76, 80, 82, 82n66, 82, 83, 84, 86, 106, 107, 112, 115, 122, 123, 124, 126, 127, 129, 132–34, 134n102, 136, 137, 143, 145. *See also* figure 36
Leslies's Illustrated Weekly x, xiii, xvii, xxi, xxiii, xxiv, 3, 9, 9n12, 10, 13, 60
Liteiny, Petrograd street xviii, xix, 38, 42, 43, 44, 75, 128
Lvov, Prince Georgy Yevgenyevich, politician 49, 56, 56n48, 58, 70, 79, 92, 95, 111, 136

Mariinsky Palace, Petrograd 63, 63n57, 76, 95
Mars, Field of, Petrograd 27, 27n23, 39, 41, 42, 45, 44, 75. *See also* figure 42
McCormick, Robert R., journalist xiv, xv, xv n21, xvi, xvii, 6–7, 7n8, 7n9; Thompson's 1915 trip to Russia with 6–8
Mewes, George, photographer 42, 42n39, 98, 147
Miliukov, Pavel Nikolayevich, politician 24, 24n19, 49, 55, 56n46, 57, 61, 70, 72, 73, 77, 79, 81, 84, 87, 88, 143, 147
Miliukov note 24n19, 79, 84

Moika River, Petrograd 45, 45n40
Morskaia, Petrograd street 19, 23, 38, 39, 45, 56, 75, 76, 78, 124, 125, 138
Moscow ix, 21, 26n20, 54, 72–74, 92, 116, 128, 143, 145
munitions, Russian 8, 8n10, 20, 20n14

Nevsky Prospekt, Petrograd street xviii, xxi, 19, 19n12, 21, 23, 26n21, 27, 29, 30–34, 35, 41, 43, 45, 57, 61, 75, 76, 77, 78, 82, 83, 85, 116, 125, 127–29, 138. *See also* figures 14, 16, 35
New York World xii, xiii, 4, 24, 39
Nicholas, Grand Duke, military commander xv, 10, 10n16, 83n67, 104, 123
Nicholas II, Tsar 7n8, 10n16, 18n9, 22n16, 22n17, 38, 50, 50n43, 55n47, 57, 61n55, 65, 65, 83n67, 103, 105, 122; abdication xvii, xviii, xxi–xxii, 57–58; 1915 meeting with Thompson and McCormick 7n8; 1917 meeting with Thompson, 97–98
Nikolai Station, Petrograd 19, 19n13, 29, 31, 32, 33, 34, 38, 47, 77, 137, 138
Northcliffe, Alfred Harmsworth, First Viscount, newspaper magnate xiii, 5, 5n5, 6

Pankhurst, Emmeline 120, 120n92. *See also* figures 2, 55
Pavlovsky (Imperial Guard regiment) 28n25, 39, 39n35
Pekin (Bejing) xvii, xxiv, 14, 15, 16n6
Peter and Paul Fortress, Petrograd 22n17, 28, 28n25, 31, 39, 41, 47, 49, 50, 66, 98, 106, 122, 131, 132–133, 134, 136, 143; attack on 133–35
Philippines xxiv, 13
Photography, wartime restrictions on 3–5
Powell, E. Alexander, journalist xi, xii, 4, 5, 6
Pravda 84, 129
Prisoners of war (in Siberia) 148–50
Protopopov, Alexander, politician xxi, 22, 22n17, 23, 25, 26, 49, 62, 122
Pskov 50n43, 57, 57n49

Railroads, Russian 8n10, 16n6, 71–72, 81, 87, 87n72, 91

Rasputin 18, 18n9, 22n16, 22n17, 50n43, 62, 66, 74, 80, 97, 98–99, 98n76, 122. *See also* figure 8
Red Cross 37, 56, 105, 108, 118
Riga xxii, 66, 85. *See also* figure 11
Rodzianko, Mikhail, politician 49, 50, 50n43, 53, 66, 143
Romania xiv, xvii, xix, xxii, 8, 9, 11, 17, 18, 21, 22, 24, 90, 107, 141, 142
Root, Elihu, US politician 81, 81n65, 86, 103, 107, 109, 111, 115
Russo-Japanese War (1904–05) 62n56, 116, 118, 123
Ruzsky, Nikolai, military commander 50n43, 57, 57n49, 92, 104, 144

Sadovaia, Petrograd street xix, 27, 31, 33, 34, 36, 39, 61, 77, 78, 125. *See also* figure 35
Shanghai xvii, xxv, 14–15
Shingarev, Andrei Ivanovich, politician 65, 65n59, 96
Singer Building, Petrograd 26, 26n21, 33, 78
Skrydlova, Maria 118, 118n91
Soviet, Petrograd (Council of Workmen's and Soldiers' Deputies) xxi, 52, 55, 59, 65, 66, 68, 70, 71, 74, 75, 79, 84, 86, 89, 91, 93, 94, 95, 99, 100, 127, 130, 131, 133, 134, 140, 141, 145, 146. *See also* figure 24
Spiridonova, Maria 70, 70n62
Stürmer, Boris Vladimirovich, politician 22, 22n16, 24n19, 49, 62, 66, 122, 134
Sukhomlinov, Vladimir Aleksandrovich, military commander 59, 59n53, 62, 143

Tauride Palace, Petrograd 30, 30n28, 49, 141
Tereshchenko, Mikhail Ivanovich, politician 88, 88n73, 95
Topeka Daily Capital xvii, 5
The German Curse in Russia xxii, xxiii, 10n15
Trans-Siberian Railroad xvii, 14, 16n6, 16–17, 87n72, 144
Troitsky Bridge, Petrograd 28, 31, 41 132
Trotsky xx, xx n34, xxi, xxii, 124, 136. *See also* figure 36
Tsarskoe Selo 7n8, 61n55, 63, 66, 97, 135; Thompson's visit to 97–99. *See also* figure 2

Viroubova, Anna 98, 98n76, 122
Vladivostok xxiv, 16, 16n6, 72, 103, 148, 150, 151
Volynsky (Imperial Guard regiment) 41, 41n36, 66

Washburn, Stanley, journalist 109, 109n86, 115, 147
Wheeler, Charles, journalist xii, 6
Williams, Harold, journalist 121, 121n93, 137
Winship, North, US consul 34, 34n31, 64
Winter Palace, Petrograd 45, 46, 47, 50, 56, 62, 64
With the Russians at the Front xiv, 7n8
Women's Death Battalions 116–21, 142, 145, 146, 147. *See also* figures 50, 51, 55

www.ingramcontent.com/pod-product-compliance
Lightning Source LLC
Chambersburg PA
CBHW032022230426
43671CB00005B/169